Transformation and the Golden Keys

Transformation and the Golden Keys

A book about facilitating transformation and rites of passage

Dr Lem Ravensdale

CONTENTS

PREFACE	ix
INTRODUCTION	xix

1. Romantic Love: Imogen and the Anima — 1
2. Personal Growth and the Hero's Journey — 47
3. Transformational work — 71
4. Living your myth with attitude — 91
5. Mental Health — 103
6. Love — 147
7. Fathers and Sons — 175
8. Ancestors: The shoulders on which we stand — 193
9. My Personal Myth — 207

CONTENTS

10 | Rites of Passage 283

11 | Conclusion 309

Appendix 316

Further Reading 360

Copyright © 2020 Lem Ravensdale

All rights reserved.
No part of the book may be transmitted or reproduced by any form or means, either mechanical or electronic, including recording and photocopying, or by any known storage and retrieval system, without the written consent of the author/publisher, except in the case of short quotations being used in a review. The views and opinions expressed in this work are solely those of the author. Some names have been changed to protect privacy however they reflect real people and events.

 A catalogue record for this book is available from the National Library of Australia

978-0-6488997-0-9 (Paperback)
978-0-6488997-1-6 (Ebook)

Disclaimer
This book is not intended as a substitute for the medical advice of physicians directly or indirectly for any technique as a treatment for mental or physical problems. You may consult a physician in matters relating to your health in regards to any symptoms that may require diagnosis or medical attention. The author's intention is to offer general information in support of your journey for body, mind and energy wellbeing. The author assumes no responsibility for your personal action.

Interior & Cover Layout: PickaWooWoo Publishing Group – Bookbuilder.

Dedicated to Fiona, Josh and Rebekah
May all your dreams become your truth

And to the woman I chose to call Imogen because she was the bringer of an image, a sacred symbol, a reflection that will forever be an inspiration in my life and in the lives of others.

PREFACE

Some years ago I stood in the dead of night breathing in the salty air of a floodlit ocean at Hamelin Bay in Western Australia. All around me lay the battered bodies of dead whales and the overwhelming despair of a mass whale stranding. I was exhausted but there were still many more hours before sunrise to get through.

All afternoon I had stood with a group of rescuers in the shallows holding one of the whales off the sharp rocks nearby. Slowly the Indian Ocean swallowed the orange orb of the sun from the western sky, the silvery horizon wrapping it in her warm embrace as evening arrived. We spent the rest of the night walking up and down the beach fetching endless buckets of seawater to cool the whale as he lay propped up on a bed of sand. In the intimate enchantment of that relationship we talked a lot, the whale and I. We had all night and our lifetimes to share.

The beautiful ocean veiled by stars was alive with sharks moving through the whitecaps and the seaweed. Huge bite marks were visible on the dead whales that rolled in with the surf. Through the floodlit sky above the unfolding ocean, ghostly flocks of white birds would silently pass by flying across the scene of our Armageddon as if it had all been painted by Michelangelo.

PREFACE

At midnight – that moment between all our yesterdays and all our tomorrows - I stood there holding my bucket at the interface of beach and tumbling waves, of outer world and inner world, facing the god of the ocean and asking him why this had all happened. My tears so warm in contrast with the cold salty spray whilst other whales drifted in from the night. They were following their brothers and sisters to an end that we humans couldn't really make sense of.

Only years later would I gain enough wisdom to discern for myself a meaning behind this metaphor of nature: I couldn't save everybody no matter how much love I poured on them. Just like I couldn't save all these whales on that overwhelming night. In fact the best I could do was to find myself and find my place in this miracle that we call Life and maybe inspire a few people along the way. The beach near where I live is the margin between a vast ocean and the forest. I had to find that beautiful place to be, that margin – that place between all that is within me and all that is outside of me. Otherwise I risked burning out or losing myself and losing my way in the process of trying to save everybody.

As for the whales, their only hope was to take our kindness and when they were ready, face the ocean and the sharks as they returned to their lives beyond the reef. So too with us humans: when we are ready and strong enough after a setback, we have to get out there, get involved, face the sharks, face our own demons and dragons, and swim and thrive in the River of Life.

I have a photograph of a friend of mine. She struggles courageously trying to make sense of her world because she perceives life differently to the way you and I do. Without much of an Ego to defend herself, without a mask, her inner world is on show for everyone to react to and attack. We can take offence at the arrogance of archetypes unmodified by an Ego and

PREFACE

they attract conflict and drama and people's words enter such a mind unmoderated, the castle walls undefended.

She is looking so happy, so colourful and proud of herself in the photo holding a paddle and wearing a life jacket as she stands next to her kayak dripping wet. In the background is the island we paddled out to in very rough conditions and she is standing right next to where I cared for that whale years ago. I tried to use the metaphor to break her depressions by asking her if she wanted to be the woman in the photograph, empowered and magnificent, or one of the beached whales….like I foolishly assumed she still had a choice instead of a destiny. But the metaphor lost its power and its magic to her deep depressions which like the swell of the ocean time and again robbed her of the ability to transcend the matrix of her mind. Mostly the metaphor was meant for me.

You see, I get burned out trying to rescue people and sometimes I have to release them to the sea when there is simply nothing of me left to give. I can't save everyone. The metaphor gives some comfort to my broken heart when I let go and say goodbye. I have had to release some very special people along the way. You will read of them in my story. Letting go and grieving is a skill, something we need to learn so we can do it well in a lifetime of goodbyes. I am still not very good at it because I am still too attached to people and my precious things.

This book describes the journey of a life and of a lifetime

This book is written so that you might reflect upon your Life, to wonder at it and then to live it consciously. If lived unconsciously, Life becomes a projection outwards and onto others. It becomes a reactive life robbing the individual of experiencing what is truly a miracle. I hope to renew your confidence in Life, a confidence many have lost or had severely challenged along the way. The book is something of a dialogue between you and me, full of encouragement, motivation and inspiration. It is full of stories and learnings many of which I use on Rites of Passage programs.

Although every life is unique, there is a typical journey and the development of the mind that is common to much of humanity. Billions have gone before us, so it is not surprising that general patterns start to emerge. It took me into my mid-twenties to realise that the general trajectory of my life was not so unique even if the details were. I want to describe aspects of this journey to you through the stories and metaphors in this book.

By the end of this book the terminology and the concepts will become second nature to you and will reveal the matrix underlying what we do in transformational work and Rites of Passage programs. I might repeat some concepts along the way but that is just to help you understand and to remember. In a lifetime, all of us are inevitably going to live most of life's stages. As we encounter each stage between birth and death, we might as well live them all with abundant passion, heart and soul to create our unique story.

Authentic people simply speak from the heart, it's easy, and their stories contain a spell of enchantment that conveys meaning and wisdom and connection. On such journeys of the heart - Rites of Passage programs are only one of many - we encourage everyone to share their stories. This is my story and I want to share it with you and I would love to listen to yours even if I just have to feel it from afar. I hope we walk through the pages as if on a trek together. And maybe images will appear in your mind that we can share and wonder at.

PREFACE

Pulling things to bits

As a kid I always pulled things apart to see how they worked. I was never content with simply watching the magic, I needed to understand what was beneath it all and then, if possible, have a go at re-creating it myself. I can't just watch sport or adventure programs on TV, I have to play the sport and go out in search of my own adventures. That's just how I am.

So this book attempts to uncover and explain the underlying mechanisms of such things as romantic love, ancient and modern myths, mental health, Rites of Passage programs and male and female initiation. It establishes a vocabulary for the discussion with which we can share these concepts. And it draws the reader into the world of metaphor where the power of metaphor and colourful, picturesque speech start to resonate with the reader and become a habit of enchantment. We will take a peep to consider what is behind the theatre of Life.

I wanted to write about what I have seen and learned along the way. I wanted to describe to you the myth I live by and how I discovered my Anima and my Life's Mission. It resonates for me because it is my journey, my story. Some of the insights may be useful to you and others may seem discordant. Your life is like music. With some things it will harmonise so beautifully and with other things it will not. It may even sound like shark music when you get emotionally triggered by old memories and events.

You can learn from all of this if you begin to wonder at why feelings and emotions arise in response to such things. Perceptions are accompanied by sensations and emotions that lead us back to an inner truth and insight if we learn the mechanism, the technique to discern what the sensations represent.

PREFACE

As I will explain, whenever these sensations start flowing it is because an inner archetypal energy of the subconscious is stirring - the stirrings of schemas and complexes - and a story is being created because each of these archetypal energies has a voice. What to do with them is part of the mastery of who you are in creating a meaningful and abundant life filled with insights and epiphanies. Everything in Life comes in opposites and we need to reconcile opposites constantly in order to bring about something that is far deeper, more profound and peaceful than either opposite alone.

This does not necessarily make for an easy life because the enlightened path is alive and it leads from Enchanted Forest to Enchanted Forest, over mountains, through lakes and oceans and into the deepest caves. I couldn't imagine a greater adventure than the journey to encounter my own Soul. In reconciling these two opposites – the person you think you are and that part of you which you feel is lost, there will manifest a Man or a Woman on Mission, with gifts for a needy world and with a personality, character and physical image completely transformed.

Talking in pictures

This skill of working with metaphor enables us to speak the language of Nature, decoding her symbols, what she is trying to say and seeing where Life beckons because we now have the 'spiritual eyes' to see. Symbols abound throughout the earth and throughout history always imbued with a wondrous energy and meaning. Learning to love the language or significance of a symbol can transform something like the images of the Codex Borgia into sacred works capable of bringing me gasping to my knees in muted humility and reverence. They are masterpieces of information beyond my understanding yet I am still crushed by the significance of the Codex, of such magnificent symbols and the power they must have had.

With Spiritual Eyes – eyes of the heart - Nature becomes a friend, a mirror to look into and a place of enquiry and processing. And picturesque speech paints pictures that speak heart-to-heart, and not so much mind-to-mind. To some degree, it bypasses mental processing, mental filters and just arrives in the heart for the receiver to experience from their own centre of gravity. Metaphor – symbols in a sentence - is like an apparition, a hologram that appears within another and magically speaks in a known language, because the resonances, the impact, are of the receiver.

Myths and Sacred Work

Myths are just metaphors in story form that describe aspects of the journey of Life. Like layers of a sandwich, within each myth can be found profound psychological truths, practical advice and soulful insights. They are alive with information to reflect upon. But by far the greatest and most important myth is the story you tell about yourself, about who you think you are and who you want others to think you are.

There is gold in the stories of others. Like a metal detector used to find lost jewellery and coins on a beach, the quality of your questions, your ears, your eyes, your instinct and empathy will dictate what inner gold you bring to the light as you sit with another in conversation.

When the Knights of the Round Table agreed to set off in search of the Holy Grail, it is said that each one entered the dark forest by their own unique path. They made a conscious decision to enter the forest alone, striking out on unfamiliar ground. In your own quest to find abundance of Life, you must choose to create your own unique path through the Enchanted Forest. At times you will encounter and follow another's path to see what you can learn along the way. But ultimately **you** get to join the dots of your unique journey and give it its meaning. A Guru's path will only lead you to the Guru and the Guru's paradigm. You must eventually create your own path, your own truths and your own story, the myth you claim to live by.

Meanwhile the inner world is your very own crucible of transformation. Here you can dialogue with archetypes, shift energies and work with your dreams. These workings are then taken into the outer world in your rituals, ceremonies, in your prayers and in creating your altar or your sacred work in real material form as in painting, dancing, sculpting or ritual art. With these practices we can truly change our lives shifting the energies and situations that have become blocked and troublesome along the way. Anyone can do it and transform their story in the process. It is actually normal. It's the way we were meant to be.

The Witness

All the while there is a part of you that watches, both in your ordinary daily life and within your dreams. It is free of worry and stress. It simply watches and wonders. It is the Witness to your Life. It is you, the Universe, looking on without judgement...just wanting to experience everything, denying nothing. If we were not here as conscious observers, would this lessen the miracle of Life? What does our presence contribute? What happens when we stand and observe the wind rippling the surface of a pond or silently witness a sunset and thus become part of it all?

Through the act of **perception**, we become part of the ongoing celebrations and ongoing rituals of all that is. Perception creates a relationship between the observer and the observed - a oneness and a synaesthesia in the moment -and relationship magnifies all aspects of Life. We can transcend this human existence by expanding our definitions of words like 'ritual' and 'sacred' to allow other things to have their sacred rituals too as when we allow the myths to speak and come alive and enlighten us. We could shift our centre of gravity to capture something of what it means to be the Moon with her own sacred rituals of growth, renewal and how she blushfully shies away, her celebrations dancing so gracefully with the Earth and the Sun and the ocean tides. Love it all. Let its magic wash over you even if so much of it is beyond human comprehension.

We can be in relationship with it all by staying present and conscious and grateful just to be alive. The passing of Precious Time becomes a celebration of Life. And Death is no longer the Grim Reaper, but a sweet Angel who has come to take us back to our first home amongst the stars.

Fiona with eyes full of mischief. We all need spiritual, soulful eyes to see the magic. Then life beckons.

INTRODUCTION

Morning Time

I am kneeling before my bedside table. It contains all my very precious things. There are photographs of my dear ones on the wall above and paintings I made of my inner world once upon a time. In the gathering dawn, I light a candle there each morning and let my eyes wonder across the sacred objects. Each one has its own energy, evoking unique feelings within me. It's a place of resonance. As when Howard Carter first shone a candle into the tomb and treasures of Tutankhamen, the objects on my altar reflect in my eyes and dance with the golden candle light. There is a light in my heart each morning too, all aflame with wonder and love and passion. Here I meet with my ancestors, my gods, my memories, my voices. Here I find my power and whisper my prayers for the day really only asking that my day be alive with Life, mystery, insight and the unexpected.

When we were kids living in Africa, Mum taught the four of us to pray. She said, "Go and stand alone by a tree and talk to God." It was so simple. And the trees were beautiful. Mango Trees, huge Avocado Pear trees and purple-flowered Jacarandas. It was an electric atmosphere because God was all around me, meeting me in the stillness. And over the years I began to feel the heartbeat of God, to feel the caress in the wind and the smile

INTRODUCTION

in the sunlight and to free God from a man-made concept of a God in Heaven.

The Path of Abundance

Humanity has a relentless search for meaning, clarity, wholeness and to explore its potential. The mind asks: "Who am I?" "What am I to make of all of this?" Yet all around us is a living miracle of abundance to which we are mostly blind. And we can be equally blind to a miraculous world that is going on within. The Ego wants to define its own version of abundance and to write its own self-serving life story. But true abundance and happiness is on another path which ultimately you yourself have to cut through the forest. You can only walk another's path for so long otherwise it is not your own authentic journey. This path of abundance is one of a life in service to a greater Mission, to the Greater Good in some form.

Yet many set off to the pub as if it were their Life's Mission to numb this calling. They delight in the next pint, the huge flat screen TV and a bowl of hot chips as if they had discovered Aladdin's Cave. Meanwhile, outside the window, a figure in black - a Ninja - scurries silently past on a quest to subdue dragons, solve the riddles of life and fulfil his yearnings courageously facing the many challenges scattered throughout a lifetime. Neither person is guaranteed of success or of a safe return from the chosen journey. I am not even sure if either one holds more intrinsic value or which one will ultimately come up with the greater insights or outcomes.

Anyway, I am not going to sit around at the bar for very long waiting to find out because although bars are nice it seems to me that a real life of quality occurs everywhere else except in a bar. My son Josh was working as a barman some years ago to earn money as a university student. Two young ladies came running out of the toilets and whilst one poured a line of white powder on the bar counter, the other applied a straw to her nostril. Josh, ever the professional at moments like this, nonchalantly wiped the cocaine off the counter with his dish towel and rinsed it off in the sink leaving the young ladies reeling in shock. I thought that was hilarious.

In our forties and fifties bizarre dramas colour our lives, dramas that many of us never expected. Our very Souls warned us along the way but we live those years somewhat distracted and unconsciously. There are stirrings of romantic love, emotional upwellings, and creative energies that cry out to be expressed. When I read of the great contributors to metaphysics, mythology and psychology, many were beset with ever greater challenges as they grew older when we would expect them to be blissfully retired. Many died with their work unfinished. Such is your Life's Mission: it is a direction, not a destination...it is never really completed. Maybe, if we are doing things really well, it is not so bad to actually die on mission and maybe leave some kind of legacy in the hope that people use this pathway to create their own. Every person's gift needs to be expressed because a gift unexpressed will only impoverish humanity and create neuroses.

In looking for certainty in an ever-changing world we try to still an emotional pendulum that swings between hope and disillusion. Many would settle for a set of beliefs and rules to find meaning, some kind of mental matrix or daily discipline. Or maybe a religion so as to start the day in prayerful communion with no other than one of the Gods and to ask for a clearer vision of what the plan is for the day. Life unfolds regardless and I hope this book helps you to see why.

INTRODUCTION

Social contracts and overwhelming change

When I was teenager, I was exiled to a boarding school far removed from the ones I loved. I was still trying to find my identity and my place in the world. I developed some skills to survive but my personality was pathologically shy. And today it feels like I am in a game of football where, once the ball is kicked and the game starts, the rules seem to change every minute and even the goal posts keep moving. There is fear every time the referee blows the whistle because it means someone broke the rules and must suffer a penalty. And ignorance of the changing rules is of course no excuse: the game with its bewildering penalties goes on relentlessly. Self-reliance, self-belief and self-awareness have helped get me through these times of overwhelming and unrelenting change.

For me it was important to understand what a **social contract** is and to be aware of this concept whilst trying to make sense of the modern world. Governments can no longer fulfil many of the social contracts with their citizens that got them elected. There is simply not enough money to do so without creating debt and inflation. The problems are too complex and the power each government inherits is often corrupted power and self-serving regardless of how nice the leader is. We become fearful, frustrated and angry citizens, and with ineffective governance across the globe, we abdicate our own self-governance to find our comforts and happiness in alcohol, cooking shows, travel documentaries and singing competitions. Others choose to riot in the streets. We watch citizen against citizen on the news: one clothed in a police uniform, the other clothed in tear gas, attacking each other like dogs at a fence. Both have children, both have lives, and feelings and loves and dreams. Someone told them to look inwards at each other and hate what they see and to attack this image with bricks and rubber bullets. But they are just people in slavery to different belief and value systems.

Society, culture, money, justice... these are just constructs of the mind we all buy in to for various reasons or rebel against. They are not the real things, but their consequences are real. On a personal level, if you and me choose to believe in beautiful things and put our trust in them, maybe we can change the world to a better place. That's all society is, its money, its systems – a belief and a trust we all bought in to by choice or by coercion. Newborns in nature buy into their system because it is untainted by the distractions of human thought and it contributes to survival. Us humans deprive our newborns of their innate right to a beautiful primary caregiver when the adults domesticate them with the prevailing society and then set up the core wound for their own offspring.

Looking inwards like this is not the best way to bring about cultural change in communities and organisations. To change people's hearts and stop the infighting, someone needs to get them to look outwards to the bigger picture, to the greater good. Maybe even to the miracle itself. This is how cultural change happens, not by pointing fingers or shooting bullets into the team. I hope we can teach this to the adolescents today. I hope this book helps you look down past your feet to much deeper things and to look upwards past the clouds to a conscious universe above. Changing just yourself is enough to fulfil your social contract with life. All the rest that unfolds in the process is just a wonderful bonus.

The elders and their wisdom

With a new common enemy, basically the collapse of nature and society as we knew it, many now shift their centre of gravity from the former things we all worshiped like materialism and the modern day party at-

INTRODUCTION

mosphere and look outwards to the New Age movement to feel safe and secure. That's great, but it seems wise to enter this new frontier with wisdom and understanding lest we project too much outwards living unconsciously and thinking we've found our Rescuer. We forget how the global migrations of early and modern man into new frontiers caused mass extinctions within a few short years wherever he and she found themselves and expressed their human nature. To help explain, treat and prevent the imbalances within people, community and nature, shamans were invented. They arose from our own genius within. I have no doubt that many shamans - gifted or otherwise - may have been the least balanced of their entire community since to become one seems to involve trips through death, hell, drugs and other worlds. But they were masters of inner world stuff and valued for their contribution to society. Those of us who venture into the inner world often bring back as much fruit as the many scars we accumulate on our journeys. And for some the journey is all too much to endure and they may lose their way or the mind may fracture and the journey terminates at a psychiatric ward. Whilst the shamans and gurus abound and fill our lives with magic, fire and wild leapings we also need the oversight of a few elders to keep it all in check. As you will see, without eldership in any organisation, even in a family, Shadow becomes rampant.

It has been lauded as something like the end of an age of left-brained, logical, patriarchal governance and heralds the advent of a right-brained, diffuse thinking, matriarchal age. Yet there are pitfalls in any approach without elders keeping a close eye on Shadow, any Shadow in either gender. For as we ascend and draw nearer to the light, our Shadows grow bigger, not smaller. We are called to even greater awareness of Shadow as we realise how its Shadow Mission is 180 degrees in the opposite direction to our Life's Mission to serve the Greater Good. Shadow serves the

INTRODUCTION

Greater Bad. That's just how it is. I know us men have got a lot to answer for through thousands of years of patriarchy, but by way of example the inspiration of the Anima, and indeed many things feminine, can just as easily seduce many a man like myself and leave him marooned on Calypso's Island with his Life's Mission lost in stagnation. And what man or woman has not felt the heat or been burned to a crisp by the destructive aspects of a Shiva or a Kali?

Lack of respect for true eldership and the oversight by elders means that Shadow simply runs amok and unchecked in organisations and in society corrupting everything, turning gold into straw and into worthless lead very quickly. Today, elders and eldership can take many forms including poets, playwrights, musicians and mentors even feedback forms or a well facilitated TV interview. In olden times it was the court jester, the advisor and the elders that all helped to keep the sovereign in check and on track. Shadow, like a tiny rudder, can turn a huge ship… but it is the steady hand on the wheel that ultimately steers it to safety. Choose your New Age activity well that it bears the right fruit. Basically if you want to evaluate anyone or any pathway, just look at the fruit that gets created along the way.

So do your inner work as you engage with these forces that are unfolding in your life and in the world so that you do not move forward without due diligence and consciousness. Basically keep reading widely and informing yourself so the blinkers fall off until you eventually transcend the confines of knowledge for the freedoms of wisdom. If you do your inner work, the rest will take care of itself because "…as within, so without…" It's all your journey, every bit of it, every step, every thought and feeling and every choice you make. When a person owns their projections and takes them back off this outer world, nothing is ever someone else's fault and we reclaim our power to change things. Then you can '**trust the process**', trust in whatever unfolds.... because Life backs a man or woman on Mission and will keep its half of the sacred contract blessing your honest efforts in the process.

Taking Action

So what are you waiting for? Don't just live on platitudes. We don't even know what all this change means yet, and it will take a lot of time to become apparent. So embrace Life anyway and get out there and live well. It's your life that is ticking by moment by moment. Live it with all your heart. Grow plants, save water, learn to talk to your goldfish and respect your dog more. Take action. Foster great attitude. And approach life as a sacred gift. Born out of the sufferings of the First World War, where soldiers and their horses suffered in equal measure, Hugh Lofting was inspired to write his stories of Dr Dolittle in 1920. Humanity's core wound of a global war and epidemic disease was transformed into a gift of compassion, health and understanding to our fellow sentient travelers, to the animals, when Dr Dolittle learned to be in relationship and conversation with everything from Alpaca to Zebra Fish.

Keeping your half of your social contract with Life

It might seem hard to understand at first, but one aspect of the way forward is in reconciling opposites, not in replacing one with another, not in suppression or denial or mixing them up into a homogeneous blend. There is a synergy and a balance in creating a third element in proper relationship out of two opposites. To suppress one, or deny one is to create a neurosis out of an unresolved paradox. People say that the Sun has set and it is time for the Moon, for the feminine element to govern us as if it were some panacea, without adequate respect for Pandora or indeed the positive aspects of the Mature Masculine. Good governance is a state of synergy which also must give due attention to the undesirable energies we would otherwise like to repress, deny or remain blissfully unaware of. Unattended, these energies just simmer and boil over. Cooking shows are a perfect metaphor for such things within.

For thousands of years women's' circles and men's circles have existed to process so many issues, free of the entanglement and complexities of co-gender groups. Co-gender work in any form can take Shadow to a whole new level in cascades of pent up energy. And Shadow enacted in this real world has real world consequences. So it always reassures me when I see that an individual has made peace and connection with people of their own gender.

In his book: "A Circle of Men" Bill Kauth includes a short article written by Danaan Parry. It describes a poignant moment years ago when two opposite gender groups met after days apart on a retreat in nature doing inner work. And despite the longing in their hearts to reconnect, they admitted with honesty, maturity and insight that both genders still had more work to do. For men and women to be together in their authentic power and co-create the synergy such relationships are capable of without the insidious and destructive presence of Shadow takes a lot of maturity – maturity of these nascent energies within. As spoken by one of the woman folk, using her courage and the Lamp of Insight so typical of her gender, the time was "...**not yet**..."

I say, regardless of who governs in this new age, give due regard to the divine aspect and strengths of your opposite gender - within and without - and in this way reconcile the opposites through respect, wonder and love. The Divine Marriage of masculine and feminine elements is a stepping stone along the pathway of our transcendence and heralds the time of balance and wisdom: the time of eldership.

Myths

In the western world, the challenge today is for each one of us to develop our own spirituality, a personal myth and mythology to live by – it is more truthful, courageous and authentic that way - to shoot from the hip and declare where you stand. It's about spending a lifetime crafting your own story and your own authentic path instead of following someone else's. We are driven to do this because a man will do just about anything to know that he is on some divine mission… that his life had meaning and was spent doing what it was intended for. We seek this affirmation from our fathers and we seek it from God. If you are like me, you will take a moment even just once in your life to sneak past these two aspects of the masculine – God and Dad - and affirm yourself with a whopping great, kick-asse, self-affirming story…otherwise I would still be sitting gazing out to the ocean waiting for their approval.

Dragons

Maybe it is time for you to light the Lamp of Wonder and Curiosity, to look to the bizarre activities of your own gods **within**. Then you will understand better what is happening **without**. And you will be able to better navigate the oceans of your lifetime. You can yet regain the magic pen that writes your story instead of surrendering the pen to others. You can hunt Shadow and Dragons, not to kill them but to befriend them, hear their stories and in this way release their energy and treasure back into your own life. No voice and no Dragon inside us wants to die. Instead, it wants to be heard preferably to negotiate a deal with the Ego. Otherwise its energy will just resurface later like a beach ball when it is pushed under water. And its golden treasure will remain undiscovered.

Mission

Working out one's life's mission is a fundamental part of the journey. My mission is that I create a world of wonder, adventure and learning through connecting, encouraging and empowering. That's my mission at the moment. I can change it whenever I feel called to do so. My ego's higher purpose is to step aside a bit and to serve this Mission. That's why I get out of bed each day at 4 am and go scurrying off looking for adventures and golden threads to follow or to wonder at the stars and a new dawn. And I will show you in this book of stories and metaphors how you can do this too.

Keeping my feet on the ground: The Razor's Edge

I realised that to be effective, I have to be careful to live hard, work hard and play hard in this real world and not get too mixed up or lose my way whilst I am on my relentless inner journeys of heart and soul. It gets confusing and dark in there sometimes. And I can't take the safer option and just bliss out in meditation each day because my unique life would then slip through my fingers unlived.

So I strive not to cross-contaminate my inner world with my outer world even though one is just the consequence of the other. I try to live them in parallel, walking along the space in between - a place I call The Razor's Edge - so that I can process things quickly. It's like the beach between the forest and the deep, deep ocean. If you could look down the Razor's Edge, you would find the Dalai Lama sitting there cross-legged, smiling and childlike in a state of balance and self-processing any disturbances of

INTRODUCTION

his inner or outer worlds in the blinking of an eye. There is a real place where I sit with this metaphor. It is along the thin dam wall of a secluded weir near Burekup in Western Australia on the beautiful Collie River. I sit there amongst the dear memories and echoes of when our children were little and played in the surrounding forest. I can always think back to that place and energetically regain my balance sitting on the dam wall separating a deep expanse of crystal clean water on one side and the cascading rapids below.

It is indeed possible to process things in a moment while others commit to years of psychotherapy and wrestling with energies just as Jacob wrestled with an Angel all night in the Biblical story in Genesis. We've wrestled our Dark Side forever and always will until we reach the peace of enlightenment and transcendence. We will always be Theseus killing our boorish Minotaur within. We will forever hear the wise genius of Daedalus warning Icarus not to fly too high lest he become lost in the hubris, lose his wings and fall. But let's learn to process these things with a touch of urgency like I imagine the Dalai Lama does and not spend years howling at the moon over some distant wounding...sort it out, there is much work to do and if you haven't noticed, the time seems rather limited.

Meet my friend the Forest

You see, after my brief prayers at my altar, there is a real forest in which I walk each morning with my dog Scout and where I can renew myself daily. It is not easy to keep my inner world separate because in wondering at life in the forest each day, following the kangaroo tracks and snake trails and talking to the trees, ants, the birds and the sky, I take that same wonder into my working day and become eternally distracted by shiny things. I find myself talking to inanimate objects as if they were old friends. If the stapler falls off the desk, I burst into tears and run to give it a hug. When I grew oyster mushrooms at home, I raised them like they were my own children. There is wonder everywhere. Ordinary life becomes a profound experience. I see the divinity in others and take their conversations and questions seriously leap-frogging the superficial noise of chit chat to give honest and what appear to be unexpected answers.

Mum taught us the Polish custom of **'A guest in the house is God in the house'**. But it scares people if I treat them as divine, smiling too deeply into their eyes or if I try to wake them in any way from their slumber. I see my own awakening when I read the journals of my teenage years and re-visit how deep my feelings were in that difficult time so alone at boarding school. Eventually I learned to express better this spirit of wonder and curiosity that was always jumping up within me: I tempered my exuberance with respect... a measure of respect and acceptance for others' journeys as one would respect an artist and not get too critical in the artist's presence.

Five senses, an emotional body and a cinema screen

My friend lost her sense of taste when she fell over in an accident many years ago. Imagine a tasteless world. But many of us still have the five senses as a gift to make sense of Life. My senses interact with this physical outer world gathering information to create my version of reality. It is a very faulted process which corrupts and limits the incoming data. But it is what I have to facilitate my journey along the miracle of life. It is a miracle anyway regardless of my limitations or my interpretations.

So it is humbling to think that I interact with the vast field that is all creation through just five faulty senses. My eyes only perceive the world as solid because they haven't got the magnification to see past the crystals of sand to the swirling energy that it is all composed of. I have a faulty inner cinema screen, my imagination, on which to project it all. Here, the sensory inputs are mixed with beliefs, feelings and associations of all my mental schemas forming new complexes. All my mental entities and concepts are encoded with emotions and stored in memory. And each one is able to resonate as if garnished with tuning forks poised to pick up resonances from outside that bring all of this into streams of thought.

It's all a story contrived in this way. But I must honour my story as my own work of art - the complexities and agreements that are uniquely mine in defining what is truth and reality and what has shaped such things along my personal journey. I have to remember every day that life really is a miracle and not to despair when my doubts and cynical nature creep in. In my outer world, I have to keep motivated and maintain a great attitude to keep myself as a man of action. And I try not to send so much of my inner world out there to the outer world that I become dysfunctional, or scare people when I express these concepts in conversation. I try to check how open their worldview is before I start talking because some people seem to be fixated on talking only about the weather. Yet with creative genius, you can expand even a weather report conversation into three dimensions quite easily.

Fostering our innate freedom and authentic expression

We are born so very innocent. A friend of mine was standing in the glow of a moonlit night and his little daughter, who had only just learned to speak, asked him to lift her a little higher so that she could hold the moon. What an eternally precious moment. He shared the story and I have never stopped being blessed by it.

I saw a child step out of the car the other day. She was about 6 or 7 years old. Her mother was fussing with collecting all their belongings from the car so she could lock the door and continue on their way. The little girl, oblivious to her own existence and free of any self-consciousness spontaneously did a perfect cart wheel. Then she stood there, distracted and experiencing the joy of her own world, of this moment, her hands and face lifted up to a sky filled with sunlight.

What a blessing to have a parent who lets a child explore the world by always saying "Yes!" to Life – and holding the child in a positive matrix by rarely using the word "No!" I hear parents saying "No!" all the time. From now on it is probably going to annoy you too every time you hear it and look up from your coffee and magazine to watch another parent squashing a kid instead of guiding the child. How wonderful for anyone to have the skills to hold another of any age within a positive social environment so that it is both safe to explore and safe to return. It means being older, wiser, kinder and if necessary stronger for others, for young and old alike. Can we practice maintaining this kind of relationship for just a moment, or for a lifetime until it is part of our very being?

With the right social environment, people can really talk, and share and feel affirmed and heard. It is a skill to be able to track another's feelings and help them organise their emotions and the stories they spin whilst in real time holding and acknowledging these same emotions and feelings. We must resist negating or suppressing them with logic regardless of how irrational they may be until they have been heard and acknowledged properly. Maybe that is all the speaker needs…our gaze, our attention and our ears. Emotions help bring things out of the unconscious and into the light and allow an archetypal energy to be heard. In this way, we provide the safety for a child or an adult to explore the world or to explore new concepts and conversations knowing there is a safe social environment, a safe place or person to return to or to look back to for reassurance when

INTRODUCTION

things seem a little shaky and uncertain...and when the conversations get too deep.

I wish I could build a beautiful monument to the cartwheel girl with her arms outstretched to the sky. It would remind everyone to live more, to play more, to delight and to wonder more. But I knew the little girl's mind would soon be fully domesticated by the system in which we raise our children because I had done this to my own. She would be given a fictitious paradigm to believe in by her primary care givers and her parents so that she could be functional in the fictitious game called society. She would enter the distractions of this modern world and end up in the dark forest like everyone else trying to re-connect with a Soul and an original, authentic self whose voice speaks to us constantly but whose voice we no longer recognise. The glimpses and encounters we have with our unique Soul go unnoticed or undervalued because we do not know the profound implications of following where the Soul beckons. The Soul beckons inside, shining a Lamp of Insight upon your inner world. And it beckons outside to encourage you to live your Life's Mission and express your unique gifts to a needy world.

On one extreme, you can stay safe and conservative and not experience much of this. On the other extreme, you could go mad if you let it overwhelm your world. A conservative life will drive you neurotic anyway because things will start to swing first like a pendulum, then like a wrecking ball and unwelcome energies will build up and break through sooner or later attempting to resolve the paradox, the conservative stalemate. Another way is to reconcile the conservative and the madness to create a third alternative: a sense of wildness that the little girl had- an instinctive way of being. It is most simply found by heading into Nature for a time.

There, Mother Nature will release you from your unnecessary suffering as if releasing captured wildlife - a squirrel maybe - back into the wild.

Spiritual Eyes to see the magic

Without what I call 'Spiritual Eyes' to follow the calling of your Soul, life steadily becomes a two dimensional wasteland. The Ego foolishly fights the process for years on end instead of getting on with the program: stepping to one side and allowing the magic of other dimensions to happen. We feel a heart-sickness or become restless, angry, dry, depressed or frustrated. Dramas and neuroses unfold. Profound woundings from our past break back into daily life at the strangest of times.

There is a memory I have of trekking through the remote northwest of Australia. I was climbing a dangerous rock face of a very steep hill and was beset with the images and presence of my father. I was completely overwhelmed with tears that blurred my vision and robbed me of my strength just when I needed it most. And there were cries from deep within my heart. I heard them there at the rock face almost as a stranger witnessing the cry of another. These very images were of my strength from a time when I had first glimpsed it: when as a little boy I needed my father's strength and first saw it there in him, in my father. I had found my own strength over the years and I even had it as I clung to the rocks. But these images took me back to a disempowered time and for a moment I nearly fell into an emotional black abyss and very nearly fell from the rock face. As within, so without...

And so we create an entire personality to shield ourselves from the pain, a personality that limits and imprisons us from living fully. There is a feeling that there must be something more, and there is. That is what happens when the Soul lies unexamined for too long. Sooner or later it awakens into one's life by tapping on the head of the Ego, usually with some seriously hard knuckles to grab the attention. And it asks the Ego to step to one side a bit and watch the magic unfold. It guides the journeys that lead to the Gift.

Your Inner Guide

Your Soul is your true Soulmate but we project this onto another human because as a man just feeling her stir within is so intoxicating. So in the western world we don't understand the concept very well. Why would you deny yourself her love and inspiration which only wants to electrify your life and bring your unique gifts and unique Mission into being? Here is where abundance lies, the abundance of Life, a life well lived, your unique empowerment and the fulfilment of your deepest desires… those fulfilling desires beyond the mundane ones of Ego.

If you ever get to read the ancient tale of the Fisher King, you will discover a man who transcended his mundane world bringing about its complete healing and regeneration by simply asking a very curious question at the right time in his life. He asks it consciously when he was given a second chance after failing on his first attempt. And the question is pure magic. It will transform anyone immediately simply in the asking. The question in the ancient myth is: "Whom does the Grail serve?" what this means to modern man is "Where do I find abundance and fulfilment in my life?" This immediately puts a person on the right pathway, into a little boat of enquiry that sails along a winding tributary leading to a mighty river. This river is the River of Life and in it is your Life's Mission which in this analogy is actually in the sailing. The guide for this journey and the bringer of the gift is your Soul, what Carl Jung called your Animus or Anima. In my book we will go and find her first because being a man I had to find my Anima to then release her rocket fuel of inspiration into my life.

Greatest need greatest gift

Some years ago I drew a picture that represented my greatest need when I was a child. When I drew it I was in the company of sixty men, sixty warriors undergoing a male initiatory weekend into authentic masculinity at an old ex-naval facility in Fremantle Western Australia. And it is a profound picture because it also represents my greatest gift to the world. That is often the way it is with us human beings. Your greatest need becomes your greatest gift to the world. Nelson Mandela was imprisoned for 27 years and he comes out of jail preaching freedom...freedom for millions. My picture is of a little boy sitting in the palm of the hand of a much bigger and much older man. And he is listening intently to the wisdom, advice and mentoring that the older man is giving.

As a child I cried out for help to make sense of an ever changing world. I was born in South London only fifteen years after the Second World War had ended. I was raised there for six years in the vibrant community of Polish refugees trying to make a new life in England after the war. They could not return to their country, to Poland, because it had been lost to communism, a country they fought and died for and core to their sense of identity. After the Germans and the Russians had finished ploughing the Polish countryside with their tanks, trucks, bombs and bullets there was not much for my Polish family to return to besides persecution by a communist regime. They had already lost their beloved family farm to the Russians at the start of the war and I often wonder what stories the farmhouse witnessed as it lay there slowly crumbling like the rest of Poland.

INTRODUCTION

Forty years later my aunt made a very hazardous journey through some lawless and very radioactive regions of Belorussia to see what had become of the farm and probably to see if the tap water glowed in the dark. She found herself standing in a very bare and nondescript field with no sign of any farmhouse, no roots, no remnants of her personal history tying her to the land. It would have been hard trying to make sense of a moment like that. I imagine she blinked a bit, swallowed hard and looked around listening to the laughter and voices and dreams of her childhood until the emotions and reality overwhelmed her and brought her back her solitude and the desolation at her feet. But her gift was to become a science teacher and she committed her life to bringing knowledge, love and fun to thousands of school kids in London filling them with dreams and visions of their own empowered futures and a sense of belonging.

Lost in this new world

Like so many indigenous peoples and like modern man today, we Poles in exile had lost our sense of identity, our stories, our connection to land and local myths, our way of processing life due to the lost connection to nature, culture and to our rural existence. The first lines of our national anthem say that Poland will never die as long as we are standing... as long as I am alive.

Yes, it is true: all songs, all stories, and even the very gods themselves will only live as long as their names are spoken, as we tell stories and as our songs breathe them into existence once more. We need to resurrect the Storyteller within us for it is the Storyteller who connects us to all that is, to the wisdom, history, insights, and connects us to the land and to Life. And we need to write new stories too that encompass change without losing our past so that we stay grounded. Multiculturalism is pure magic but not if its people have lost their stories or are in a lost state of mind.

And when I listen to the modern songs and the stories of today I can see the emergence of new gods and new energies. They relentlessly seem to plough through the very fabric of society and community and the way things used to be. Instead of wasting too much energy on worrying and complaining about an inevitably changing world that we can't keep pace with, we can harness some of this energy to accelerate our own transformation, inner growth and development. This is what it means to create an Ally: by harnessing a perceived negative energy and channelling it to good use instead... taking anger or fear or loneliness and putting it into some good and decisive action. For example, you could transcend your depression or anger by channelling its energy into fixing the leaking garden tap that has wasted water for 5 years.

If change is relentless in the world today, how about we transform and transcend our very selves so that we can be big enough to accept the immensity of Life?

The Alchemist's Forge

There is a fire in everyone's heart – a place of transformation. Those who want to can take up the tools of an apprentice and can begin to learn the craft of forging golden things for their lives, golden insights. It is a place where a Blacksmith would go to hammer out issues in the sweat and heat of this magical forge. The Glass Blower creates the intricate, majestic and colourful shapes in clear glass out of what was basically only sand. Here the Alchemist learns to turn every situation in life, all the straw and all the lead and base metals into pure gold. Time becomes Precious Time. People become fascinating aspects of God, of a Conscious Universe. Nature becomes a place of daily communion with something alive and with a unique and beautiful voice. And all of life becomes a miracle.

INTRODUCTION

Every breath, every second becomes a miracle, a celebration of life in all its forms, in all of its unfolding.

Paradise lost and paradise rediscovered

So this is my gift that I bring to my world and to the world of others. I create a world of wonder, adventure and learning. A world of transformation. And I do this by connecting, encouraging, empowering and in teaching. I see elements of this journey starting at the age of nine when the teacher challenged us to invent something. So I created a tiny machine with an electric motor that could scribe and sculpt blackboard chalk. I was thereafter referred to as "The Professor" and imagined that one day I would become a great, wise and knowledgeable teacher.

I can only look back in wonder at the journey even if I am not maybe that great, or wise or knowledgeable as I had hoped. It fills my heart with overwhelming love for the little boy who climbed all those hills and mountains to encounter the bigger, older wiser man in the picture I drew. I found my Self on this journey: so many elements of a disowned self, pieces of my wholeness hidden away when the innocence of my childhood was broken in my domestication. It happens to all of us.

And I came to realise that I was actually a small element of a conscious universe looking back upon itself. I came to realise the one-ness of it all, of this miracle in which we live. As I look around me and witness the unfolding of this universe, there is this larger conscious element looking back at me and beckoning me ever onward to deeper experiences, to deeper insights. It is a world of connection and relationship to all that is. The picture I drew of the boy in the palm of an older, wiser man was just a metaphor for all of this, for a conscious universe of which we are all just a part draped in human flesh. It speaks to us and watches as we sit in the palm of its hand.

The Biblical narrative describes this loss of one-ness, a loss of symmetry and harmony. Then follow many chapters describing epic stories of loss and gain before a divine order is re-established. Such is our own sacred journey: our attempts to find our wholeness, our one-ness with a conscious universe, our Paradise Lost.

Nature is a reflection of the Soul

Carl Jung believed that without nature, without a rural existence, man was already in a neurotic state, in a paradox, estranged from such a great and necessary presence. Many indigenous communities take their young boys away for a time into nature to embed a sense of connection and relationship to all that is. On this Rite of Passage, each element of nature, be it an animal, an insect, the sun, the moon, a star, a fish, is given its name, its story and its proper relationship to the boy is explained. The One-ness of relationship to self and to others and to the cosmos is created. The boy becomes embedded within this living matrix of nature, of existence, of life. This is how nature comes alive. It stirs and becomes alive to us and to our consciousness in the telling and wonder of such things. This is why nature is a place of communion and connection and relationship to those who allow themselves to resonate there. And it speaks to us constantly. With such a web of connection and relationship to all that is we are never alone in nature or in life.

And when we realise how much nature loves **us**, we can go to her for wisdom, guidance and insights. We can go there to perform our sacred rituals, our ritual theatre. That is where we go to process our life's issues and our dreams from the night before. Here we deal with issues of the

INTRODUCTION

heart and psyche and come back renewed to a secular world bringing life, and vibrancy and passion to quench the thirst of communities who seem to be almost dying in the system because of a two dimensional existence. Inasmuch as my Soul is my inner guide and teacher, Mother Nature is my outer guide and teacher too... they seem to reflect each other and commune together, like they seem to know each other so well and spend a lot of time together trying to figure out what on earth to do with me.

Resonance

Tuning forks resonate with others of the same pitch and set them in motion. Within us is a vast array of tuning forks that resonate with things in the outer world. The mind organises concepts and its perceptions of reality into groups of related information, into entities called schemas or complexes which bristle with tuning forks. And by saying just one word or by my behaviour I can jiggle, poke or stroke an underlying complex within you because I caught your attention and bowled something into your tuning forks. Then these things tumble into the river of thought, with emotions and story, the reactions, responses and dramas that all unfold. We need to learn the Art of Resonance because it is a skill.

The emotional body resonates with each perception encoding all our memories and schemas with emotions that colour our world with emotional melodies. Every time a tuning fork is set in motion, underlying schemas flow into streams of thought releasing their packets of emotions. So tracking an emotion leads back to an underlying schema, a complex, an archetypal voice and its story.

Nature and people are giving off signals all the time. These enter our minds and resonate with our tuning forks within. In turn we resonate with everything around us whether consciously or unconsciously. That's why, in making first impressions, or in acting as a leader, in public speaking or in relationship, sending out the right signals is so important because people will resonate with the signals and react accordingly. Sensitive people resonate very strongly. For some individuals they are so sensitive or so sensitized by their mental state at the time that the resonances of everyday life can be overwhelming and they need to withdraw periodically or permanently dampening their resonances with medication.

Alcohol is a great way to dampen the resonances of an overwhelming world. Much like a fur coat helps to keep us from feeling the cold, the entire planet wraps itself in the comfort of a blanket of alcohol on the weekends and basically goes unconscious. I am reminded of how in 1945 the Russians were just days away from capturing Berlin. And with the great Fuehrer dead, Goebbels running around poisoning his family with cyanide and an apocalyptic Judgement Day looming over all his staff in the underground Bunker - like a Russian snake about to consume a German mouse - a huge party started up inside the Bunker so they could forget their worries. It was an epic party. In mythical terms, Dionysus the ancient Greek god of wine, ecstasy and frequent madness possessed the Bunker that night. Berliners are still famous for their parties to this very day but Dionysus has gone global. Weekly all over the world there is a profound alcohol-induced psychosis and a tuning fork disorder of great proportions, a self-inflicted shamanic journey with very uncertain outcomes and for all too many it ends like a night out purging on ayahuasca and an inevitable walk of shame.

Emotions colour our world and resonance is the music

We never really know what resonances are activated in another because the array in a person's mind is so vast and complex and generated by a lifetime of subjective experience. Therefore, one's intention and the resulting impact can be as exciting and as hit and miss as a game of Battleships and the transfer of concepts and data is only ever approximate at best. I hope the stories, concepts and life skills in this book will help with your resonance to yourself and to your outer world so that you create and pick up the most beautiful harmonies.

A harmony is a relationship – a good one. And a dissonance might sound a bit hard on the ears but if it is held for long enough, it will break through into golden insights and great outcomes all by itself and in its proper time. In music, a dissonance and a tension is created just before a release of the melody into rapture and flow. Brazilian music is a delight of this tension and release. So too in Life, energies build up before a change or an insight. Learn to hold them like a conductor holds the orchestra in the pitch of suspense with just a tiny but mighty baton while he stands there quivering on tip toes. Your inner Magician was born for this.... for it is your inner Magician that understands and channels energy and the energies of a group.

There are many stories of a naturalist or a wildlife photographer whose resonance is so natural and peaceful that they get to play with the cubs of a cheetah, the young of the chimpanzees or swim with sharks. If their resonance were otherwise, they would stand out from the matrix of nature as hostiles and become unwelcomed and feared as the rest of humanity is. But they conduct themselves well, resonating themselves into a relationship with nature and then they don't get eaten in the process.

The Magician and his tricks

So I wanted to share with you some of the experiences of this Magician and his magical forge of transformation. I always thought that as we learn how a magician does his tricks then the magic would disappear. But it is not so with becoming a master magician in the magic of life because you then become a custodian of the magic. The audience is not only ourselves and those that love us, but all of humanity and the very universe itself. If you take one step towards life, then life will take ten steps towards you. Life always backs a person on mission. Life will always back a hero on the Hero's Journey. Life Beckons. But she also sends Helpers when we most need them.

Learn the magic, share the magic and watch it constantly unfold in your life. The Magician is the genius within and you will feel your own genius resonate as you spend time reading the unfolding pages. Your Magician will love some of it and hate some of it but take whatever you need and use it to change the world......basically by changing your own world and in so doing, changing **your** half of all relationships into pure gold and pure joy.

The Dark Night of the Soul: when the going gets really tough

Just about every hero's story ever written contains a moment when all seemed lost but was pivotal to some brilliant outcome. If you have ever reached the point when all seems so lost, and your life's battle is collapsing into defeat, this is where your Alchemist must suddenly leap towards the forge shouting: "Don't worry! It's just the Dark Night of the Soul!"...and before you know it the forge turns the dark moment of defeat into overwhelming life-changing victory. A tiny mouse scurries onto the battle field and with some magical proclamation, judo throws the power of angst, failure and a huge fire-breathing dragon into the celebration and festivities of redemption, of resilience, of another battle won and another challenge overcome. And like the glitter of fireworks come profound golden insights to light up the darkest sky transforming all the dark energies into brilliant Allies.

INTRODUCTION

I think of Robert the Bruce watching the repeated attempts of a spider to complete its web before his victorious battle at Bannockburn. And I love Shakespeare's version of Henry V's rousing speech before defeating a French army nearly ten times as large. So now I don't worry much anymore. Chaos and calamity are just Dark Nights of the Soul – a birthplace for something brilliant, a place to fire up the forge and get to work. Problems, difficulties and challenges are all vital material for the forge, for the manufacturing of pure gold. As long as we fully engage with Life, this base material will abound. And then... Oh! How rich we can become.

Problems, calamities, chaos... throw them all into the forge. Turn all that straw into gold. This cake recipe calls for all the ingredients of a disaster to be baked in a magic oven that only makes golden cakes. It is a time to practice your brilliance because your Magician was born for days like this. And in this way you learn to thrive on the magic and opportunities of every train smash instead of suffering it.

Holding yourself to a new standard

When Roman armies were on the move and when engaged in battle, each cohort had its own standard, its own emblem displayed on a pole so that it could be easily seen and used for signalling and as a rallying point for the cohort. As a symbol it represented many things including the governance of Rome, the Roman people and the cohort itself. Should it fall into enemy hands or should the standard bearer be killed it was considered a disgrace of the highest order and armies would fight to regain a lost standard.

We all march with a persona held high before us for all the world to see. And we behave and create a story that defends this persona lest anyone catch sight of the real person behind the mask. Yet we march with our own unique symbol whether people can see it or not. The challenge is to let this be elements of your authentic self so that like units of the Roman army, you've got a standard worth fighting for, and, in this case, worth living for.

Your own epic movie

I hope that the metaphorical language I use will help create useful images on the panoramic cinema screen that is your mind's imagination. For it is on this screen that you gather an array of inputs to create your version of reality. And like any movie, behind the scene is a whole cast and crew that contribute to the production, to a fascinating show that is your life's work. The best movies are absolute epics...filled with birth, death, passion and humour so embrace them and don't deny them. You will see elements of yourself in the stories that follow. And maybe this will inspire you on your own epic journey.

And when at the end of your life you write the last sentence, and in that moment of hesitation before you put in that final full stop and basically die, may you hear the two words that every child longs to hear – and many wait a lifetime to hear - but this time spoken by your bigger, older self.... by a conscious universe. May you look back on it all and simply hear and say the profound words: **"Well done."**

INTRODUCTION

The Dark Night of the Soul

I have done some dumb things in my life and they always seem to end up with a Dark Night of the Soul. I was trekking with ten Nepalese soldiers – the Gurkhas – in the very treacherous ranges of the far north of Australia when I thought up a crazy plan. It seemed like such a great idea at the time. With me was the owner of the adventure company, Colin Hendry, a distinguished soldier in his own right from twelve years of combat experience in the Rhodesian war and then four years as the commander of the Sultan of Oman's personal elite troop.

We were hot and tired from eight days on the steep and treacherous Kimberley ranges of Western Australia, sleeping on the rocky ground and catching fish along the way. Slumped against our rucksacks in the shade of a tree, the soldiers delighted in showing me footage of their training which happens day after day, month after month right through their 25 years of service. So I couldn't help but notice how one group of men in their video seemed to be so bored with storming yet another building, bashing down the doors and peppering the rooms with bullets. It must become so mechanical when you have done it a thousand times. Almost yawning, four men sauntered over to a battering ram, picked it up and destroyed a door whilst their mates casually wondered through the splintered wood and calmly emptied magazine after magazine seemingly at random into the interior.

So Colin and I hatched up a plan to create a bit of a buzz in the journey. We would create a snake bite scenario and see how they coped with the situation and the casualty evacuation. But we didn't warn the guys, we just ran it as if it was real. I used a small pair of scissors on my penknife to make two small nicks in my forearm and set about flailing the bush as if bitten by a snake and then collapsed in a heap. The fiasco that unfolded will haunt me to the rest of my days. I proceeded to fain my own death with the poor soldiers crying by my side as they hastily built a stretcher from their walking sticks and a tent and tried to carry me to a suitable landing site for a helicopter.

When I miraculously came to life and we congratulated them on their excellent work they were understandably furious beyond any fury a man should ever want to experience. They explained that they were moments away from cutting my entire arm off with their machete-like Kukri knives to stop the flow of venom. Colin and I slinked away to a shady rock pool around the corner and floated in the cool water there for ages wondering what on earth to do. They did forgive us eventually but there were two dark and lonely hours of total mutiny in the face of such a betrayal of trust. Their act of forgiveness created a brotherhood amongst us that endures to this day and won us a bottle of whiskey when we presented the stories of our journey at the end of the trek.

Moments like this, I call the Dark Night of the Soul...when all seems lost. It happens in every hero's story when the battle seems lost and hopelessness abounds. But it is precisely at that moment that something magically changes and everything turns into overwhelming victory.

So with every team I lead, I explain to them about Tuckman's concept of group formation theory (forming, storming, norming, performing and mourning). Every group is going to face some kind of challenge sooner or later. If you pre-warn the group about the concept of the storming phase, ie: when some massive challenge or low point occurs, it makes things a whole lot easier when the shit hits the fan. I tell the group that we should immediately recognise and indeed welcome the arrival of the Dark Night of the Soul because if we recognise it when it happens, we won't become so unbalanced as when we experience it unconsciously like some kind of crisis coming out of the blue. If a team calmly deals with the Dark Night of the Soul, they become intensely bonded and will go on to shine from that moment. It is the making of a great team, so why should we fear it or panic when it happens? Best to put the kettle on both to celebrate and to think and see the crisis for what it is: our time to shine.

Other examples that come to mind include when three of our soldiers got struck by lightning on one trek, when the entire dinner for ten hungry Gurkhas fell over into the sand during the commander's evening briefing, when a teenage girl on a school camp went over a cliff on a mountain biking exercise and we had to call in a rescue helicopter and drop a paramedic in to rescue her... ironically after all that drama and expense the hospital found her to be perfectly normal and she was immediately returned to the camp uninjured.

On another trek in the remote Australian northwest, my friend was climbing a ridge alongside me and a rolling boulder cut the end of his finger off. "Don't worry, Chaps!" I cried..."it's just another Dark Night of the Soul! He's not going to die, it's only his finger!" So the Gurkhas passed up a first aid kit to me and we bandaged his finger on the precarious hillside. Others made tea and we had lunch whist waiting for a rescue helicopter to take him away. I remember the chopper pilot shouting to us on the radio:

Pilot: "What's that great big white cross you've got on the hilltop?"

Me: "The soldiers have marked your landing zone with rolls of toilet paper..."

Pilot: "Well I'll just hover here while you get rid of it..."

You see back at his base the staff knew he was on a rescue mission and if he returned with his chopper covered in toilet paper they would really think the shit had hit the fan.

If we lose someone we can always talk to them in sacred space.

We processed the Dark Night of the Soul well and within a couple of hours started making our way down the cliffs to the valley below. The soldiers were quite sad and so they painted a face on a nice round rock to symbolise our lost team member and carried it for the rest of the trek. Every night it sat in circle with us by the fireside and was offered a portion of rice and a few sprinkles of whiskey, and always lively conversation.

Sacred paintings of my mature, authentic Masculine, my Feminine in the form of my Anima, and the Divine Marriage bringing the two symbols into balance and wholeness.

1

Romantic Love: Imogen and the Anima

The Animus and the Anima: your Soul and your Inner Guide

So I will start with the curious way that I found the absolute Holy Grail of personal development. I might as well give you this golden key up front so that at whatever moment you spot it, you can immediately harness its energy to put the rocket fuel of transformation into your own life. Carl Jung said that an apprentice studying archetypal psychology really graduated into the Mastery School of self-actualisation and transcendence once the student began to assimilate concepts of Animus and Anima into their life.

Basically the apprentice had stumbled upon a stash of rocket fuel or plutonium... enough to transform the world. Or blow it to pieces. I am a man, and I can only really speak for one typical of my gender. So this is how I discovered my Anima - a special feminine element of the psyche. In a nutshell: this is how I discovered my source of abundant inspiration, my inner guide and probably the greatest energising principal any man could ever wish for. It's what Carl promised and what I now believe in. But, oh my God, it is not a journey for the faint hearted nor will many understand it when it befalls a man or a woman.

The Death Café

Six years ago I came across a curious notice in the local newspaper. It was something like: *"Come to the first meeting of the Death Café where aspects of death will be discussed over biscuits and tea. If you would like to talk about such things join us at the local primary school on Thursday night at 6.30 PM."* Well I have seen so much death in my life that I was like a bee to honey with this one. And on Thursday night I was there early to find out who on earth these creepy people were convening around such a ghoulish topic in the sleepy city of Bunbury Western Australia.

Fearing the worst, I took a dear friend along with me lest anyone try to wrestle us down with chloroform and steal our kidneys during the evening. But, no, it was a delightful gathering and actually they occur innocently all over the world. Our Death Café continued for six weeks before falling on its own sword and dying out completely. It passed away from natural causes because we had basically talked the subject to death.

The most enduring thing I got from the Death Café was a woman called Imogen. She was the most bizarre creature I had ever seen. Beneath a crazy head of hair in colourful, braided dreadlocks and with skin alive with ink still wet from a local tattoo parlour there was this face with eternal eyes. Eyes that made you constantly overbalance and fall into like some eternal sea. But deep within those eyes I could see elements of the giant sort of popcorn machine you find at your local cinema. There was some kind of firework show going on in there amongst reflections of all the psychology books I had ever read.

Because of the energetics of her mind, I am not sure if Imogen ever finished a single sentence that she started. In fact she never has. The listener is forced to finish each of her sentences by interpreting her embodiment of the meaning. Imogen sees life in terms of energy. So ImogenSpeak, the language of ImogenWorld comprises sentences that describe the energy of things plus... if you wait long enough and don't finish her sentence for her... a bodily expression to complete the sentence. And polar opposites abound as she talks. She even calls me by my English name, Mark, which is so foreign to me. So most people just listen in wonder, unable to make head or tail of what Imogen is trying to say.

Well I am a patient man. And so I waited for her in each sentence. And I learned ImogenSpeak. And I learned about ImogenWorld. And from my first meeting I came home and exuberantly told my dear wife Fiona about the Death Café and that I had found my Soulmate.

Soulmate; noun: 'a person ideally suited to another as a close friend or romantic partner'

Now to all you men out there let it be known that this was a fatal error of epic proportions. Never talk to your wife about a Soulmate unless SHE – your wife - is your Soulmate. Pretty soon, that vacant look in your wife's eyes, those probing questions, that fidgeting with the knife and fork and Tabasco sauce turns to a steady reddening of the complexion and then smoke coming from her ears. Such is the nature of blissfully unaware Soulmate talk.

You see, I spent the next six years having coffee with Imogen at a local café overlooking the beach. These were such delightful and enchanted conversations that time became a mystery. But what the hell, I was only having coffee, it's not like I was sleeping with Imogen. As time went on, I came to realise that Soulmates act as inner guides for each other and inevitably will encounter each other's core wounds. Then the role of Soulmate can become by far the very most brutal and painful of experiences a human being can ever endure.

I never realised that the word: "Soulmate" would activate a seething tigress in my poor Fiona's archetypal zoo. And I was bewildered why she would gently tear strips of flesh off me when I returned from such coffee outings and why she would slowly roast me on the rotisserie of guilt and questioning until I realised she absolutely hated Imogen. I just could never understand why.

The trouble is that unbeknownst to me, Imogen, being a single mum, went home and told her children the same thing. She had met her Soulmate at the Death Cafe. Five years later I found out that, of all the men in Imogen's life, I was forever referred to as "Boyfriend Mark".

Imogen's story

Imogen's life story starts off in the crucible of a brutal home, a brutal conception I imagine. And it unfolds into a story of redemption but through ascending stages of total and utter mayhem, disaster and destruction. Like various stages of a nuclear explosion. No wonder she talks in terms of energy. The redemption is that she has not got a mean bone in her body and is so functional and accomplished. We once ran a 21 kilometre half marathon together talking all the way in a howling gale. But we won the happiest runners award for the day. That must say something. People said we were absolutely shining. The funny thing is that of course the people themselves now were shining too. And they would take that shine back home to their families and to their lives. Maybe we lit a small flame in their hearts that day. Maybe we gave them some love and hope and connection that still ripples on somewhere....maybe even out to the stars.

On a good day, the social environment Imogen creates is one of absolute peace and love. To go to her home is to enter a place of beauty, balance and harmony. Despite what the whole family has been through over many turbulent years, the six teenagers and two adults that share Imogen's beautiful home hardly say a bad word to each other. It is just so normal there. Even the cats and Imogen's playful little dog are your friends and delightful together. The home is ornately decorated with Buddhist statues, beautiful lamps and alive with succulents and plants that symbolise Imogen's qualities of being able to endure the thirstiest journeys of the human spirit.

You see, Imogen cared for a severely disabled child called Amy. Amy is not Imogen's child, but Imogen has enough love for the whole world, in fact for the whole universe. And Imogen would sit there day by day showering all her love on this little girl. Day and night her love for this girl appeared unconditional. I would sit there drinking tea with Imogen whilst she held this child in her arms lost in their world of connection. It was obvious that there was something very, very special here. I was drinking tea on holy and sacred ground.

One day ImogenWorld hatched a crazy plan to take the little girl to a floatation tank so that this beautiful child could experience weightlessness for even just a moment in her life. This child was paralysed. Her skeleton was fashioned on a pretzel design and her voice was not capable of human speech. Instead she spoke with sounds that more resembled the chorus of birdsong in the morning. She was 9 years old and she was therefore a heavy and limp weight to carry. And she had an assembly of pipes that entered her abdominal skin so she could be fed by syringes of liquidized food.

In the surreal room of the floatation tank, with temperature control and pinging gongs of meditation music, Tibetan chanting and subdued coloured lighting, somehow Imogen carried this dear child in her arms and lay with her for an hour in the warm water. There she watched the smiles come and go across the child's eternal face. That's beautiful. And Imogen was the one who taught this child to open one eye under water in the local swimming pool whilst keeping her from drowning.

I will never know how Imogen does it. But ImogenWorld is all about simplicity. And her simplicity enables her to do complex things and things most people could never do. I learned that ImogenWorld was immense. And that this scatterling of life was also immensely powerful. I discovered that Imogen's best friend was Imogen and that Imogen had compartmentalised elements and stages of her life into her own masterpiece of ascendancy. I also discovered her dark side, her Shadow and the Kali energy that would occasionally wreck all that she created. I just happened to be a very small part of her journey. It became a journey that cycled through Heaven and Hell so many times I lost count. But it was worth it.

Cupid's romantic love: an arrow that entangles things which are better kept separate

Well one day life got a bit tough for Imogen. Nothing that she couldn't handle but being a typical male I answered her call for coffee thinking I could help fix things. Imogen actually needs no help because in ImogenWorld things just seem to fix themselves. But seeing her vulnerability at that time, I fell like Alice in the Looking Glass down the rabbit's hole and my life would never be the same again. In one moment, and not expecting to do so, I fell in love with Imogen and I think the doorway was when her vulnerability and her authenticity met my immense sense of compassion and empathy.

Now I don't know why, but when the Universe came into existence, the flow of time, the flow of its unfolding and the expansion of consciousness seem to go only in one direction. Excluding black holes maybe, but basically it all keeps moving forwards and expanding. Generally you cannot force the universe to go backwards. And so too, you cannot force consciousness back into a box. If you did, you would create a Jack-in-the Box. Eventually it is all going to explode outwards and probably in an exuberant mess. If you put a lid on a boiling pot, it is all going to boil over. Falling in love is nobody's fault. It can happen in a moment, in a glance across the room. Many things in my life were never ever going to be the same again. And Imogen was going to be forever special in my life regardless of the ebb and flow of romantic feelings. I just had to explain it all to Imogen and also to my Fiona with whom I had spent nearly forty golden years of faithful marriage. And then probably to a host of other interested parties like my children and my dog Scout.

But I knew exactly what it was the moment it happened. I understood the Rocket Fuel of Inspiration that all Romantic Love brings to a man's life because women have been an inspiration to men since recorded history. No one is to blame for falling in love because most of us do this all the time consciously or unconsciously with people, animals and all manner of things. What we then get judged on is what we do with this love once the energy is unleashed upon our world. And herein lays the golden key to becoming the Master of your Mission, and of your Soul's gift to the world of all your inner work and of abundant energy for decisive action. Stick with me and it will get clearer as I tell you how events unfolded.

In the treatise of Romantic Love by the eminent Jungian Psychologist Robert Johnson, the wonderful youth Tristan is faithfully delivering

Princess Isolde to his Uncle the King...a good and wise King worthy to marry such a delightful girl. A love potion is slipped into their evening dinner and drinks whilst sailing across the ocean to the good king. And Tristan and Isolde fall helplessly in love. And, trust me, it is an epic and tragic whirlwind of forces and drama, of passion, betrayals and death. This is how Romantic Love can overcome us mere mortals and unleash power that we are mostly incapable of dealing with.

When people win the state lottery, they inherit money they have no idea how to deal with. The money that they have lusted and longed for all their lives burns them to a crisp in two years. Such a couple is left divorced, destitute, worse off than before they won the millions. The power of so much money needs to be dealt with in a more sacred way lest it dissolve people completely. So too with romantic love and it's neurotic and psychotic nature.

The God of Divorce

All around you, in this rapidly changing world you will see unstoppable and often destructive or disruptive forces moving through society. The 'God of Divorce" is the name I gave to the disruptive forces that assail relationships these days and cause such a high failure rate. He is clever and he is very, very powerful. He tried to destroy my marriage but we somehow managed to appease this God by expending a megaton of energy swimming the other way from perfect storms or sacrificing cuttlefish shells to the ocean in ritual appeasement. It is said that an unresolved paradox is the cause of all neuroses. Think about that one for a while, it's worth remembering. This is why a love triangle is so neurotically destructive and it would seem that the simplest way to resolve a three way paradox is for one of the players to leave.

If only it were so easy for one of us three to leave. I am a compulsive rescuer who never leaves anyone behind and so pledged my life and soul into getting the three of us through this intact somehow. Remember the metaphor: I was one of the many who tried to save the whales relentlessly beaching at Hamelin Bay. And I was groomed by my mother's bedtime stories as a child to be the knight in shining armour who rescued the princess entombed in her castle. All around you, you will see the relationships of couples erupt into an epic series of dramas and betrayals because romantic love has been unleashed either within the relationship or without. The ensuing expenditure of energy is beyond anyone's wildest imaginings and way beyond most people's endurance. However, the sooner you return to normality and peace, the sooner your learning stops. The pain of inner growth grinds to a tattered and dilapidated halt in a cloud of smoke…gun smoke mostly.

The conflict spirals and the affair spirals, the Secret Squirrel texts at night and secret meetings and bizarre synchronicities, the passion, the fire in the eyes, the comparing and contrasting of narcissistic lists of values and preferences as people encounter authenticity for the first time. And then they encounter the throwing of furniture, the "FUCK YOU!"-s and the flying cutlery. The dramas swing between extremes. Just one misplaced bit of punctuation in a well-meaning text can cause disharmonies to erupt into brutal confrontations. And Heaven help anyone if such a text is inadvertently sent to the wrong person. Then it's a grab for the material assets, half a house, half a DVD collection and who gets to keep the dog and the goldfish. Ask the dog or the goldfish and they want neither of these two maniacs. Instead they watch the **war of control** and drama and plates and cups fly between the kitchen and the lounge room like watching a Wimbledon tennis final.

Fortunately, I had already studied a lot about romantic love. I knew what to do with it. Most people seem to have no idea. Not surprising, because it is an overwhelming energy anyway and has to run its course regardless. The thing is, you see...*conscious* people know how to set a course for the Bowling Ball of Romantic Love to roll down and hit the right skittles. *Unconscious* people end up getting run down and squished by the massive, rampant bowling ball that can wreck a whole city, indeed an entire kingdom. There are countless thousands of love stories to this effect.

Fiona. At the age of 2 she lost her own mother to breast cancer. Her mum had been a child health nurse. Fiona became a paediatric and child health nurse and lactation consultant working in the hospitals and with the Aboriginal medical services. Her greatest need for a mother had become her greatest gift to the world.

A Comb for the Tangles

I have been happily married for over forty years. But once in my life I fell in love with another woman and spent two years and more trying to untangle all the elements that got tangled up in the process. It cost me all my energy, and it broke my mind maybe four or five times. But I did it with my marriage stronger than before and the woman as a dear friend.

We tangle things constantly in life... things that should never be tangled. Once things get tangled, a paradox is set up and it has been said that a paradox unresolved is the cause of every neurosis. For example, a love triangle is a very severe paradox and filled with neurotic behaviour. It is usually resolved by one of the three leaving the triangle. The cost emotionally, physically and financially is beyond enormous. Don Miguel Ruiz in his book 'The Mastery of Love' said that we pay a high price for our social encounters of love and of sex. But we are willing to pay the price because the mind can become so needy. He explains that the mind creates all these needs and forces them upon the body because it thinks it is the body. The mind itself actually has no needs at all besides love because the mind is not even a real tangible thing. The body's needs are very simple yet the mind is so insensitive to the body, to its dearest friend. And the essence of who you really are is not the mind and not the body but the Life that passes through you, the force which the whole universe is infused with and is made of. So don't mix up these three elements – the mind and its stories will deceive you *every time whilst you repress, deny and mistreat the simple needs of your unconditional friend, the body.*

Robert Johnson spoke of tangled things when he said that as a therapist he would first have to determine what was tangled and then help to untangle the mess. Everything has its proper place. And if the entangled elements have too much emotional charge, or if they cannot be undone in this world, they can be dealt with using ritual, ritual theatre or by putting the elements into a sacred space symbolically for safe keeping by the gods. You can always symbolically burn things in a fire, talk to a tree or throw an object infused with meaning into the deepest ocean. This is why I have an altar by my bed where I can commune with my ancestors and my gods. And there are many things there on my altar that I cannot resolve in this world...my mother's ashes, my grandfather's war medals, my romantic love.

In discussing tangles, specifically men creating tangles with the various types of women they will meet in a lifetime, Robert Johnson asks us to imagine the chaos when a man (and conversely for a woman) tangles some of the following elements: when a man confuses his daughter with his wife and is too intimate with her or confides in her to an inappropriate level when he should be sorting out these issues with his actual wife. Or if he confuses his wife or partner with his mother and seeks to be mothered instead of establishing a mature relationship with this woman. Some men confuse their partner with a slave. Some men believe their daughter is their Soulmate. Some people confuse women with Sophia, the Goddess of Wisdom and believe everything a woman says. Some men confuse all women with Aphrodite, as sex goddesses and cannot see their humanity and the complex nature of women.

TRANSFORMATION AND THE GOLDEN KEYS

> *Once you look for tangles, you will find them everywhere, in the Animus/Anima fights of intimate relationships, in the Oedipus Complex of sons needing to rescue their mothers, in the ego-inflated narcissists that believe they really are God and the centre of the universe. Drug addicts defend their drugs and their addictions as if defending a lover.*
>
> *We all need some kind of Golden Comb to separate the tangles and put them in their proper place. This is why setting up the paradox visually using ordinary things like the salt and pepper shakers on the kitchen table, or creating it out in a forest using sticks and leaves and rocks can be so insightful. One need only ask the question of the paradox: "So...what needs to change here?..." and the resolution comes in a flash, in a mini epiphany, a flash of insight that by rearranging the salt and pepper shakers or the sticks and rocks, profound changes unfold in the real world because we answer the question ourselves and find our very own solution to the paradox.*

We all come from the crossing of two ancestral lines

But let me rewind a bit to describe the intersection of two ancient ancestral lines from whence my siblings and I fortuitously entered this miracle of life. I have put photos of my mother's side and my father's side on the wall above my altar so that as I kneel there praying for forgiveness, deliverance or a good asse-kicking, I can look up and know on whose shoulder's I stand and that I am never alone.

You see, Dad was born in Smyrna, Turkey, the son of a British ambassador. He was also the official playmate of Prince Faisal of Iraq when Dad's family moved to Baghdad. Prince Faisal chose him from an official line up of all the foreign diplomatic corps children. So a royal limousine picked Dad up each day and took him to the royal palace where he and Prince Faisal would spend the day zooming down the corridor in any number of the Prince's vast collection of pedal cars. Dad was a complete rebel, but basically he was upper class in the colonial 1950's. Riding a 1000cc Vincent Black Shadow motorbike in his tight T-shirt and bulging muscles, he met Mum at architectural school in London. She had been awarded a scholarship to further her studies as she was a gifted child whilst in the Polish refugee camp in Devon. The day Dad walked into her classroom, she fell instantly in love with him. Five years later after watching the endless succession of his four children being born from this lowly Polish refugee, and his beloved motorbike transform into a family car, he chose a path of freedom, adventure and infidelity and about four years later fled to Zambia 8 degrees south of the equator in the middle of Africa.

Some years ago whilst sitting in the room in which I was born in South London I read their heartfelt letters of reconciliation. I read of how Mum left us in the care of some young ladies as babysitters and flew to Africa to see if she and Dad could try again. In Dad's photographs of her visit she looks like Audrey Hepburn in her white dress, elbow-length gloves and a beautiful hat tilted to one side. Mum was so very beautiful. Dad didn't know it, but he was capturing images of his Anima, his source of inspiration. Her hair reached all the way down to her ankles. She had the face of Nefertiti. But her poor spine was the shape of an anaconda, an s-shaped railroad track of pain and suffering and inevitable lung collapse and heart failure. Such is the nature of scoliosis and malnutrition as a child prisoner in the logging camps of Siberia's brutal Taiga forest. She grew up on cabbage soup that the adults gave to baby Halinka. In those camps, if you didn't work you were not entitled to food. She was so tiny then... maybe two years old. Yes the Russian army invaded one day and destroyed their paradise, their family home, their small farm in eastern Poland. I have a photo of her entire family posing for the camera taken months before the Russians invaded. I always wondered what happened to the little dog in the photo, the one my uncle – the delightful 12 year old boy - is holding. You can't take little dogs with you when you are being herded at gun point onto the cattle wagons of steam trains heading thousands of kilometres into the vast, cold unknown.

Dad grew up in Turkey, Egypt, Libya and Iraq. He went to boarding school in England and as a 13-year old never lost a swimming race in his entire school career. What I mean is that he used to race against the 18-year old boys when he was 13 and never lost a race. He was brilliant at all sports. He simply had to win. When you grow up amongst the Arab street kids you either win or you die. It's simple. He used to beat us in every point on the squash court. He was merciless. We hated playing him in any kind of sport. Like if he hit a softball with a baseball bat, you never found the ball again. After an hour of searching the African bush alive with snakes we would all just go home.

So from the age of six, I grew up in Zambia after Mum and Dad got reunited. One minute I was standing in my grandmother's kitchen chewing on a pickled gherkin surrounded by Polish family and listening to the endless Polish drama of displacement. The next minute the whole lot of them including the kitchen and the gherkin had disappeared and I found myself displaced, in Zambia, and surrounded by Africans, monkeys and snakes and wondering how does a six year old mind process such things?

My first pirate ship

When I was a teenager, our little town of Ndola situated close to the Zaire border decided to host a crazy regatta at our local dam. I spent a week building a fantastic pirate ship for the event out of huge inner tubes from the tyres of an earthmoving vehicle and lashed them together with lengths of bamboo to create the deck. It was brilliant. The sail had a huge painted face of a pirate and could be rolled up and down. It had a type of catapult for hurling massive sponges at other boats, a gangplank at the front, and a wonderfully loud brass siren powered by a hand crank. The crow's nest was manned by a sizeable Pink Panther doll sporting a kamikaze bandana.

But as I worked in the garden on the pirate ship one afternoon, Dad called me over and said, "Listen, Lem. We are going to win this thing. I want you to help me build the fastest boat ever in the history of mankind." And in no more than 45 minutes we had built it. We split lengths of bamboo to create two hulls, like two small canoes. With a few more bits of bamboo we turned them into a catamaran. And with waxed canvas cloth and a staple gun we had them clothed in waterproof canvas in the blink of a dragonfly. Two bamboo paddles appeared after a few clicks of Dad's magical staple gun and we were ready to rumble.

That weekend the pirate ship which I had built set sail with a drunken array of the happiest pirates in the world, namely my two brothers and all our friends and a crate of beer. As usual, I was not with the fun group: I had been waylaid by an adult again, namely my Dad. We sat one in each hull, paddle in hand ready under the Starter's Orders. Next to us chaos reigned supreme. Amidst cheers, the pirate ship sent a relentless torrent of soaking wet sponges - steeped in Bilharzia parasites and beer - onto the surrounding flotilla of boats and rafts. Whilst they traded insults and various projectiles, Dad and I left all this noise, fun and confusion behind and finished the lap around the dam so fast that many boats had barely left the starting line. And why would they... it was where all the fun was happening!

The Pirates.

I stood on the shore that day, dry, lonely and miserable whilst Dad punched the air, skipping around with glee at yet another win-or-die victory over those Arab street kids of his childhood. But I was a lovely child. And my smile was just a smokescreen for the pain of loneliness in my heart that day, the longing to be with the fun group, as this kind of separation insidiously crept into my world. Adolescence can be such a lonely and self-conscious time creating a persona that can then spend a lifetime masquerading in looking socially functional.

Oh loneliness and longing.... these giant companions that walk beside me and seem to vibrate with every step I take. I feel them like the wings of a giant butterfly that sits upon my heart. When I subsequently matured into an intensely lonely 18-year old in Zambia, I was employed to run movie films on the Rio Carnival at a Brazilian exhibition in an international trade fair for a whole week. I became possessed by fifty spirits of the Samba. And when people come to my house, they will inevitably hear the beautiful tension and release of Brazilian Samba in the background. They think it is coming from a boom box or a radio or my phone. It is actually coming from my heart.

My personal symbol of Romantic Love: my magical Butterfly of Longing and Romantic Love

If you could crawl up to the edge of my heart and peep over its massive cliffs, you would come to see a golden wonderland of Samba and Carnival. The splendour and pageantry, the music that never stops. I have percussion that Carlos Santana would wish he could play his electric guitar to for just one moment. He'll have to wait a bit because I am still intoxicated by my never ending samba. The whole place sways with each heartbeat of love and romantic abandonment. The women are the goddesses of the Rio street carnival and the men are bronze warriors of the deepest darkest wildest amazon forests. And they sway and dance and reach out to the world. This heavenly place is the home of a Queen. She looks like a Rio Carnival Samba Queen but is best imagined as a sexy super hero with golden angel's wings. She has become transformed into a goddess by my eternally fickle butterfly of Romantic Love.

Energised by the music of his people, the fickle butterfly would fly from my heart each day many times and whatever he landed on would become golden and magic. Instantly bonded to such things, I was actually totally out of relationship with whatever the real thing was under the golden illusion of Romantic Love. But it was beautiful and totally intoxicating. The butterfly could land on anything and it would glow. My heart would swell with love and passion, ready to risk life and death for whatever the butterfly happened to sit on. It could be a human, a car, a poem, a book, a tropical island, a song, a superstar, a bee drowning in a pond. The Butterfly, deep feelings of loneliness and longing, reaches out from me constantly bathed in a romantic melancholy searching for connection.

Capturing my Butterfly: an encounter with my Anima, my Inner Guide and my Soul

So when it landed on Imogen of course she glowed and in a cloud of Pixie Dust turned into something like a fairy queen goddess. Now when the Titanic was sunk by the iceberg, people in the water had two choices: either to grab something that floats or to grab another human... and other humans do not float. So I grabbed the butterfly and swam immediately back to my house to paint a picture of what the fairy queen goddess looked like. Imogen was left blinking and floating in the water.

You see, Imogen had no concept of Romantic Love. All the men in her life had helped her create a concept of love that resembled a badly tossed salad. Her salad of love contained handfuls of drama, violence, control issues, drugs, abandonment, destruction and all drizzled in mayhem. She had processed a lot of these issues at the local tattoo parlour so you could work out some of the scribblings and calculations of her mind just by trying to make sense of the designs on her skin. Like it was some kind of personal jotting pad for journaling and analysis. Now this latest man in her life had just disappeared around the corner clutching a handful of paintbrushes.

Chasing my feelings to create the symbol and the picture of my Anima

On my kitchen table the alchemist set to work to capture THE MOST important and energising principal he could ever wish for in his life. It was the goddess which I glimpsed in Imogen's eyes, my Samba Queen, and I had only one chance to capture an image of it. And I knew that if I could paint this picture, the Butterfly of Longing would return to my heart and he could rest there. All the sweet nectar he had ever drunk on his million romantic flights of fancy would become the sweetest lifeblood for my own thirsty world. You see, for a man, the feminine element, the goddess I glimpsed as a reflection, what Carl Jung called the Anima, becomes an overwhelming source of inspiration and insight. She really is rocket fuel in a man's life. She becomes the inner guide to a vast inner world and to riches beyond our comprehension.

If you look up into the night sky and could comprehend the immensity of all that is, well that immensity is also within. And it is easier to feel this 'within' as deeply personal and everything out there as separate from self. But indigenous people knew to take their youths to nature to make the outer world deeply personal too. Then the relationships, inner and outer, are set up as a complete matrix. It is only a tiny fraction of the internal archetypal world that awakes from the inner world of dreams and then gets out of bed to make sense of the outer world, of another day. And we call that tiny thing 'me'…my Ego. By contrast, my Anima, the goddess I had glimpsed as a reflection in another through the medium of Romantic Love, would help me navigate and understand my inner world and would relentlessly and powerfully bring my Life's Mission to manifest in the outer world.

Untangling what is best left untangled

Now I want to thank all of you women out there for being the golden mirrors into which we can search to find the reflection of this Holy Grail along the path of ascendancy and transcendence in the lives of men. If I could paint the picture, it might give me my only chance to let Imogen be Imogen without the burden of my Anima projected on her. Then my

Butterfly of Longing and Romantic Love could stop its restless search because it had found what it had searched the world for. I would be free of the entanglements of a romantic illusion and could relate to Imogen as a human being again.

The magic Butterfly lands on anything and shouts "Lights, cameras, action!" and with a trembling of his wings we get so hypnotised by Romantic Love that an ordinary walk in the street becomes like a psychedelic trip in Las Vegas. At the end of the day, a real human is ALWAYS going to trump an illusion even though we might not like it when it happens. Reality is more magnificent than the images your computer is projecting out to you. Behind each image is a complex computer and a cast and support crew, millions of dollars and shipping containers of equipment – real things -that go up to make the illusion. And maybe the most empowering way to exist within a world of illusion and underlying reality is to reconcile the paradox and see them both and enjoy them both - seeing through the illusion to the reality underneath – knowing that a sacred illusion is at play.

Traditional arranged marriages versus the romantic love marriages of the western world

I know a lot about the Nepalese. In fact, I speak their language and sing their songs. In their traditional culture, marriages are arranged between families long before the two partners get to meet or even get to know the other exists. It is a pity that this is judged so harshly by the western world. I can see that it is simply brilliant when done properly. So many issues are resolved offline and before the partners meet to create the allegiances of family so vital to survival in a marginal world.

An uncle will take the young man on a journey to the prospective bride's house. She will often be unaware that this young man is about to propose to her as she busily sets about making tea and serving food. If things are looking good, they will subsequently be given 30 minutes together alone to talk and discuss this ambush of impending marriage. And either partner has the right of refusal. But to say no is to refuse the proper flow of thousands of years of culture, of the flow of their songs and stories and religions, and to go against the wisdoms of all involved who set this potential union of individuals and families, of destiny, in motion. She may sob her way through the wedding but soon an ancient peace within the relationship will appear and the flame of romance will slowly be kindled within the traditions and cultural rightness of it all.

Love in the Western world

In the western world our gods simply pull out the safety pin of an overwhelmingly powerful bomb of romantic love and drop it onto two people and then watch the drama and collateral damage unfold. But there is always a better way, one of the many Golden Key's in this book. I believe that the secret to an enduring, vibrant, passionate and real relationship is to learn to love twice. If Romantic Love comes first, learn to see through the illusion to see the real person beneath, to love that one too as a real, vulnerable and often faulted human being. A real human is actually godly enough.

We are created from an idea the universe had 15 billion years ago at the biggest conception event ever… and called quite appropriately 'the Big Bang'. Everything is made of vibrations in this cosmic tapestry, energy fluctuations in the multi-layered fields that are the very fabrics of all that is. But there was consciousness in the first vibration if you believe in a conscious universe. With this concept, consciousness is encoded in every atom, every subatomic particle, possibly as just another field pervading everything and everywhere. It's all around you and inside you right now. And it is in your loved one too creating a one-ness of everything because we are all cut from the same cloth, the fabric of the universe. We are just the stardust of that first light, that first vibration in a field - or all fields - that made the first atoms, then the first stars and then made the minerals, the planets and you.

Two lovers can build a foundation for relationship based on an authentic Reality Love that is different to Romantic Love. In the Nepalese culture, they first experience the love and relationship of real people, and then get that chance to love again and elements of romantic love appear in time. I call this learning to love twice, but it means leaving the intoxicating chemistry of oxytocin, serotonin, endorphins, dopamine and noradrenalin to second place on the podium.

Usually, in the western world, Romantic Love happens first ie: without a bit of good governance, logic and a reality check. Those involved have fallen down a godly rabbit hole that leads to both Heaven and Hell because they are off their faces on the rollercoaster of emotional hormonal chemistry: the chemistry of Romantic Love. And there are psychological consequences of projecting a divine image on another... onto a mere mortal and putting them onto a pedestal. It is bound to end in tears, or serious challenges, or massive personal growth. If done well it could be the most wonderful delusion that could last a lifetime. But it is done quite badly in the western world and often results in broken cutlery, traumatised offspring and giving your hard-earned assets to very wealthy divorce lawyers.

Visualising my Masculine and my Feminine Archetypal elements

So what did I paint? Well it absolutely complements the painting I made of my fully masculine element, my bronzed warrior in a forest. I painted him after undergoing male initiation into relationship with my innate masculine energy at the Mankind Project. But my beautiful Anima appears in her painting with such serenity, an irresistible woman with braided black hair and a white/red headband, a garland of flowers. She is wearing an elegant and softly flowing deep blue dress and has huge golden and delicate wings as she quietly looks down gathering a bouquet of flowers from an abundant and dappled meadow.

Oh, how my heart broke with wonder and awe as I gazed upon her whilst cleaning the paint from my trembling hands. Meanwhile, outside the eastern window of my kitchen, the most bewitched full moon began to rise. She spread her blue cloth of light amongst the stars and called upon the gods to give her the hand grenade so she could drop it with maximum chaos upon my kitchen table. My dog Scout watched - bewildered - as first the firing pin landed with a thump in the garden.

Fortunately I have always fancied myself as a reincarnation of Bruce Lee and I caught that hand grenade in slow motion just before it hit the kitchen table. It exploded anyway... I mean, who was I to think I could cheat the Moon? But it was nothing that 3 days of scrubbing, cleaning and vacuuming my mind couldn't fix. Or so I thought.

Well actually I knew that this would all be like an atomic bomb of energy released into the lives of Fiona, Imogen and I. But I remembered the words of Robert Johnson that the first job of a psychotherapist is to find out what has become tangled in a person's life... things that should never have become entangled in the first place.

When lovers fight

I knew what the tangles were and I knew I had to disentangle them as fast as I could. Little did I know it would take more than two drama filled years for all three of us to work it out and separate all the issues and energies. We went mental... everything from mini-vapashnas to a 4000 km road trip where Fiona and I nearly lost the car bogged to its axles in the quicksand of a tidal mud flat in the middle of nowhere. Many Dark Nights of the Soul including my 800 km solo road trip through the early hours of the night, a trip to nowhere, a trip to Death, to the loss of my mind all over some simple misunderstanding.

Just another Dark Night of the Soul when the Calypso-Dawn Treader got totally bogged in a tidal flat up north and we nearly lost the car to the incoming king tide. Any problem we now face is referred to as, '...just another bogged Isuzu D Max..' because we know we will always get through somehow.

In Jungian psychology, these fights are all Animus/Anima confrontations of the disowned and unconscious masculine and feminine elements within. Forgive the sexist tone here but by way of illustration, in a conflict spiral, if a woman comes at me with nit-picking masculine logic, I will respond with my bitchy and irrational feminine. She will witness my ugly feminine and I will witness her ugly masculine. She has grown balls she has no idea how to control and I have totally lost my logical mind for one that is irrational, illogical and ultimately hysterical.

But the fights can be wonderful too when we can see that it is simply Shadow dancing right there before our eyes wanting to be understood. It is a rare couple that can hold the space for each other while over the years the woman steps into her power and the man explores his feminine. My advice to you is that when you fight, explore your contra-gender element that inevitably steps in to do much of the fighting. Where is that projected element failing you in your partner? As the smoke clears and you get to reflect on what happened, give each other a huge big hug. The initial issue is rarely important. The resulting conflict spiral is just your own pent up Shadow energy.

Robert Johnson describes this well in the myth about the beautiful maiden Psyche, her newfound squeeze and romantic crush Cupid and her nemesis Aphrodite. Hysteria beset Psyche's every task in this story. She would first fall apart overwhelmed by a conundrum set for her by Aphrodite. Then magically she would get her shit together and resolve each paradox when helpers from the masculine provided the resolution.

What a sweet and wonderful story is this journey of Psyche, a damsel in distress, and our masculine nature that always wants to fix things. Men especially want to fix women. But women would much rather simply fix their feelings using a man's or a woman's ears as the tools. I asked Fiona once how does a woman fix another woman with a problem. She said, "We don't. We just sit and listen…and then after a while we ask insightful questions."

I have to squint to see the twenty four intense months. In fact, I wince. It feels like twenty four years. They are thick with the smoke of sage smudge sticks, incense and alcohol. Tears regularly soaked Scout and the carpet. And I remember cleaning up a vomit trail of red wine that started in the kitchen, continued via the bedroom and into the lounge. And the perils and time wasting of texting soon became apparent. All the love, all the hate, all the thousands of texts – oh my god...a nuclear bomb has got nothing on this.

Learning to hold a woman in her emotions

All three of us got through, because I refused to let go. Like Ernest Shackleton, I wasn't going to leave anyone behind. In retrospect this is a miracle. And the heartfelt and authentic conversations along the way were just pure gold. Watching Fiona ascend into her strength and self-love was the most privileged experience of my life. But to do this she had to grow past me and to transcend me. Whereas for me it involved holding a woman in her intense emotions. Basically it's like holding the Sun and getting totally roasted. I asked her for a set of oven gloves if I ever had to do it again. And I had to hold her so many times that I almost became immune to the smell of my burning flesh and my clothes on fire. I had to learn what it means to hold a woman in her emotions and not try to fix her. A woman will fix herself if we let her be heard and if we can stand before the tempest and the fury and the tears and not run away or throw it all in her face. Some would say that it is impossible to make a woman happy – she will do it herself – but we can create the safe social environment of understanding and love and listening that she needs to achieve this.

If you want to get skills in surviving a battle zone, go to the Middle East and you'll come back an expert. So it is with relationship... stick it out with endless heartfelt discussions, and you may just come out with what we did: beautiful and brutal honesty, a lack of Ego taking offence at anything that is said, a love and respect for each other's journeys, and a huge dustbin for story, principally the story of our inner Judges and Victims. Now we listen to story, and then as necessary dump it in the bin where it belongs and dust our hands off ready to talk about positive and useful stuff like how we plan to live another day in this miracle we call Life. Above all, we discovered a little bit more of our wholeness.

Emotions, feelings and moods

Emotions are like chemical and neurological fireworks of varying intensity. They happen in response to a perception when neurotransmitters like adrenaline, oxytocin, dopamine, endorphins, serotonin, and a host of others get dumped in the system. But they happen in a moment, in milliseconds, and in general they push the body's nervous system either towards stress...the autonomic nervous system of Fight and Flight...or to being chilled with more parasympathetic tone.

An **emotion** often has not just the emotional component, but a physical one as well like breaking out into a cold sweat with hair standing up on the back of the neck, or a change in body posture, a change in breathing or facial expression. Once we add story to the emotion, once we start all the mental chatter and analysis, we get a **feeling**. All of the body senses will alter as the emotion becomes experienced as a feeling. If the feeling stays for a while, a **mood** may manifest. Moods are long lasting mental, emotional and physical states and whether positive or negative will cause a shift in connection one way or the other. Mostly they disconnect. And often the initial cause becomes lost in an ocean of mood while the mind sets sail in an ocean of story. There is a whole spectrum of mood – from elation and mania to depression, anger and fear.

Up until the age of thirty and beyond, I drowned in all of this stuff. I still drown in emotions, feelings and moods but I developed a sense of humour and some coping skills to get me through and keep me functional... a sort of functional emotional train wreck much of the time. But I learned about emotional energy, how it flows in different emotional channels. And I learned how to create a switch to divert emotional energy into the good channels, the happy channels and to divert it into useful action. So I am not so ruled by my emotions anymore. Instead I harness their energy, using them as an Ally. And I don't take their associated messages so seriously because I know I have the power to change their story and thus change the feeling to a more desirable one.

Seeing your contra-gender element in another

I could never understand why I kept defending Imogen through all this drama of the highest order. Why are we still great friends to this day? Well Fiona gave me the most beautiful completion to this puzzle. She said that if I were a woman, I would be exactly like Imogen. My disowned feminine elements were so similar to this Imogen that I had glimpsed myself in her. Not just my feminine aspects, but my inner spirit guide, my Anima, my Soul. She had been my mirror. I could let go of the goddess Imogen now. The projection of Romantic Love was in its proper place and things were far less entangled.

But Imogen does cool things. And she's my friend. So I still have tea with Imogen and we laugh about the drama and we wonder at the immensity of Life and our friendship together. And if I ask Fiona if my feminine side looks as wild and crazy like Imogen, she says: "Oh yes. More than you will ever know." And truth be told, Imogen had already told me many times before that her masculine element looked exactly like me -was me – because she had not yet withdrawn the projection. I just didn't understand.

And I wonder if she may still need to extract her symbols and images to let me be a mere mortal again.

Ritual Theatre and ways to process Life's issues using metaphor

I love sacred processes and Ritual Theatre. It's where you set up some sacred process - say using people or leaves and sticks in a forest, cuttlefish and seaweed at the beach or salt, pepper shakers and the Tabasco Sauce in a restaurant. You can arrange them so that they represent a situation or are symbolic of something and then run the ritual or process eg: throwing your wedding ring into the ocean whilst shouting at God, or seeing what needs to change when an overbearing Tabasco sauce bottle (Bad Dad) keeps yelling at the salt shaker and three sugar bags (Little Jimmy and his three younger siblings). I use it in all the Rites of Passage facilitation work I do.

So the next day I took my dog and paintings of the Warrior and the Anima with me on a forest walk to process these issues of the heart in a symbolic and sacred way. My dog Scout is a white Retriever. Scout is no stranger to his Master's shamanic world. At the last Equinox he watched patiently while Fiona and I practiced balancing sticks on an outstretched palm whilst standing next to an arrangement of our sacred objects on a hillside in the forest with lovely music playing through a boom box. A young family stumbled upon us and fled immediately down the hill in mortal fear. Scout understood. But the subsequent three months were the ones where keeping our personal balance became absolutely vital to our survival and we had the symbolic imagery to relate back to. It was like opening a portal, setting a theme, a portent of things to come. Each Solstice and Equinox we set a different theme and celebrate it on the day with its own unique ritual. From there the theme and the magic unfold.

Creating an impromptu process for insight

It wasn't hard to interpret the symbolism because I do transformational work all the time. Symbol is everywhere. And within the liminal world of treks and Rites of Passage programs, symbols become more apparent and take on more meaning, just like the nature cards do that Fiona and I use in our Candle Ceremony every morning. We were taught the Candle Ceremony years before on a couples retreat led by John and Rhonda Gaughan and it has endured and evolved into our unique time for connection each morning especially when we added nature cards – pictures of aspects of nature – to choose at random from a pack and reflect into each day rather like a Rorschach inkblot test.

I found a suitable clearing in the forest, a junction of three paths and put the two pictures of Animus and Anima together on the ground. Scout sighed and lay down to see what would happen. Actually it was quite bizarre because in a complete circle around this spot lay the tattered feathers of a forest dove that had been recently dismembered by a passing raptor. So it felt like a place of sacrifice rather than one of synthesis. Maybe it was a place of dissecting the elements so that a phoenix could arise.

Anyway, gazing upon the images I could see the completeness of male and female elements making a gateway and within the gateway was a place of Transformation. A lifetime's journey seeking wholeness was going to involve reconciling opposites symbolised here in the form of male and female elements of the psyche in a crucible of transformation.

Male and female union makes children. Children are droplets of the universe, treasures like gemstones. This place of Transformation, of archetypal alchemy advanced the consciousness of the universe one click at a time just like when more conscious elements - ie: children - are born into this world to grow and experience Life in order to become islands and aggregations of consciousness.

I knew without a shadow of a doubt that I had entered a portal of transformation. Nothing would ever be the same. All I had to do was stay conscious and experience a process, a journey as it relentlessly unfolded so as to change myself, my beliefs, renew all of me and hopefully learn a few things along the way. I was a leaf swept up in this surging River of Life.

Bush Art and Sacred Processing

> *I was out camping with a few families and we set off on a short walk across the forest to find a campsite for the night. The boys in the group were in total disarray with their backpacks haemorrhaging sleeping bags, sweet wrappers and clothing all along the trail. At the back walked an autistic boy who was obviously struggling because he had way too much stuff, his shoelaces were undone and his socks didn't match. But this young man gave the group a most profound moment of pure magic the next day.*
>
> *It happened during a process we call Bush Art. In a clearing in the forest I settled the group of children and asked them to go quietly, find a spot and start to assemble sticks and stones, flowers and grass litter into some kind of bush art, something that represented their current situation or their family or whatever came to them at the time.*
>
> *In this way they would access their natural genius: that part of us that can manifest things in this real world that otherwise simply would not be. Creation is something we all do but many people*

ascribe it only to the gods. And I must agree it is a very godly thing to be able to create. We get a 100% success rate with children and adults in this activity. At the end they proudly explain to the group in turn what their creation represents. And I always ask them gently if there is anything about their creation they might wish to change because asking this question sometimes gives the artist a profound insight. It is a very moving and sacred process of deep psychology, this Bush Art, so the group has to give each speaker utmost respect as they describe their creation in turn. Basically, the ending has to be facilitated well because sharing is a vulnerable moment.

So the autistic boy created a perfect chicken out of a piece of paper and stood it amongst a collection of tiny pebbles. Next to it he had created a perfect frog out of paper sitting on a lily pad and with a fly at the end of an extendable tongue. He explained that the chicken was a very loveable creature but the chicken's life was easy because everyone took care of the chicken and gave it the little pebbles to eat each day. And the frog was also a loveable creature but it had to be cleverer than the chicken because it had to hunt for its food and catch flies. The boy was the chicken because everyone helped him get through each day, but he wanted to be more like the frog and stand on his own two feet becoming more self-reliant. So I said to the boy that the chicken might always be a part of him and was there anything he would like to change about this dynamic. He unfolded the frog and placed it over the chicken and said that in becoming more self-reliant he would care for the chicken, for his less functional but loveable part.

And I once had a boy who was addicted to gambling and didn't want to partake in the Bush Art activity because he couldn't connect with the process. That was until I reached into my backpack and handed him a pack of cards. And using these cards he created a wonderfully cryptic picture of relationships between his classmates at school which kept us enthralled, and all the boys guessing at who was the Queen of Hearts and who was the King of Spades.

We can use sacred practices, ritual art and ritual theatre like this to process so many of life's issues. It works especially well for those situations where we cannot deal with actual people or events because they have passed away or the situation happened long ago or in some distant location. That's why people set up shrines so they can go there and talk to those who have passed away, or set up plaques to commemorate historic events so they can commune with the history. Robert Johnson advised that if we interpret a profound dream, have a profound insight or a profound inner experience it is best to go to the forest and in some symbolic or ritualistic way re-create and revisit it there using such mean so as to make it real in this world and release its energy to us.

This practice has totally transformed my life especially because I choose to believe that nature is alive. It has released immense energy back into my world. One day, when my wife and I were under immense pressure in our relationship, we stood by the ocean and each threw an object into the water – in my case a cuttlefish shell –to appease the God of Divorce so he would give us a break because we loved each other and had had enough of his chaos. And I guess he has a sense of humour because he listened that day.

One of the boys built a stone cairn up to an impossible height balancing stone upon stone until it defied the imagination. It repre-

sented his ancestral lineage and the shoulders on which all these great people had relied in turn as a resource for the next generation. And when I asked him the magic question, he picked up yet another stone and with all of us holding our breath in stunned silence he proceeded to balance this stone on top of this mind-boggling spire. And he said this represented himself as the next in line, the next resource for the generation to come.

Some little Vietnamese girls created a most beautiful funeral shrine for a very dead and crisp but colourful butterfly. Another girl re-created her childhood home – a farm – that she missed dearly because she could not forgive her parent for selling off her version of Heaven. Another girl decorated her friend with ferns and flowers because her friend had been sad that day and needed honouring and cheering up.

My wife and I always choose a theme for each of the four solstices and equinoxes of the year. The theme for one solstice was to be all about transformation. So we built a giant mandala in the sand at the beach working right through the moonlit night with a shovel, string, star pickets and a diagram we printed off the internet. And we walked the mandala in silence as the dawn broke in a haze of incense smoke and gentle music to seek clarity and resolution to whatever we brought into the mandala. For me it was to gain a healthy respect for the God of Alcohol and not to consume it so unconsciously. There followed three months of the most intense transformational changes we could ever imagine until we begged for mercy. But many other people walked that mandala because it stayed in the sand for nearly a month before the ocean and the winds reclaimed it.

The next equinox had a theme of balance. So we stood in the forest at the time of the equinox surrounded by sacred objects, incense and music balancing some walking sticks on the end of our fingers in deep silence and connection to the cosmic phenomenon. There followed three months of total chaos so we had to practice finding our inner balance until the skill was burned onto our very souls. Other themes explored the feminine, the child within, the sacred, health, the taking of action and having great attitude. With such themes, we developed ourselves over the years in a sacred dance with the Sun.

Such is the power of bush art and sacred ritual. And I wake up to it every day because we have our separate altars in the bedroom where we assemble and re-arrange those objects and symbols that are sacred to us. Each altar is alive with meaning, dynamics, emotion, and history. Here is where I have placed my mother's ashes, my grandfather's tiny diary and war medals, my talisman from male initiation and my Egyptian ushabti which is thousands of years old. This is where you will find my vision board, my hopes and dreams.

TRANSFORMATION AND THE GOLDEN KEYS

Bush art. Sacred process and ritual processing. Simply create something from your heart and let it speak.

My advice to those people struck down by Cupid's arrow

So my advice to you is that if you feel romantic love for another, step back or peer more closely and feel or hear or see or instinctively know some reflected golden energy that is your own. Then run... quickly... and build it or paint it or sing it or write the poem or dance it or whatever helps you get at least a tiny hold on the contra-gender element that is either your Animus if you are a woman or Anima if you are a man. Find the symbol that represents it. These things come as a symbol (eg: a beautiful winged woman with an associated butterfly for me) or a word (eg: Solidity or Discernment) or the majestic Eagle of Fiona's Animus. Then keep it somewhere sacred like as a tattoo on your body, a concept in your mind or an object on your altar.

My Butterfly of Longing and Romantic Love will always fly away and land on things, but I am conscious of this now. It was just searching for my Anima and for connection. And now I can play with this dynamic. I wrap his romantic wings around my own heart, wings of self-love. And then I feel a glow from the presence of my Anima and I wrap her wings around me and the Butterfly. And then I wrap myself in Mother Nature's wings... the wings on which I fly when I am facilitating Rites of Passage or trekking in Nature because Nature is alive and her energy flows through me when I am on Mission, trusting the process and facilitating life changing journeys. The pain and longing and drama of Romantic Love ceases and I can get on with loving reality in all of its forms increasingly free of my projections. The longing was simply the cry of a butterfly far from its proper home.

Amy's story

How Amy's earthly journey ended came as quite a shock. I had spent the day bobbing around in the ocean doing a surf rescue course and was heading home when the phone rang. It was Imogen in tears. Amy had died unexpectedly at her mother's house and Imogen had rushed there to find the ambulance officers and people in the house all devastated. And poor Amy, no longer smiling, no longer breathing. She held that lovely child to her heart and wept and wept.

A few days later I went with Imogen to spend some very precious time with Amy at the funeral home. And we both hugged her tight and tucked her blankets around her. Imogen was so accepting and peaceful that day. She said to me: "Amy is gone... she's not here." And because I believe in the One-ness of the Universe so strongly, I said, " Yes, Imogen... because now Amy is everywhere." Her body was melting back to Mother Nature whilst her spirit was melting outwards to merge with the cosmos from whence it came to us nine years before.

How do you deal with the loss of a loved one such as Amy? You deal with it in sacred space. You go to the forest and build things and talk to the trees and the sunset by the beach. You make a shrine at home and decorate it with pictures and flowers. You place some of her precious things on your bedside altar so that you can feel her presence very near. And you can sit by candlelight and talk to her there. These are the sorts of things that Imogen and I did to process what our minds could barely comprehend but which our hearts understood so well.

Imogen cared for another terminally ill girl in the subsequent months after Amy passed away. One day she dropped by my house to tell me to come and help her with washing this dear child. Imogen intuitively knew it was going to be this 9-year old's last day on Mother Earth. So I drove them around to a facility where children with special needs were cared for. Barefoot in the shower room, Imogen and I rolled up our trouser legs and set about washing this little girl with the shower spray as she lay in a sling suspended from a hoist rather like the angel she was soon to become. We washed her little toes, her fingers, we washed her hair, her body which moment by moment was succumbing to pneumonia and congestive heart failure. By the end of it, the little girl was clean and warm and beautiful, smelling of all the scents of fragrant soaps, hair conditioner and body lotion. We put fresh dressings on her sores. And then, as if by magic, all of the ladies who staffed that facility started coming in to the room one by one to love and hold the girl they knew so well whilst one of the ladies platted her hair for the last time. The outpouring of love and the heartfelt goodbyes were an honour to witness. And with that timely job well done, thanks to Imogen's legendary powers of intuition, the child was returned to her home for the evening and passed away peacefully in her sleep that night. Imogen had enacted a Washing Ritual that must have extended back through many cultures for countless thousands of years. "Washing Away the Smell of Death" she called it. And it was washed away with an outpouring of countless gallons of love from all those women. It was an honour to witness more love being poured on this child in one hour than many children receive in a lifetime.

We constantly change roles in Life

So many things shifted in me through all of these experiences. For example, many times in my life there has been a profound and deep shift in my inner masculinity: when I first kissed a girl or when I first made love, when I first held my own children and when I said my wedding vows in the golden glow of a Catholic wedding service. But what shifted with the current drama was the concept of "Husband" which had become weighed down with nearly forty years of baggage. That role was forever changed, or parked permanently in a Sacred Place because in many respects it was holding me and Fiona back and wasn't serving us too well anymore. I didn't want to lose it entirely. I just wanted to make it a whole lot lighter to carry. Even for Fiona, the word "Wife" seemed to make her jump. We had grown so much from our early years together and now related to each other so differently. Or maybe it's just that the world has changed so much from our conservative days in Africa.

People shed roles constantly in Life. A son will eventually defy his father maybe for the first time in late adolescence. Some sons will release pent up energy by tearing bewildered strips off Dad in a powerful tirade. Although painful to witness, this inner eruption of molten lava may help burn away the projections of father and son. Then they can become more real to each other as a son steps beyond the confines of this relationship to establish his own path. If processed well, it can help create a less enmeshed and encumbered life. But a son can also fix it with his Dad more gently, more beautifully, both saying sorry and forgiving each other for the transgressions, or just in honouring each other's gold. And if Dad is no longer around, it can still all be done in sacred space.

Gathering Golden Keys for your toolbox of Life Skills

So I have given you one more golden key to put rocket fuel into your life: that while sneaking through the window for a visit with your Lover, you might glance across her lace-draped room, past the bottles of intoxicating perfume and pheromones to catch a glimpse of yourself in her mirror... the one where she sits each day to paint a captivating illusion of the Divine Feminine with mascara, eyeliner, blusher and sensuous lipstick. Romantic Love can be a gateway to discovering your Anima. Wonder at these things. Wonder at the Sacred Marriage of masculine and feminine elements within you and outside of you. Wonder at Soul Mates and Soul Guides, and Soul Journeys. Wonder at Romantic Love and how you are going to dance a lifetime with elements such as these. I don't wonder alone... as I walk in the forest on one side I hold the hand of my Anima in all her beauty – the winged maiden in my painting. And on the other side

I hold a gentle leash tethered to a contrite butterfly, an exhausted butterfly but he's home now to rest a while.

The Candle Ceremony

A bamboo flute gently calls to me in the darkness. It is my alarm clock calling me back across the peaceful divide between my archetypal dream world and this outer world of a brand new day. I look back to search for my dreams before they melt away into my inner world taking with them their wealth of insight. The wooden flute reminds me of the barrel of self-love I need to immerse myself in before opening my eyes. And in the light of dawn I look from my pillow upon my altar of precious things, my sacred objects and vision boards. There lie my paintings and my Nepalese flute, also made of bamboo, which sings and accompanies the flutes of the magpies in the forest each morning outside my window.

But it is time for the Candle Ceremony. I wake Fiona and, sitting in bed, we light the candle that with a flickering cone of light brings out the sparkles of her eyes and warms our faces reflecting off the steaming cups of coffee.

We talk about our dreams and help each other process their meanings and insights posing open-ended questions and holding sacred space for as long as it takes. Then it is time for a check-in to state how we are feeling that day. There is no interruption from the other because whilst one is speaking, the other is simply listening without judgement and hence without fear. These moments can be beautiful. They can be brutal. It was after one such Candle Ceremony that I stumbled off to my office and wrote:

'Her heart was singing and beating its wings and her eyes sparkled as she spoke of magical times still seemingly within her vibrant hands. And then her eyes lowered and faded in the candlelight. Reality had settled upon her, the living memories lost in sepia tones. Almost in stillness she said "But….oh…that was a long time ago……"'

We then wish each other a special wish for the day in turn and these are just a lovely gift, a time to wish each other the Sun and the Moon, a precious day, to wish each other laughter or a blessing… anything a magic wand could bring because it always brings a smile.

And then we look inside, into the matrix of our minds and describe what is going on in there. For me, I go to my Spanish Galleon and see what the men are up to. Fiona goes to a cottage in the woods and describes the world and activities of her women within. At times they are all in the kitchen baking, or playing in the sunshine on the veranda. Sometimes her strong masculine presence is there reassuring her in the form of her grandfather or her Eagle. And sometimes her cottage is just a smouldering ruin because I have been mean to her or broken her heart.

I looked into my heart one morning and my men were huddled around a fire and all wearing animal skins. "There are wolves about…" whispered one of them. Immediately they all said "Well, let's call them over to join us…" and the Spanish Galleon, the Calypso-Dawn Treader, slowly but steadily became inundated with tame wolves who covered the decks and made their home peacefully there. And in the oceans the sea creatures, and all sea monsters, and all dragons on the land were at peace with the men on the ship because the men understood that all of these things were their friends, were indeed part of themselves, part of my mind and they had nothing to fear. Anything they had previously feared had now become a source of treasure.

And in the Candle Ceremony the next day, I saw a chicken jump on the deck and announce peace to all of my inner world as it wandered off and fell asleep peacefully amongst the wolves. It heralded such a profound peace that I recognised the little chicken as my Anima, my Soul Guide in disguise.

Our candle ceremony.

Lastly in the Candle Ceremony, we shuffle a deck of picture cards that have such lovely photographs of all kinds of aspects of nature. We take one or two and let the cards resonate within. Our minds can then describe the meanings that the cards evoke and their wisdom for the day. It is a skill to let these images activate our inner tuning forks, bring up emotions and schemas for us to spin story and meaning from this ritual.

And then we blow the candle out and head to the forest, or to the beach or to the gym or to the telescope because it is a brand new day. Life beckons. And the magic awaits.

The moment my ego reached out and grabbed this baby crock, I realised I had wronged Mother Nature.

2

Personal Growth and the Hero's Journey

Get involved with real Life. Don't just sit by or get lost in addictions

These insights often happen later in Life because there is a massive river in which a lot of swimming must occur first so that you can understand and survive these Life transitions. And by "you" I actually mean your Ego which you would normally identify as your "self". And the river is the River of Life. A lot of people will be seen sunning themselves on its shaded banks doing very little whilst this vast aqueous miracle flows slowly before them. Some are lazy, some are ignorant, some are too scared and some are recovering from the grazes and bumps of going headfirst over a series of life's rapids - a mini Niagara Falls.

Some are drunk on their addictions sipping yet another bottle of Shiraz while turning their eyes into their heads to praise its bouquet as if speaking in Tongues. We all worship our addictions creating rituals around them, specialised and ornate equipment like hash pipes and Octoberfest beer mugs and of course there develops a unique vocabulary for each addiction. And we defend our addictions as if defending a lover. But Life ticks by relentlessly as we party on mistakenly thinking the party never ends.

Be in this world, play hard, but do it mindfully, with a bit of emotional intelligence, a bit of consciousness....keeping our emotional balance even when we have to do the tough stuff like carving the roast when we unknowingly invited vegans for dinner. This is why I loved the Samurai Game we played in San Francisco when I went there on a week long initiation with the Shift Network to discover my relationship to the feminine.

In the game, two teams of warriors challenge each other. And you play every move as if it is your last moment or your last chance on earth. So you play beautifully, with all your heart and soul and mind, beyond any game you ever played before in total mindful connection with your opponent and with yourself. If you play it ugly, the gods in the game will kill you anyway. I was blessed to play this game to its 4-hour conclusion, but others lay there dead with their eyes closed for 4 hours wishing, and wondering, and listening, and learning: they made mistakes early and lost their balance. Sometimes in life, you only get one chance. So give it your very best, in every moment, in every opportunity... you never know what fortune - good or bad - such things may bring.

Years later, I was dutiful and faithful in helping an adventure company who contacted me out of the blue needing some plastic bags. And this one simple act led to my many years as an adventure guide, trekking with Nepalese soldiers, learning Nepali and taking school groups on Rites of Passage camps. All from one simple act.

Say "Yes" to Life

The best word I ever learned from the Nepalese soldiers is the word "Yes". It happened when a young sergeant was narrowly missed by a falling boulder as we were making our way up a kangaroo track on an impossible slope of shale in the Kimberly ranges. This guy ducked the widow maker and simply smiled and said, "Yes!". It was always his first response to disaster- whether he was standing on a Death Adder or removing a fish hook from his friend's arm – to say the word "Yes" and then go on and deal with the situation like staunch the blood, return machine gun fire or shoo the snake away.

My life has never been the same since because I learned the skill to simply say "Yes" to life and let its magic flow. It helps to keep my mind and my options open. The moment I say "No" to Life, I am mostly in a negative frame of mind and my brain processing starts to become inferior. Don Miguel Ruiz said: do not deny Life passing through you, because it is God passing through you. And then you will find you hardly react at all when the unexpected happens. And when you do react, it will be from a place of better choices.

So later that same evening, this soldier had cooked dinner for us all. It was not the usual delicious dinner we had all come to expect because we had caught no fish. Most nights we had boiled curried fish, roughly chopped, bones and all, including head, eyeballs, gills and tail, served on rice so you couldn't pull the bones out before eating... You pulled the bones out from your mouth whilst you ate, mostly out of an impaled gum or throat. If a bone is stuck in your throat, and you think you are about to die, the Nepalese will enthusiastically offer you a ball of cooked rice to swallow. It worked twice for me and it cured me of any bone swallowing because I chew slowly and softly now - like a giraffe grazing on acacia thorns. And I don't play Russian roulette by swallowing anything in a fish soup until my tongue has inspected and checked every molecule.

You see, without catching any fish from the rock pools along our journey that day the men were faced with eating a dinner of rice and lentils. I proudly reached into my back pack and handed the cook about 3kg of dried beef jerky which I had made for the trip. I had salted and dried it in my dehydrator for three days so it would keep for the journey but inevitably on day four or five it would grow white fungus…by then my hunger exceeded my fear of death by food poisoning and I would eat it heartily anyway.

To my surprise the cook was not too enthusiastic. He was a Hindu and the beef was their sacred cow. But his empty tummy didn't believe in God and said "Yes" to life and to the beef immediately. So he ran off clasping the parcel of protein and then poured the dry jerky into a wok of hot oil to thoroughly fry the divinity out of the meat. You see, they don't mind eating other people's gods such as our kangaroo, but they hesitate for a respectful amount of time before devouring their own. I was told this is because Hinduism is a foreign import from India and they have suffered India's hegemony and political meddling for generations. So they are not too hung up on the religious details of angering the somewhat foreign gods.

TRANSFORMATION AND THE GOLDEN KEYS

He spiced it and boiled it for half an hour and put it aside to cool next to the camp fire where we all sat in circle. Before long, the commander was giving his evening debrief for the day and where necessary was roasting various members of the junior ranks. This is when my friend got up to tend the fire and accidentally booted the boiled beef across the firelight and into an endless patch of sand that swallowed the gravy like blotting paper. This man simply smiled and said "Yes" and picked up every piece of beef, washed it in river water, fried it and spiced it and boiled it again in time for dinner, all whilst the commander kept talking. And it was delicious.

Say "Yes" to life. If you stub your foot on a rock, drop your kid sister out of the kitchen window, or accidentally fill your petrol car's fuel tank with diesel. Saying "Yes" will make things a whole lot easier to deal with as the day unfolds. Any request from another can be your chance to show how much you care and how deep is your love. Say yes. And that is why with raising kids, I love to mostly say "Yes!" to their requests and then go on to make it happen with whatever compromise is necessary to keep things appropriate and functional. But there is undoubtedly a certain magic, flow, creativity and positive action about the word "Yes!" because really, those three letters stand for positive energy, for the entire universe moving forward. They are a symbol for life and life flowing whereas "No!" is more like a symbol for stagnation and death. And bottled up energy is what bombs are made of – it's going to explode at some stage.

Walking the Razor's edge between Inner World and Outer World

But some people strip off and take a running dive headlong into life. And all that people on the banks can see is the white of a butt cheek as if a porpoise was traveling by in the moonlight. Your Ego needs to get involved in real life. Joseph Campbell always said that we had to be in life and play it hard even though part of us must also be the Observer, the Witness. We can't simply bliss out. The Ego is there so that we can put bread on the table and functionally engage with the world and its systems.

There is a special place that I want you to consider. I call it "Walking the Razor's Edge". It is that special place of equilibrium between the necessary forays into inner world journeys and the necessary forays into outer world journeys. It is a place of balance that we can return to many times a day. If I spot a metaphorical rabbit running in the outer world, I will immediately go into Warrior mode and hunt it. The same with an inner rabbit – a glimpse of something worth exploring and I am like Alice through the looking glass chasing it.

There is this place of balance and wisdom and rapid processing of life issues that is beautiful. I am sure that with golden slippers the Dalai Lama walks on this razor sharp interface where mindfulness and mindlessness blend into peaceful existence. Here everything in the universe is exactly as it should be despite the body count on the news and warnings of diabolical weather and all the global fear. Your Ego has to walk on this Razor's Edge like a tightrope walker clutching a Balancing Pole of Humility to keep it in check with balance, wisdom, respect and a certain peaceful demeanour even in the face of life's many disruptions.

Ego fragmentation and subsequent renewal

The Ego, the Self, needs to have the tools to reform itself anew after each of many, many Life transitions and insights and experiences. Without constant personal development your Ego might fall to pieces and not have the glue or the muscles necessary to put itself back together. If this happens, Humpty Dumpty falls off the wall and all the king's horses and all the King's men get covered in yolk. The Ego is so very fragile, often reactive and scared and searching for answers.

Just like a caterpillar, energy builds up in and around us prior to a life transition. Then we enter a cocoon phase of Liminal Space during which everything inside and outside becomes more fluid and like cocoon mush. In this matrix of diffuse thought and diffuse connections, the linear mind falls asleep so that a new way of being and relating can be established. And at the appropriate time a butterfly emerges, a new Ego. You HAVE to understand Liminal Space if you are ever going to learn to transform yourself or other people. More on that later, but so much of this can be found in Bill Plotkin's wonderful and life-changing book 'Soulcraft'.

How I began to study life skills and personal growth

I stumbled upon a lifetime's path of personal development when working in England as a veterinary surgeon. The career in veterinary surgery added an immense range of colour to my River of Life. It filled its waters with such a diverse range of animals, many of them human, and experiences that are priceless and eternal even though I mostly got paid in bottles of wine or a dozen eggs and some pork chops. Sitting in South London one day I followed a powerful instinctive urge to jump on a train and go into the city. And once again my life would never ever be the same. I had to solve a very serious problem and the story is quite interesting.

You see, the problem -or let's call it a dynamic - had been set up in my head many years before. The dynamic is all about my insecurity surrounding love. If I love you, I never, ever want to say goodbye. It tears a big hole in the fabric of my mind and I fall through. At times I have felt like I was never coming back from this black abyss because the falling wouldn't stop. I have stitched up the torn fabric in my mind quite well now and placed warning signs close by that tell me to stay away from emotional farewells. I have said so many farewells and many of them forever because like I said, I am no stranger to death.

My childhood in Zambia and feelings of abandonment

Anyway, when Dad first got to Zambia, he bought an old and very rambling house in the middle of the tiny city of Ndola. I can remember that when I was six years old, my mother taught me how to make mayonnaise one day using an egg, oil and a fork to beat the mixture into nice thick consistency. The trouble is we all knew the house was haunted and I would be left for hours at night beating this mayonnaise in a very distant, deserted and dark kitchen full of shadows. Meanwhile, my siblings were at the opposite end of the house behaving like chimps on Amarula juice. Sweating and whimpering with fear, I would beat the mayonnaise in a frenzy so that, at the appropriate thickness, I could drop the fork and run, run, run down endless corridors to the safety of the TV lounge.

It was a house with as many stories as it had shadows. I want to share some of them with you, the stories and the shadows. Like how mum used to send me and Tom barefoot out into the heavy monsoon rains, the sky alive with sizzling lightning, to collect buckets of rainwater from the gutter pipes so she could wash her beautiful hair in it. But the lightening was everywhere, so close, just blowing the town and our eardrums to bits. The courtyard was the Circus Maximus for a magnificent cockerel called

General Custard. He had six inch long spurs on his legs and a velociraptor's beak that tore great strips of flesh from our screaming bodies - worse than one of the scenes from Jurassic Park where you have to close your eyes, tuck your knees up to your chin and hide behind your popcorn. Tom nearly lost an eye to General Custard's beak.

My oldest brother Pete kept huge monitor lizards in an enclosure in the garden. He would release them in his bedroom and they would absolutely wreck the place because they love to climb trees so they find bookshelves are a bit more challenging. But I wince when I remember how in a flash they would clamp their jaws on my finger and never let go. If anyone came to the rescue, they had a very efficient way of repelling such a person: they would clamp down on my finger twenty times harder so my screams became an impenetrable force field. I would involuntarily kick out at anyone who dared come close to help even though they held the necessary pair of pliers to set me free. And I am sure the lizards were chuckling as they dangled from my finger. Later I will tell you how the front door and veranda got covered in pints of Pete's blood. But Pete is a story worth devoting a whole chapter to and I promise you the ending is nothing short of spectacular by any standard.

Dad was an excellent long distance runner. He never let thieves escape. He would chase them down the moonlit streets of Ndola like he was chasing a trophy in athletics. I remember the night Dad caught a thief in that house and beat the living crap out of him. He then held him captive in the corridor outside the bedroom Tom and I shared. The police arrived later to take the thief downtown for yet another tenderising at the police station. It's very confronting for a child getting out of his bunk bed at night to stand in pyjamas blinking and trying to make sense of the human carnage. Like that stuff was only supposed to occur in the dream world of nightmares.

Pola told me a story that happened some years later when we had moved to our new property called Halina's Farm 8km out of Ndola on the Misundu Road by the Zaire border. Hearing gunshots at night, she fled the house and was cowering in the furrows of our strawberry fields expecting to get killed. Meanwhile Dad ran off to rescue our neighbour who was under attack by Zairean bandits next door. She remembers Dad pumping 9mm bullets into the fleeing mob using a handgun his mother Audrey (with my aunty Darlene's help) had posted to us from Canada concealed in a sack of flour with boxes of snub-nosed bullets. Thank god we didn't bake the stuff. And Pola remembers the blood trail the next day that must have snaked its way through no man's land to some witch doctor's hut in Zaire where the operation might be successful but the patient would most surely die. Now a bullet would need extracting… and then the patient burying… and probably a chicken sacrificing. The witch doctors always had better luck working with chickens than with things like gunshot wounds.

Boarding school

Every morning, Dad would drive us to Kansenji Primary School where we got a great colonial education. But one day Pete disappeared on a bus. He came back three months later sporting khakis, a bright red blazer and some fresh welts across his butt from the many beatings the Catholic priests gave him at his new boarding school. We all eventually went to that boarding school and learned about corporal punishment and the shining of shoes and making of beds. It was Saint George's College, 830 km south of Ndola in Rhodesia across the mighty Zambesi River. Tom was only 9 and I was 11 when Mum drove us down for the first time to

TRANSFORMATION AND THE GOLDEN KEYS

drop us off at school. She travelled at 160 kmph mostly in third or even second gear in our new Toyota Corolla. From my observations I am not sure she really understood what a car's gearbox was for.

This car was the love of Mum's life. And it was also the ultimate empowerment of Pete's manic bipolar disorder when inklings first manifested in his adolescence. Well they also manifested as burn out marks along Misundu Rd, smoking brake callipers, terrified, white faced siblings screaming and holding their bums, a 100 kmph head on crash with a cyclist that created endless meters of skid marks along the road, a crumpled bicycle and the chief of police's son in a ditch alive but rather split asunder.

Anyway, I digress. Tom and I were presented by Mum to a nice looking gentleman called Mr Parsons in the foyer of the school outside his office. The staircase led up to the dormitories above where boys, mostly 10 to 12 year olds, were getting busy with another night in a concentration camp masquerading as a school. Mum kissed us goodbye and dried our tears with her own moist handkerchief from her gloved hand. She gently closed the front door with a last parting look which the child within me will never forget. Then Mr Parsons took me and Tom briskly up that staircase. We each dangled by one ear from his cruel and calloused hands - our feet bumping limply up the stairs.

There is a certain smile mixed with a grimace and a delight and a fire that is unique to pure sadists and many of us got to know it well. We would look back over our shoulders whilst Mr Parsons tore our bums apart with his selection of willow canes. From that day on and into senior school I learned that the only thing I had left which could withstand the loneliness, the bullies and beatings was my brain. I must say that my first mental breakdown was at the age of 11 maybe a few weeks in to my first term at the school. I had never witnessed such brutality and bullying in my life. I tried asking for help but there was no one to ask it from.

Well, a nervous breakdown can be a cradle for brilliance because sometimes your brain comes up with a breakdown truck to rescue the part of you that's on its knees with engine aflame. Like soldiers on a battlefield never leaving their injured behind, a stretcher arrives and loving arms pull the wounded on board and head for cover. And here my alchemy started as I discovered ways of mental and physical survival.

The purpose of Heroes in our Lives: Projecting our Inner Gold on another

We all need heroes to invest our inner gold in, to inspire us to greatness and to get us through the tough times, the Dark Night of the Soul. And when we are big enough, or when our golden projections become too heavy or burdensome for the hero to carry, we get this gold back and transcend that stage to another. Then we go looking for more heroes, another rung up the ladder to hold on to whilst we find our footing.

My hero was perfect. It was of course Bruce Lee. He smashed so many mirrors in the movie 'Enter the Dragon' that the 7 years of bad luck for each mirror broken added up and he died way too young killed not by an armed ninja but by a mere headache pill. I suppose each of us meets our unexpected nemesis sooner or later. The whole world still had their gold invested in him so we all took it pretty hard. And then there followed a sort of vacuum of heroes for a while. But we eventually got over it. Some people even swapped Bruce for rap artists and break dancers.

Even so, I am eternally loyal to Bruce. He is carrying my gold somewhere in Heaven and must surely be getting tired by now. Once I told my friend

Imogen that with all that bad luck stacked against his karma, Bruce Lee was reincarnated as an ant. She texted me back, "Really?????" So I texted, "Yes, of course...and if you are ever in the forest and you see an ant with a pair of nunchaku's...that will be Bruce."

Defying the system and breaking the rules

My best friend Scooby and I created our own mini Shaolin temple at the back of the huge school hall. This area was out of bounds and had a panoramic view over the entire school and the nearby botanical gardens. There we practiced our version of Kung Fu each day and Bruce's cat-like screams... very badly because we only had vague memories of Bruce Lee's fight scenes to go by and our voices were breaking.

And at night I would sit in the dormitory cross-legged and meditating before setting off as a Ninja, all in black, to creep across the moonlight throughout the surreal school buildings. The school was built like a medieval castle, the many chapels, and enormous library all with wooden and creaking floors. Nothing can match the feeling of practicing silent footsteps across the ultra-creaky floor of the empty, massive hall under the cover of darkness and then the silent escape through one of the rear windows landing outside like a cat cleaving the shades of night.

Defiling the sacred

Well, actually stealing sips of altar wine from the sanctity of the many chapels was also quite cool. We were filled with the excitement of tomb robbers... Raiders of the Lost Ark. In the darkness I expected God to tap me on the shoulder and with a clearing of his throat ask me, "...er... what the Hell do you think you are doing?... That's the holy blood of Jesus you are drinking... and it's meant only for the priests...!" Then God would have had a heart attack as he witnessed my friends unlock the holy tabernacle and help themselves to fistfuls of consecrated wafers - munching on them like nibblies to go with their glasses of sweet altar wine.

My relentless inner longing for connection

So what was this dynamic that became established in such a traumatised but resilient mind? Well it was the insecurity surrounding love. If I could be banished from a loving home to this lost and lonely place, then surely, like a banished goat in a desert, I would forever wander thirsty for love and connection but with no evidence that it would ever be enduring should I find it. A longing and a melancholy took up residence in my heart as my Butterfly's wings started to beat – a Butterfly I only really understood some 40 years later. Remember: melancholy is the song a lonely butterfly sings far away trying to find its home, the home of the heart, a place of connection.

I would gaze through the bars of my classroom window into the botanical gardens below the school. On weekends, us boarders could study in the lonely, deserted classrooms and I often would sit there watching distant couples strolling slowly by. With each day, my insecurities grew and grew. When I left school, I only slept with two women before I met my future wife Fiona. Both were one night stands. I was 18 and starved of female company. So I proposed to both women. I had to be honest recently and tell my Fiona that actually she was the **third** woman I had proposed to, not the first. She took it well, but almost swallowed her teacup.

All relationships have a price and because we long for connection so much we are often willing to try to pay that price. Kings give away kingdoms for such things. At 18, I thought I had nothing much to lose. My unlived future seemed a small price to pay in exchange for the wonderful company of a human with two 'X' chromosomes.

The first woman was at least 20 years older than me. She dragged me back to her place from a nightclub to help me discover what being a man was all about. But most of us know that takes at least a lifetime, if not many. Anyway the gateway to manhood and real greatness is a doorway called Humility not a woman's vagina. But I learned about rejection the very next day when I stood at the reception of her crowded workplace holding a wilting bunch of flowers. She gently asked me to leave whilst the bewildered staff looked on.

The second woman I simply lost... as in I lost touch with her. I didn't have her number. And I arrived too late at the hospital. She had been discharged the day before. You see, her Dad forced her into an abortion. I have no idea if the child was mine or not but SHE had been mine if only for one night, and the heart's longing for people such as this never ends. You just want to say sorry and hope they are safe and well, and hope they found love somewhere. I have cried my tears for her. Beautiful girl. We met as young fun-loving strangers on a deserted roller-skating rink one night. She was too scared to go to the toilets in the darkness to have a pee on her own. So we walked there hand in hand and I waited for her bashfully looking at my feet which were standing on holy ground before her open toilet cubicle.

So my love was wonderful but its foundations were built on the insecurities of a child banished from a loving home. Like a koala bear I clung to Fiona but that never works very well because Fiona is not a koala. In fact it was fueling a very deep depression and anxiety in me. It was a heavy kind of love for Fiona to carry and I have apologised a thousand times.

Make personal growth a lifetime study

So that day in London I set off to find a cure for my profound depression and insecurities. Bumping along the Underground, how was I to know that I would somehow find myself at the top floor of Foyle's Bookstore in central London. In front of me was an entire spectrum of self-help books. And I picked up my first two - my first two of thousands. One was entitled 'Elation and Depression'. And the other was simply entitled 'Jealousy'. Last year I read 160 books. But that's too many, the mind struggles with such a paradigm overload when you do this. It gets too far ahead of the Ego fragmentation/renewal process. And the bedside table is so stacked with books that there is no place for the coffee cups and you can't see the alarm clock. And there is no guarantee that all these books, stacked like playing cards in the mind, won't come crashing down from time to time. Anyway, that day in London I had started my journey of personal development.

Continual Personal Growth – Golden Key gathering - is essential

Now the golden key I want to give you here is that although there are many paths through transcendence, lifelong personal development is part of the essentials. If you have emotional intelligence, self-awareness and a host of people skills, you will negotiate life in all its forms a whole lot better. And with an array of skills, you will have a far deeper experience of life. And you will have the skills to reform an Ego that has been dissolved and dismembered in liminal space. Sometimes a rapid succession of profound events may be encountered and it takes great skill to re-form a shattered Ego repeatedly and keep up with incoming missiles. All I can say is thank God I had so much material and insights and tools to fall back on. And if your partner is also up to scratch on the tools, on the terminology and language and understanding, you have at least half a chance at getting through the inevitable relationship dramas or to limit their damage.

Developing your own language and words to capture golden concepts

You also develop your own language and terminology regarding these matters within each group that experiences them. These special words and phrases become so useful. That's what language is anyway: a means of transferring information in units of symbols. This book is full of them and the world generates new ones all the time. Things like The Dark Night of the Soul or Walking the Razor's Edge. If two people sit together and start complaining or 'awfulizing', I refer to this as 'Milking the Toxic Cow'... buckets and buckets of poisonous milk that goes into their hearts and out into the world to make everyone sick.

Golden Glasses and Toxic Cows

> *Once upon a time in a forest far away lived a little boy and a little girl. They were the most miserable children. Every morning, they would wake up and put on a pair of scratched, dark glasses and go out into a very scary and miserable world. Everything they looked at was dark and hard to see clearly because the glasses they wore made life so difficult. And to make things worse, the two children would sit together and talk for hours about how horrible life was. It's as if they sat there milking a cow whose milk was made of poison. And they would milk bucket loads of poison from the Toxic Cow and would share it with anyone who would sit and listen to their miserable conversations. Of course the milk made everyone very sick indeed.*

One day, they were walking down a forest path, milking another Toxic Cow in their conversations and awfulizing about everything and everyone. Suddenly they saw a shape in the tree above them that called out to the children and said, "Little children. Stop milking the Toxic Cow and listen to me for a moment." The children were stunned into silence and they peered through their dark glasses trying to make sense of the dark shape that they saw. "What you need is inside the magic treasure chest at the base of the tree. Open it and your lives will be changed forever!" said the dark shape.

They inched forward and opened the treasure chest. From inside, a golden light flooded the forest. The little boy reached in and picked up two pairs of magic Golden Glasses. "Put them on!" said the voice.

When the children took off their dark, scratched glasses and put on the Golden Glasses, the whole forest came alive with light and wonder. And in the tree above, the dark shape had become the most beautiful, colourful bird that chirped and danced for them in delight. When they looked around, their entire world was now golden and when they looked at each other they saw how beautiful and perfect they themselves were.

And the bird said, "Life gets better when we learn to think better. Life is perfect and wonderful but it all depends on what glasses we are wearing. When Life seems scary, or you are worried or sad, it is not Life that is the problem, it's the glasses that you choose to wear. Every morning, before you even open your eyes, reach for the Golden Glasses and put them on. And in the day share them with others who are feeling down until they can find their own. The

TRANSFORMATION AND THE GOLDEN KEYS

> Golden Glasses will help you see that all of Life is a perfect miracle. And you are a golden miracle too."
>
> From that day on, the children lived in a golden world delighting in even the tiniest of things. And in their conversations they never milked Toxic Cows again. Instead, when they spoke, it was golden words about a golden world, a beautiful life and beautiful people. Dark glasses bring only fear, anger and sadness. Golden Glasses bring love, laughter, happiness and joy. Life is Life – a miracle. But what we see depends on the glasses we choose to wear.

Jack of all trades – an apprentice to all dimensions: creating length, breadth and depth

My relentless sense of curiosity led me to study everything I encountered on my journey through life. And you will see glints of this in these pages and in the bibliography at the end of this book. The eminent swordsman and Samurai Ronin, Miyamoto Musashi, taught that we must be acquainted with every art, know the ways of all professions, following a path of training and doing only useful things in life. Miyamoto also had pearls of wisdom like, "Distinguish between loss and gain in worldly matters." I like that one. It speaks of wisdom and tactics. In weighing up values, we make choices which have consequences and these add up to create our destiny. We need a mental weighing machine which can also weigh up matters of the heart in a moment or over time to see what we value most.

Now, I can see the value of specialising in just one thing and mastering it. That's cool, like becoming a famous pianist for example. But I do worry about what happens to the corpse of self-sacrifice and self-denial in all of this, what Robert Johnson called 'the unlived life'. And I can also see the value in being a Jack of All Trades and being a Master in that too! Consequently I do everything. And it works for me because I am addicted to variety and get bored so quickly. I don't like watching people performing on television, I want to be the one doing that thing: swimming in the River of Life not just watching it flow by. On my deathbed, every cell in my body will be saying, "...At last!....now we can rest......!"

People who do not read or study can lack a certain depth which might be required to hold others someday. So I try to create depth and variety in my knowledge by being widely read. At least I am never short of things to talk about. So I studied Life and I studied the mind. On the way I also got a Chemistry and Biochemistry degree and then a degree in Veterinary Science. These are mind-expanding things to study anyway and I will give you an example of what such things can do for your life.

Witnessing the Miracle of Life

In a Zoology practical experiment I witnessed the miracle of seeing a chicken embryo grow cell by cell over the course of a weekend. We had to peel a small hole in the shell so we could focus a microscope onto the embryonic disc below. Then using paper and a pencil we had to sketch the unfolding miracle through the two days. Muscle blocks gathered in perfect symmetry. Soon a primitive spinal cord and brain appeared in the dance and folding of tissues. Then an eye was watching and witnessing me, the artist sketching away and co-creating this miracle on the other side of the eggshell portal. I gasped as the blood cells and muscle tissue in the chest came to life and started keeping the tempo of a beating heart filled with all the hopes and dreams of the universe as every new heart is.

But oh, the wonder! To understand bacteria, and viruses, protozoa and all the animals and insects. With trembling hands we dissected dogfish to study their cranial nerves. We witnessed Life through the prism of DNA creating endless diversity, converting an alphabet of amino acids into a storybook of proteins. We came to understand the abundant nature of cell types and tissues in the body from histology to gross anatomy and the biochemistry and indeed the quantum physics beneath it all. I wondered at all the physiology, pathology and pharmacology. I learned how to harness these elements and manipulate the endocrinology of animals to create new life in breeding programs, learning how to deliver puppies, kittens, lambs, calves and foals and the techniques of necropsy for the dead. In this way I came to appreciate the matrix of the universe and its manifestation in so many forms peering through telescopes, microscopes and bubbling test tubes. The human mind and man's place in all of this was yet another horizon, another study in the ways of being and collating it all into paradigms.

Moments such as these of mutual perception and one-ness are discussed so brilliantly in the book 'the Spell of the Sensuous' by David Abram. If you read his book, and Soulcraft, and some of Don Miguel Ruiz you will enjoy a lifetime of living in the miracle of life.

Wander about wondering

There is so much to wonder at. Wondering gives us insights as we expose our brains to new horizons. And in practicing we embed the skills. Go to a bookstore or a library and you will find that the books choose YOU. They jump into your arms. Don't stop reading. Don't stop playing the personal development CD's in your car, the podcasts or watching clips on YouTube. Your mind needs an overwhelming amount of good stuff to overcome the scripting that holds you back. Before podcasts became popular, I would have played entire CD sets, some of them 17 CD's long, over 20 times in my car on veterinary calls out to the remote farms east of

Augusta along the southwest Australian coast dodging kamikaze kangaroos all the way. The car literally brainwashed me with good stuff.

Life skills create attitude and attitude is everything

There were wild cattle out there on the farms and I would line up 300 or 400 to pregnancy test. I would go like a machine for 4 or 5 hours in the dust and the sun and in the rain and the mud working those cattle. It was the University of Life - all the CD's playing in my car - that gave me the inner strength to keep going. To be good at pregnancy testing cattle, you have to have the fingertips of a grand pianist, the heart of a Lion and the brain of a cow psychologist. You also need muscles that never surrender.

Dressed in heavy overalls and gumboots and shoulder-length plastic gloves, the day is spent sprinting up and down a cattle race, going from the death-defying encounters with shit-scared cattle in the forcing pen to the arm-wrenching encounter with the rectum of each cow in the head bale. Locked inside the cow up to your armpit, you have to move with the 700kg beast as she writhes and bucks and drops trying to break your arm or elbow. But inside her you can feel for an embryo or even a fully formed calf that will try to suck on your fingers, turn its head or withdraw its hooves as you touch them inside the cow.

Mostly I loved this work. And also I was absolutely terrified. As if the cow in front of you is not dangerous enough, the cow behind you that breaks through from the forcing pen into the raceway is definitely going to kill you. She will charge full speed down the race and crunch your bones like a packet of crisps against the cow you are pregnancy testing. So for this reason you are always looking backwards. And if she comes like an express train at you, you jump hard and high to get on top of the rails. I had one express train cow ramp the one in front suspending me in midair on her shoulders until I slowly tumbled sideways from the sky to the earth below. I had another scoot my heels along the top rail and both my knees were nearly dislocated as my shoes encountered upright posts on their travels.

Thirty years of this from Africa to England to Portugal and finally Australia. But everywhere, the books and the CD's, all that learning came along with me and gave me strength and the resilience to continue. What is a man without great attitude anyway? Looking back I often used to say that attitude is everything. Well, it certainly kept me alive, kept me taking action and helped me climb a few mountains of challenge and achievement. And the knowledge – man's interpretations of reality – helped my ego negotiate this man made system and accept the advent of a time of wisdom as my hair slowly turned white.

Building a mandala for a Summer Equinox ceremony. Meelup Beach Western Australia. By candlelight, a group of us men walked it in silence that evening.

3

Transformational work

The Midlife Crisis and how a man can discover a better way to be

But there comes a time in every man's life when a voice wells up from deep within his Soul and it confronts him in a feminine voice. Robert Johnson describes it as the Hideous Maiden in the tale of the Fisher King – a mythical story about one of King Arthur's knights. It is the voice of the Midlife Crisis which confronts every man usually from the age of say 40 or 50. An old and very ugly hag points an arthritic finger right between the eyes of the man at this time and says, "You are not as good as you think you are!" Immediately the whites of his eyes appear as he tumbles backwards into a very challenging time of self-examination, self-evaluation and introspection.

Well, try to evaluate a lifetime of broken marriages, kids that hate you, a materialistic pseudo existence living on a corporate gravy train and a beer gut the size of a laundry basket: the mental Weighing Scales of self-evaluation tip immediately to the side labelled "Complete Disaster!" Meanwhile at this time of life, his wife has lost her gentle veil of oxytocin, discovered her masculine side and is standing up for herself with what sounds like a critical voice. So if he tangles things up a bit by projecting the Hideous Maiden all on her, she transforms from the Sweet Maiden he once fell in love with into Medusa.

Yes, some bits of your lifetime may be good or great but overall, finding yourself on the final 100 metre sprint in life, maybe your last hurrah, most men undergo a profound liminal shift. They eventually get in touch with their feminine side, become more gentle, grow their hair long, wear flowery shirts and buy a very powerful motorbike. All such liminal shifts seem to have an outward manifestation, like maybe the wearing of a bandana, a bracelet, a talisman or any kind of body bling. Tattoos, piercings, leather jackets, a bright red Mohican hairstyle even. How about a new wife (younger and preferably foreign), a new dog (Labrador to pull the chicks if you're single), or metrosexual shoes (pointy and extra-long).

Well for me, with a lifetime of personal development behind me, I found myself somewhat tattered and strewn with bullet holes but intact enough to notice an advertisement to attend the New Warrior Training Adventure with the Mankind Project at an ex-Naval camp on the coast of Fremantle... basically to undergo male initiation into a more mature, open, honest and authentic form of masculinity. Most men will feel a sense of terror as the date for this initiation approaches. But there is an undeniable primal calling to front up at these things in many of us. The fear is great. It pulls back the drawstring of the bow, energising the liminal charge which has in fact been building for years. And when you get there you encounter a very, very precious and dear person. You discover your Self – a self that has been waiting for you all those years.

The concept of Liminal Space and Liminality

So let me explain what liminal space is, because so much of transformation hinges on this concept of liminality, and you have to understand it well. The simple analogy is that a caterpillar enters a cocoon phase before a butterfly can emerge. Not my romantic Butterfly, just a more beautiful person. Again, I refer you to Bill Plotkin's brilliant book called "Soulcraft".

Before a major paradigm shift, energy builds up. Then a surreal experience creates a liminal space for transformation. The liminal space can be as simple as an intimate conversation over a coffee table with someone's big beautiful eyes to peer in to. It can occur on retreats or on a tropical paradise holiday or in an Ashram in India. It can occur on a mountain top or whilst experiencing an epiphany under the painted sky of a golden sunset.

'Liminal' means 'Threshold' because a change is about to occur. In this surreal space, the linear thought patterns of the rational mind become more plastic as diffuse thought patterns take over. Bizarre connections are made, new possibilities emerge. Everything and everyone becomes alive and we all start to glow and disclose things about ourselves we might never otherwise say. It's the threshold of transformation, a tipping point. Things change, beliefs change, people change inwardly and usually outwardly too. Someone may preside over the liminal space, and this could be anyone, a facilitator, an elder, a symbolic statue even.

Liminal versus liminoid

Now contrast this to the *liminoid* experience of drugs, alcohol and a smoke-filled dance floor that is cranking on a Saturday night. Pure Heaven, pure bliss, filled with gods and goddesses, creations of our own projections that laugh and gyrate in a sensuous and erotic frenzy. This contrived shortcut to liminality has its physical, social, financial, emotional and spiritual price. All relationships do.

It is presided over by three people: the D.J. sets the tempo and the Bouncer evicts anyone who dares spoil the illusion of Heaven. I mean drunken, drug crazed demons don't go rampaging through Heaven in the Bible do they? The Angels would Taser them as they tried to leopard crawl across Purgatory, bolt cutters in hand towards the Pearly Gates.

The Dionysian energy of Ecstasy - which normally, and without drugs, would be the feeling of Bliss and Heavenly connection glimpsed in a sunset for example - is dished out by a very powerful and plain clothed priest called the Barman. He dishes out goblets of Dionysian madness, of the feeling of ecstasy. As a biochemist, I know full well that even the tiniest drop of alcohol is the swallowing of an addictive, carcinogenic psychotic with diuretic qualities and an impending physical, social and financial headache. Many a magnificent ship's captain, many magnificent men and women, have been sunk by the iceberg of alcohol.

Anyway, the liminoid space of transformation on the dance floor goes absolutely berserk at a specific time, usually around 10.30 pm. You can really see a ripple in the crowd and suddenly its game on! Women, who are usually renowned for their ability to converse with each other oblivious to the world around them (hey, just ask any jogger who has been forced off the pathway) suddenly grab men or each other and the whole place starts gyrating. Dionysian madness erupts in plague proportions like Ebola Virus. Clothing is cast off. Children are conceived in the toilets. And through this evening and maybe through the night, liminoid changes will occur but usually to an inferior and regretful level. The walk of shame. The feelings of guilt. The headache. The devastating bar tab. The lost mobile phone. Oh, I've had my share.

The sham of the liminoid illusion would all disappear if the music failed. Like if someone trips over a jack plug or spills a beer into the amplifier.

Same if the bar closes or there is a power cut. The liminoid spell is broken, reality immediately intrudes and real people face each other for the first time that evening... and feel at least a little bit awkward at the madness they were sharing just a moment ago. Now where did I throw my shirt, pants and underwear...? And where can we go to continue this enchanted night of madness?

Going on a trip

Liminality. Go and study it for a while. And contrast it with the poor quality Dionysian energy of **liminoid** experiences and their dismal outcomes. Shamanic peoples have used mind altering substances for so many years to enter a different energetic dimension for a diverse range of purposes. I have studied a lot of books about them but I personally can't use mind altering substances on my brain because it would simply melt under their influence. I really don't believe I would ever be coming back in any coherent form. I know it works for a lot of people and they get the profound insights they went looking for under the guidance of a Shaman. And for some, they can rationalise their drug addictions in this way. Just it was never an option for me. And you will see why later when I tell you about Pete and his bipolar disorder. I do drink alcohol and coffee. I have smoked cigarettes, but that's about it for me.

The Mankind Project and Male Initiation into a relationship with my mature masculine

Anyway, one cold dark night in July 2007 I pitched up terrified but determined at a remote ex-naval camp by the ocean in Fremantle. Strong men met me at the gate and my life was never the same. The connection to my mature masculine self, finding a new way to integrate myself, my Life's Mission and the realisation that I truly was a gift to this world set me up for many years of transformational work within this wonderful organisation.

Through more than 57 psychological processes and insights my whole psyche was transformed in less than 48 hours. The details are all secret of course as all such initiations are meant to be. But from a motley crew of 23 initiates who first arrived like flotsam and jetsam washed up on the beaches of Fremantle, we all stood together arm-in-arm proud and strong and shining, a Band of Brothers ready to take on the world when we returned to a homecoming celebration a few days later. It's cool. And it's a place to learn leadership and your own personal leadership of self. And then the epiphanies never seem to end even as many transcend the organisation, this portal to self-discovery and into a new way of being.

Self-Image and the Golden Mirror

For example, I was sitting in a sweat lodge with men of the Mankind Project, buck naked and I swear my skin was about to turn into pork crackling. I looked inside my heart and saw a very faulted self-image... a mirror all rusty on the edges and scratched, cracked and broken. I realised this was the mirror that other people held up for me to look in to when they told me I was bad or had been horrible or when I had failed in some way. Next to it was my golden and beautiful authentic mirror. The one I had been born with. And I picked up my golden mirror and cleaned it with my tears and polished it with the fabric of my mind until I could see a beautiful reflection of my true and golden self in my very own Golden Mirror. And I could see how others had stolen this mirror and used it to control me, especially if I gave it away to those I had fallen in love with. If they were happy with me, then I was a good man. If they were unhappy with me, then I was a bad man. All my power was cut to shreds on broken and faulted mirrors.

The Golden Mirror is your own golden self-image. Keep it close, polish it each day and look within it through Golden Glasses before you open your eyes in the morning. In the sweat lodge that night I broke all the other faulted mirrors of my expected self, of my ideal self, of my perfect self, of my faulted self. Now I look within to my own Golden Mirror. It's precious and I treat it so. I never speak against it. I keep it close. I don't give it away. I don't let others scratch it or try to smash it. I have taught it to poke me in the ribs and remind me of who I am whenever I am distracted by the mirrors others hold up for me.

And when I engage other people I always hold up a golden mirror to them. I always look for and speak to the best in them. The gold and diamonds are in there somewhere, inside everyone. We just have to dig deep enough to find them. I want them to respond to me from the best of themselves, so I hold up a golden mirror until their hard eyes melt and their faces start shining. In transformational work, I sometimes have to be an impassive mirror so as not to affect the work they are doing within. But in social engagement it is very much about reflecting back to them their gold and their value so that they respond from that place, and some will find their golden selves they lost a long time ago.

And as I crawled out of the sweat lodge half dead from the heat stress, I lost my way in the darkness and crawled across the red hot rocks somehow without burning any of my bits. But I collapsed on the cool sand outside and wrapped my arms around me, my Golden Mirror safe and close within my heart forever more.

The Golden Mirror

> *Very early one morning I stood outside in the darkness on the cold wet lawn and pointed my telescope to Jupiter. There I saw the four moons circling this great planet. And I looked with awe and wonder at the two bright orange bands of clouds, like lines, across the planet... clearly visible from across space... from so far away. And later, as I stood in my outdoor shower surrounded by ferns and plants in the hot steamy water, I really felt how much me and the plants and the water and the planets and moons and space were all one thing, all alive, all a manifestation of Life, of vibrations that started billions of years ago.*
>
> *Our essence is billions of years old. We are a miracle called Life and we are part of this matrix that is everywhere. We just need to remember that as we go out into the busy world each day. If you fill yourself with love and this understanding of One-ness, and open your spiritual eyes, the magic will meet you there as you journey through the day. It always does because it is a state of being, a state of connection and relationship to everything and everyone. Then things come alive all around you and all aspects of Life become a bountiful resource... it's not like you are doing this all on your own.*
>
> *After I have spent time at my altar in the morning and filled my heart with its energy, I go jogging for mile after mile along a road that overlooks my infinity pool, the Indian Ocean. And I say a prayer of love for everyone I meet along the way. I truly pour out love on each and every one. And if they want to talk, I will stop and let*

things be perfect between us before it is time to move on again. In this way, and to my great embarrassment, I was once overtaken three times by the same pedestrian.

Inside your heart is a Golden Mirror. It is the beautiful authentic reflection of who you really are. You are a miracle, and you are perfect. Right here, and right now, you are big enough, strong enough and wise enough especially when all you really need to do is take the next breath and trust in Life.

My truth is the truth of my own innate divinity, my own miracle of existence, my perfect essence as a human aspect of this living universe. It is the humbled realisation of the magnificent beauty that I am.

Each one of us has this Golden Mirror within, but we lose sight of it so easily. We look to many other mirrors:

- *the Ideal Self – maybe the person I want to be*
- *the Perfect Self – maybe the person whose got every single duckling in a row*
- *the Expected Self – what my parents, friends or society want me to be*
- *the Shamed Self – when I am led to believe that I am inherently bad at my core*
- *the Guilty Self – when I believe I have made a mistake*
- *the Victim Self – when I am thinking: "...poor me..."*

Over time we all develop such mirrors in our hearts. But all too often it is other people who hold up a corrupted mirror and try to force this image upon us, or force this mirror into us. Look only to your Golden Mirror because it is made of Truth and is filled with abundant self-love. Never give it away to someone else lest they

> *scratch it or use it to control you. Polish it every morning before you open your eyes and go out into a busy world. Bring this Self to all that you encounter in the day and let this Golden Mirror be connected to all that is, as an integral part to a living universe, to the sentience of Nature, to all of humanity.*

Creating an immense Inner Tool Box of Life Skills and my Calypso-Dawn Treader

So I was gathering some very useful tools, life skills, Golden Keys, concepts, metaphors and symbols that all helped me navigate a wonderful yet bizarre and unpredictable existence. Using them I could navigate my inner and outer worlds. It takes balance to do this and maintain an equilibrium lest we get too enmeshed in one world or the other. Of course, this is what you do at the start but with a bit of hindsight, you learn to tack a better course.

It's the Razor's Edge- the path which integrates all of these things in a balanced way. On one side is the slippery slope of a mundane and materialistic, unconscious existence. And on the other is the risk of falling deep within into an archetypal world of endless introspection and navel-gazing awash with liminality.

My core metaphor that I would visit each day was that of a huge Spanish Galleon, which I called 'the Dawn Treader'. I smile as I remember the pirate ship I built all those years ago for the boat race in Ndola. It grew and became more complex just like the chicken embryo I witnessed developing. And when I discovered my feminine side, and feminine archetypes, I renamed it "The Calypso-Dawn Treader". At each of the four cardinal points stood an archetypal figure which I first came to know when reading Gillette and Moore's wonderful book about male masculinity called 'King, Warrior, Magician, Lover'. Those four plus a little boy in the Crow's Nest and a Wild Man full of abundant masculine energy below decks sailed the oceans of my mind each day. And the little boy had a dog called Miso, pronounced 'Meesho' which means 'Teddy Bear' in Polish. I could look here early each morning with my coffee, candle light and Fiona tucked up close to me in bed and there I could see how all of these aspects had woken up for the day. I could see turbulent oceans or calm coconut Islands. I could check in with each aspect of my masculine world, my inner matrix: was my Warrior brave or fearful, my King present or absent, what magical splendour was my Magician working on and where were those curmudgeonly little fellows: my Judge and my Victim?

Our Egyptian journey through the stars back home

Miso was a fat Golden Labrador who enchanted us and our two children for 7 short years before he lost the use of his hind legs prematurely from a prolapsed disc. Fiona, Rebekah and I sent him lovingly to the great Kennel in the Sky, past the god Anubis, using a syringe of Green Dream euthanizing solution. I imagine Miso paused momentarily in front of Anubis to have his soul weighed against the benchmark of a feather on his way to be forever with the Dog Star, Sirius, in the heavens. This was the final celestial journey through the stars of the Egyptian pharaohs from so long ago. Anubis welcomed Egyptian souls into the afterlife. And Miso was an ancient soul. I think of him as I look to Orion, peering through my telescope into our southern summer nights in Australia... the Hunter with his faithful hunting dogs, Sirius and Procyon.

A dog really is a man's best friend. Every adventurer needs a dog. If only all companions were so good in their greetings. Dogs fill their greetings of us with unconditional love. That is more love than all of us humans combined because our love is so conditional and fuels the War of Control that insidiously pervades every relationship, and almost every conversation. I had first encountered Miso as my spirit animal during a visualisation process with the Mankind Project and I will forever be called by that name by all the men in that organisation. And whenever I returned from those initiatory camps Fiona would ask me if I had seen Miso. And I would reply, "Yes… he was looking good." And then we would both burst into tears and hug each other.

Checking in with myself each morning as I awake

Anyway, I now could look inside each morning to the Calypso-Dawn Treader and see what my inner world is up to and how it is affecting my outer world. In times of personal crisis, dismembered by life's events, I have seen my core inner archetypes band together as brothers in trying to hold together the timbers of the Calypso- Dawn Treader floundering on the rocks. Their courage and love for each other is so immense - enough for me to discover my self-love in a profound and metaphorical form simply by looking towards this powerful inner symbol. The love was undeniable in the faces and actions and the shouts of the men below decks trying desperately to save their flooded and sinking ship. I have seen it best during Dark Nights of the Soul.

Sometimes the Calypso-Dawn Treader is becalmed in a peaceful and idyllic bay and I know that all is well and I am within some comfort zone of life. Sometimes it has people on board. Other times it is watching my Warrior hunt down the Judge and the Victim through the corridors of the ship, and then making them walk the plank into a sea infested with sharks. They float behind half dead on slender threads, but they are archetypal and hence immortal. They will be back on board tomorrow.

In front of my Calypso-Dawn Treader swims my Whale of Wisdom to guide me... it is the whale who holds the compass of the ship and helps it make choices and to keep centred. I dreamed of the whale some time ago: I was trying to tug Fiona through the ocean to the shore next to a big sleeping whale and accidentally kicked this huge creature... he then put his chin on me and gently but firmly pushed me underwater. My dream was telling me about my awakening of wisdom and my subservience to its leadership when dealing with my inner feminine elements of the subconscious and also with the outer world, with Fiona and with Imogen.

Discovering a symbol and metaphor for my Inner Feminine and complementary archetypes

Some years later, I was initiated into the SHIFT Network's Ultimate Men's Initiation near San Francisco. And over the five days of intense training with the SHIFT Network I came to discover my own Life's Mission to the Divine Feminine... to bring beauty into this world: basically, a beautiful way of being and doing. Everything in my life from then on would have an element of beauty in it in some form. And the effect of this in my life has been very beautiful indeed. Most of my actions have some component of beauty within them.

One night during our training, in a dream I saw a second Spanish galleon, the "Calypso', pull up alongside my own. And to my amazement it had on board five or six of the most beautiful, wild women I had ever seen. And they came on board my Spanish galleon for the best party ever. It was of course an encounter with my inner feminine elements - in this case the contra-gender archetypes of my King, Warrior, Magician, and Lover and of the Little Boy. Even the dog found he had an opposite...a little cat that travelled with the women. So to create ritual theatre around this concept of masculine and feminine elements, I bought a car, a 4-wheel drive and kitted it out for adventuring and camping. And I gave it the only name I ever could: 'the Calypso-Dawn Treader'.

Your metaphors and symbols are alive, and you can change them, embellish them and modify them as they grow and mature. And you can gather images of them in this material world and place them on an altar by your bed... or drive in them across the wilderness as I did with my car!

The men of the Calypso-Dawn Treader and self-healing

One morning after a particularly tough day I walked along the decks of the Calypso-Dawn Treader and I stumbled upon my King, so damaged that he really was limp lying on the deck and gibbering to himself uncontrollably... Post Traumatic Stress personified... a mind that resembled a fireworks display after the fireworks had all gone and only smoke remained. There is so much love between the men on my ship that the Warrior strode nobly forwards (imagine an oiled muscular frame and tanned skin) and dragged the King back to his throne. There, the Lover put Golden Glasses on the King so that he could see only a golden world. And then the Lover inserted a Golden Mirror into the King's heart so he could re-boot his golden self... in fact any sense of identity that could get him functional again... hey, he was toast a few minutes ago, anything was going to improve the situation. But the Golden Mirror started to re-boot the Disk Operating System of his mind, and it worked. He remembered to remember that he was beautiful, and he had a name, in fact many names depending on which organisation he was working with. And they were all cool. The Golden Mirror disk gave the King a disk operating system to get through another tough day. About 30 minutes later, I could remember who I was and my name and where the fuck on earth I called home.

Liminal Space and Fragmentation of the Ego can be a perilous journey

The learning here is that we all go through surreal and liminal experiences. Some involve massive challenges and they might even look like Dark Nights of the Soul. But what is happening is the Cocoon Effect - a time of learning and diffuse thinking, insights and an attempt at a return to the real world to emerge as a butterfly of new-ness. The trouble is that the journey and the return are not guaranteed to be successful. While you are away on a Hero's Journey, your cat may disown you and join the neighbours instead. You might even end up a broken and lost man or in some ashram in India and never returning to your community with anything of substance.

Acknowledging those who support us

But here is some good advice if your journey is successful and you return. Your partner usually will have this one unspoken, fundamental question as you stumble into the door from yet another heroic quest: "Am I still good enough for you?" Your beloved held the space for you while you went on your multi-coloured Vapashna, or climbed to Everest Base Camp.

Cut them some slack and tell them you love them even more whilst you download a monologue about your experiences upon the bewildered one. Remember who just paid the rates, cleaned the house for your return and has injured a shoulder vacuuming whilst you were bungee jumping in Nepal.

Drugs: psychedelics and otherwise

Years ago in the western world, Life's phases used to come upon us at an early age with marriage and parenting occurring in our early twenties. In other parts of the world, these things happened even earlier. It was when we learned to mix up milk formula, change nappies, and service the car with just a cheap set of spanners. The old people, their wisdom, stories and energies lived amongst us and helped to balance and moderate society. Those were courageous, busy years for us. Today, the twenty and thirty somethings have their unique challenges in navigating a social structure that keeps changing so fast that many struggle to find the bedrock -a solid foundation on which to constellate their lives. The wisdom of the elders is exiled to the retirement villages of our modern world where its relevance quickly becomes eroded.

In a house near Fremantle I stood before a bookshelf filled with many wonderful, soulful books about life. It was a bit like standing before one of the huge pipe organs you find in old cathedrals. This array of books was a statement, an expression of the minds of the young people who lived in this house: beautiful young people, tattooed, sun drenched skins, long flowing hair, smiles that lit up any social space. They were all searching for meaning, for the top of the mountain – a place with a sign that says: "This is it. You've made it. You have arrived."

I hope they climb the right mountains – right for them -and listen to the right teachers. I hope they see through the misty clouds to all the other mountain peaks around, many of which are still theirs

TRANSFORMATION AND THE GOLDEN KEYS

to be climbed – mind-expanding challenges they could never foresee. And I hope they sit there to touch the sky for a moment and pause to breathe in the Oneness of God, of Spirit, of all that is and to really love these journeys.

On the shelf some books on psychedelics caught my eye and I then spent a month hunting down what my troubled heart began to say. The world has been awash with drug use for a long time - skillfully and unskillfully, medicinally, recreationally and even visionary. What I have seen of mental health and mental illness, of the plasticity of the mind, I don't believe in free lunches anymore. Without some degree of mental health and stability, all is lost. Life is going to take its toll on the mind and body anyway regardless of altered mental states and altering the chemistry of your mind. So choose wisely what you allow into your mind and into your body. You may be crying out for happiness, breakthroughs and answers many times in your life. Be careful where that takes you when the responsibilities of parenting and work and income and health arise. The end does not always justify the means, and humans love to worship their drugs and addictions.

We cannot stay in the comforts and journeys of drugs too long or too often because dysfunction insidiously sets in. It spills over sideways because of the company it keeps with other drugs, with other people, with other ideas and other practices... these creep into our world because they come as part of the package deal. There is the permissiveness of unbounded experience, breaking of social norms and boundaries that it cultivates and how the heavy-handedness of drug chemistry can temporarily trump ordinary experience all too easily. Then it reinforces the experiences forever with waves of pleasurable neurotransmitters. No wonder people value the experience so highly once the spell is cast.

It borders on an extreme sport of the mind. And just as with the wonder of extreme sport, we don't readily see the costs and the consequences when things go wrong. In mythical terms, Dionysus will drive his followers mad if he is not respected. People lose sight of the God and of his power as their gaze steadily becomes fixated on the drug.

Every night we enter the dream world anyway: an innately psychedelic experience, with its good and bad trips, with riddles and epiphanies. We can learn the skill of interpreting this material to bring back what we can use in this world. We can't stay there but it's a free, nightly phenomenon we are all born with. I would rather this than look back on a lifetime of drug use for myself or for members of my family.

Yet we all have our addictions. They come in a myriad of forms and in all the pleasures we seek. We hold them as close as the lovers we are addicted to, even to the point of transcending love itself and forsaking those we should never have betrayed just to get the reward.

A psychosis is defined as a state of mind where emotions and cognitions have disengaged a person from functionally perceiving reality. An article in the Scientific American entitled: A Trip Inside the Schizophrenic Mind describes how researchers were investigating hallucinogens to model—and develop treatments for—psychosis. (Article by Taylor Beck on March 1, 2017). By definition, the psychedelics induce a state of psychosis. The researchers were in-

TRANSFORMATION AND THE GOLDEN KEYS

vestigating ways of blocking, not enhancing this process in order to help treat people with a permanent form of psychosis in order to help them become more functional in this real world regardless of their amazing visions, epiphanies and voices. But don't books, TV and captivating films also hijack the cinema screen of the mind, dragging us away from reality and freeing us from our responsibilities? Doesn't this temporarily make us dysfunctional and essentially psychotic?

Well I suppose they do, but the likelihood of possible risks involved and the severity of possible risks involved compared to those of drug use don't seem to be of the same order of magnitude unless they magically have transformed a functional human into a Couch Potato.

Get involved in real life even as you do your inner work. There is plenty of inner work to do without the shortcut of drugs which would unsettle many of us from walking the Razor's Edge of inner world and outer world balance. Life is learned by experiencing life.

When Orpheus looked backwards towards Eurydice, his wife, as they fled from the Underworld, he lost her... he lost all that was dear to him. It may just be a warning not to dally in the world of drugs too long, and not to keep going back.

Poland 1936. Family photo. Back row: Antoni and Josef, my grandfather's brothers. Anna Cesnowska. Middle row: Aunty Marysia, my grandmother and grandfather holding my mum, Aunty Wera. Reclining is my Uncle Janek with his little dog. Then the Russians invaded.

4

Living your myth with attitude

My Uncle Janek and his resilience through wartime

The God of War has always lived upon this earth. The magnitude of energy he released upon the world is staggering – the destructive energy within people's hearts, and the energy of tearing apart the fabric and order of society and the beauty of this earth. But there is such purity in what he does and I discovered this when reading James Hillman's brilliant and confronting book "A Terrible Love of War". We mortals take it all personally as his energy flows through humanity and through the berserk minds of soldiers running amok. But I reckon he destroys a million stars and planets per second across the universe without blinking an eyelid. Like a child playing with fireworks.

Janek's great attitude

But for my Polish Uncle, the Second World War was one of the best times of his life. His courage, resilience and a positive mindset brought unexpected rewards as you will see. When the Russians occupied his village at the start of the War, my grandfather went into hiding in some nearby woods and Uncle Janek would sneak out there whenever he could to bring him food. Janek must have been 14 years old then, creeping out to the woods each day. Imagine his fearful breathing and pounding heart deafening his ears, the snap of every twig underfoot like a gunshot, his eyes black and wide with fear and a loaf of bread under his coat damp with his cold sweat.

Such is the courage of the Polish heart….we are the guys who had the brilliant cavalry, the Hussars who, for two hundred years with sabres drawn would charge against any enemy who dared to threaten the safety of our homeland. And they saved it time and time again on brave horses with huge eagle's wings attached to their saddles and men dressed finer than a bridegroom on his wedding day. The military museums are full of the pageantry of military uniforms of those times - more beautiful than anything a model has ever worn on the catwalks of fashion for they were dressing up for a date with Death himself. We thought of the Hussars much as New Zealander's worship the power of the All Blacks Rugby team: invincible.

The invasion of Poland and the loss of our heroes

Well, if only the Polish cavalry uniforms at the start of World War II were made of bullet proof Kevlar. When they rode out with sabres drawn against the invading German army in September 1939, they met their bride: the God of War dressed up in the cold metal of artillery shells and machine gun bullets. And I reckon their blood and bits and all the ammonium nitrate, sulphur and saltpetre in the German explosives and gunpowder fertilised the soil of Poland for many a potato crop after that. And many a story and myth of the courage of those men and their horses grew from that soil too. A few weeks later, the Russians had a go at ploughing the soil of Poland with their tanks and artillery from the other end.

TRANSFORMATION AND THE GOLDEN KEYS

You see, the world needs heroes and leaders more than ever now. But they have all been cut down by the cowardly arrows of society and many have died far too young taking our hopes and dreams down with them. We invest our gold in our heroes in order to ascend and even to surpass them one day. But that is hard to do when they die or fall from grace lost in scandal still holding on to our invested projections. The world went numb when Bruce Lee died at his prime. And Poland lost about 6 million heroes in that short war.

Well after one twig-snap too many, the Russians discovered my grandfather hiding in a thicket and matched him with a list of persons wanted for anti-communist tendencies. He had flung some bullets their way after the First World War when Polish military forces were allied to the White Russian forces that fought against the Red Russians during the times of the Russian Revolution. So he was sent to a brutal imprisonment to the far side of Russia and no one believed they would ever see this great man again.

The incredible journey of the Polish people deported to Siberia: never give up!

At gunpoint, my great-grandmother, grandmother, two aunts, the boy Janek and my Mum - still just a baby - were shipped off on the railroad cattle trucks 4000 kms east to a logging camp in the middle of a huge forest in eastern Siberia. These prisoners of war worked hard there each day because if you didn't work you didn't get any food. That was probably a blessing because the food was just cabbage soup. I guess this is why my aunty Marysia became the best picker of mushrooms in all of Siberia. Years later, my little brother Thomas and I would have endless play fights with the piles of mushrooms she picked in the forests of England. But the

Siberian mushrooms kept Mum alive whilst she feasted on a thimble of cabbage soup and which her relentless scoliosis seemed to thrive on.

Meanwhile uncle Janek would go out each morning through the snow with a shovel over his shoulder and help an old man dig graves in the frozen soil at the foot of the camp. The two of them spent each day out there talking up a storm, and trying not to freeze whilst their shovels bounced off the icy earth. He loved those times – the company and wisdom of the old man. And I dare say the old man felt much the same. You see, digging those graves and basically working for the Angel of Death - who was relentlessly stalking the four corners of the globe at that time - they learned to live more. They learned the preciousness of life and that the Angel of Death was not always the spectre of the Grim Reaper, but sometimes an Angel of Light who mercifully took the suffering ones home to a place of peace and forgiveness and healing - a place called eternity. Here, beneath the Angel's golden shadow, Janek learned to embrace life with passion and positivity. He learned to forgive, to live and to laugh more. He learned to dance more. There was never a happier couple on the dance floor than him and his baby sister, my Mum, once the war was over. And so his eyes forever sparkled, framed within the warmest smile and all the laughter that his sense of humour conjured up - like a genie from within - at every opportunity.

But when the Russians joined the Allies against Hitler, they had to let all these Polish prisoners of war go free. The terrible memories of their railway journey to the vast isolation of the frozen forest now seemed like five star travel because they were told to **walk** back home. So Janek got the women together and hatched a plan that they would be the first ones on the road the next day using his school atlas to navigate ahead of a tsunami of humanity which poured out of the ghastly logging camps and prisons of Russia.

By foot and by any other means possible, they headed south through many countries: Uzbekistan, the Caspian Sea, Iran, and into refugee camps in India and Karachi in southern Pakistan. My Great-Grandmother made it across the Caspian Sea only to expire when she reached the other side and she remains under the sands of Persia to this day. Mum was just about dead from malnutrition, but a British Red Cross doctor took her away for some months and nursed her back to health. Some elements of this story is captured in the amazing Youtube video clips and stories of Wojtek the Soldier Bear who accompanied the Polish II Corps troops into Italy. Initially Wojtek was just as a little bear cub purchased off a boy in Iran. But he later became an enlisted soldier in the Polish army, drank beer, smoked cigarettes, carried artillery shells, helped in some of their great battles in Italy and ended up in Edinburgh zoo.

Attitude is everything: the rewards for great attitude

Meanwhile, Janek managed to join the Polish army and got posted to North Africa. Standing on a bridge one day, Janek looked up at a passing convoy transporting troops to Monte Casino and in shock he recognised his father in the back of an overloaded troop carrier. No one had heard of him since he was captured and sent to a certain death in the Russian jails at the start of the war. Janek started sprinting after the truck which fortunately stopped further down the road near a group of shops. And the joy of their brief reunion and hurried transfer of news of their loved ones still warms my heart after all those years and always will. My grandfather, occasionally with Wojtek, went on to fight in many battles including the battles of Monte Casino, Ancona, the Northern Appenines, and the battle for Bologna.

In Janek's unit there were lots of freshly trained troops still needing to be assigned to various duties. And one day the camp commander told the men to report back with which specialised unit they wanted to be transferred to for further training. Well Janek and his mates put their hands up for a job in the stores where contraband could ensure many trouble free years of abundance. But the commander was no fool and sent them to an armoured vehicle squadron instead. Janek and his armoured vehicle were sent to fight in the heat and dust of North Africa and arrived to find Rommel's Panzer divisions and the German and Italian armies in retreat and surrender.

So this armoured vehicle full of buddies, bullets and vodka was then sent into Italy still never having fired a shot in battle. And suddenly the war ended in a final deafening eruption of celebration. Thus they were forced to spend a year or two in total bliss in Italy awash with olives, wine and rejoicing Italian women.

This is how my Polish family came to live in refugee camps in England and eventually settled in London. What a journey. It makes my feet ache just thinking about it.

Dragons

I worked as an inspector for Australian Quarantine for four years in most of the export abattoirs in Western Australia. At work each day I encountered life and death in equal proportions because slaughtermen tend to be very authentic in what they say and do and of course an abattoir is a giant killing machine.

Each morning I had to start off in the lairage to inspect the animals that were penned ready for the day's processing. The lairage of this particular abattoir had a system of closed-in pens, gates and interleading corridors. So it resembled something of a labyrinth – a place you might find the Minotaur lurking in. Any human who found himself in the corridors when a pen door was opened was sure to get steam rolled by a herd of cows, bulls, sheep, feral goats, water buffalo, deer, ostriches, or emus – whatever species the abattoir was going to process on the day.

Being too lazy to climb the stairs to the overhead gangways, I crept into the corridor checking it was all clear and wondered down to a far pen. The stockman heard me coming as he had already opened the door to this pen and he yelled out, "Run! Run, Inspector!....you are going to get killed!!!" So in my white lab coat and clutching my clipboard I turned and ran with all the strength of an Olympian. But for me it was like slow motion footage of a 100meter sprint as I skidded and slipped because I wasn't wearing any running spikes. It took forever to reach the exit door and my clip board and papers didn't quite make it, but I fumbled with the latch and burst through into the sunlight outside thankful to be alive. Then I turned to look at what was chasing me: ten tiny white goatlings were hesitatingly walking up the corridor from the pen followed by a grinning stockman.

The goatlings were so sweet. Even the slaughtermen gave each one a very precious hug before pulling the trigger and dispatching their souls to heaven and their chilled carcasses to a local up-market restaurant.

We all have things we fear —the many kinds of Dragons in the Dungeon deep within. And from deep within we project those Dragons outwards into the external world and fear them there too. My Dragon projections are the big strong angry men that I fear so much because of my experiences of being bullied at boarding school. I really get triggered by angry men even now. And then I am blind to the fact that as this Dragon lives deep within me and I can often be a big strong angry man too, blinded by my own shame and in denial.

Some people think Dragons should be killed or imprisoned. But that's not true. That would be walking on a pathway of Fear instead of a pathway of Love. In life there are only two pathways: one of fear with all of its many manifestations and one of love. Dragons have hearts and feelings too...and a story. And Dragons guard treasure. The best thing to do is to go and talk to your Dragons... make peace with them by befriending them. Find out when they showed up in your life, what function they serve and what they are asking for. Then strike some kind of bargain with the Dragon, a compromise, so that you both get what you want. And all of the Dragon's treasure will miraculously flood back into your life. Facing

TRANSFORMATION AND THE GOLDEN KEYS

our Dragons means we find our courage and our power and then the Dragons and the fears do not control us as much.

Dragons are just Shadow – all that we depress, repress, deny, disown or don't know about which is very much alive and well and active in the archetypal complexes and nuances of the subconscious mind. Whatever you fear or avoid or run away from, maybe stop running, and just take a peep and see what you see.

My friend Imogen really wanted to attend a women's' circle. But in the circle she would revert back to a frightened child who we referred to as the Blanket Girl. The blanket gave the child warmth, love and security and made the child nicely invisible. So I asked what would happen if the blanket was pulled away, and she said she would be terrified... of receiving the love of the group and being overwhelmed by it. Well, we talked about this for ages but I suggested maybe it was time she talks to this Blanket Girl. And with a bit of imagination it is easy to set up the sacred process of this dialogue. Using two chairs, or Bush Art or a visualisation and inner dialogue Imogen was to get a higher part of herself to talk to the child – this could be her inner Queen archetype or a whole collection of them. She could then explain to the Blanket Girl that she really wanted to take part and engage with the women's' circle but that the Blanket Girl was making her invisible. And after some heartfelt discussion with the Blanket Girl, Imogen would promise to keep the Blanket Girl under the blanket and safe in return for some meaningful engagement with the circle by her higher self. In fact she could promise the Blanket Girl ten blankets if she wanted. And I encouraged Imogen to go to the next circle but to take a doll with her and to wrap it in a blanket and to sit it on her lap or on a chair next to her so that effectively the Blanket Girl was safe and no longer inside Imogen's head.

But befriending your Dragons is the way. They are parts of you anyway with a host of bizarre protective behaviours to keep you safe. But they guard treasure and golden insights. And the treasure you get is also the power they give you when you make them your friend, your ally.

There was a real dragon I once knew. He was about two foot high and made of red felt. Our boarding school was called St George's College and this little red dragon was our school mascot. It presided over the senior refectory, the huge dining hall for the senior students, and presided over all of our senior first team sporting events with its wings unfurled. It was a powerful, magical symbol, a wonderful little beast.

On weekends, us boarders would abseil down the face of the main building: a 100-year old castle. And on the way down we would gently cross a huge metal disc effigy of St George slaying the dragon. I remember the feeling of being like Spiderman letting the abseil rope move slowly through my hands as my shoes slid across the mythical scene. There was immense presence there in this scene of death and of triumph. Now I see it as the presence of a forceful Ego, the Ego of Saint George, and the Dragon defiant in the face of death because the rider got it all wrong. He shouldn't have fed the Dragon his lance, he should have fed it coal or whatever you coax dragons with so they become your friends. Fiona loves her dragons. She tucks them under her arm and takes them to work with her so they can feel loved and their energies can set-

tle. And my niece Amanda paints the most magnificent dragons that are always protecting maidens.

I loved two martial arts films that Bruce Lee made: 'Enter the Dragon' and 'Way of the Dragon'. In both films, Bruce beats the crap out of the bad guys. Bruce was all about authentic expression and martial arts was the medium he chose to find and express his authentic self. But if I had trained him I would have got him to pull up two chairs and a table and say to the bad guys and any other dragons he came across, "Hey, we need to sit down and discuss this in a civil manner. Now please... tell me... what seems to be troubling you?"

Four siblings and our great grandmother
She told us all about the Ottoman Empire
in which she was born. We told her all
about Woodstock and Jimmy Hendrix.

5

Mental Health

Pete

There is always a golden thread of awe and wonder and a truth everywhere, even in those things we judge as bad, evil or destructive. And I want to show you how this insight helped me understand so much about Pete – my older brother and his journey through the most fascinating manifestation of a Bipolar Disorder with its spectacular ending. You see I constantly looked for the elements of truth in all his incoherent babbling and bewildering behaviour and found that his truth was always there even if in some bizarre form.

The making of a child

In 1957, just 12 years after the God of War seemed to have taken a breather from destroying and displacing much of humanity in World War II, a beautiful child was born at a south London hospital. All children are born whole, pure and perfect because they are just droplets of a conscious and living cosmos that fall into our world still fully connected to all that is. The embryo feeds off the mother because the placenta is somewhat parasitic in nature. It will burrow into any tissue to get some nurturing just like we all do. And the newborn will always need a mother's love and care whether it's in the form of milk, a person to call to say, "...my girlfriend just left me...", or the peace and stillness of Mother Nature's forests. The greatest gift an infant can receive is the first two years in the arms of a loving mother and the third year learning to kick a football with Dad. We rarely heard African children crying because they were forever sound asleep in someone's arms held close, skin to skin, mother and child wrapped together in a shawl, in the wings of love.

But growing up in an unsafe world, a separation occurs within where so much of this child's oneness falls into a subconscious or unconscious realm – the realm we walk amongst in our dreams. And as within, so without: a separation occurs from all that is, from nature and people and the physical realm and of what we truly are. All of these disowned entities, everything we repress, depress, deny or don't know about that comprise the subconscious mind, Carl Jung referred to as Shadow. Deep down is not so much a dungeon guarded by fear, but a treasury filled to the ceiling with gold and guarded by the fear of expressing our greatness and the fear of fully embracing life. The golden keys to this treasury are the keys of insight and self-love. Self-love means getting your chattering mind to love your physical body more because your body is actually your unconditional lover. It is the Hero's quest to spend a lifetime reclaiming and talking to these elements so that they can release the golden power of oneness back into your life. Remember, every dragon actually is your friend, and every dragon guards treasure. Go there when you are ready. Talk to them. We are not supposed to kill these dragons or ignore them otherwise we will miss out on the treasure.

And once you have analysed and experienced your masculine elements, and your feminine elements both within yourself and within others, you may transcend to some kind of balance and relationship of the masculine and feminine within you - known long ago as The Sacred Marriage.

There you will discover a peaceful, beautiful, whole state of mind and state of relationship both within and without. And transcending even this, a time of eldership and wisdom awaits as we gracefully accept the honour and privilege of growing old, augmenting knowledge with wisdom.

In the cold of February, Pete was wrapped tightly in a little blanket and brought home to my grandparent's house nearby in Balham. My Polish grandfather managed to buy this house after the war with money he made from making and selling sleeping bags together with my uncle. At night time, they would drink cider and together with a Polish priest they made even more money out of gambling by playing Bridge. In this circle of men, and win at all cost, Mum as a child learned to delight in Bridge and could beat the pants off everyone. She often got me to play too sitting in the circle of women who met weekly as an informal Bridge club in Zambia. So I got to watch her going totally crazy in their little competitions. For her, the game was a celebration of survival and triumph, of victory over war and mostly a celebration of her beloved father.

Effects on the unborn

Pete had already spent nine months in her womb bathed in the stress hormones of cortisol and adrenalin. All that time he lay close to the pounding heart of a beautiful young maiden who had fallen from grace. And he could hear the voices of my English grandmother insisting on an abortion, the principal of the London Polytechnic discussing why Mum was giving up architectural school, Mum's shameful sobbing and the discussions in Polish of yet another family crisis. Every swig of breastmilk was laced with further doses of stress chemicals and then Pete, the divine firstborn child, also fell from the grace of being first born as his three siblings, Pola, me and Tom were conceived in quick succession.

Themes of harm and injury unfolding in Pete's life

He was destined for bizarre experiences of divine and epic proportions. To reveal him as the Chosen One, a portent was sent from the Gods in the form of a lightning bolt during a violent London storm. Pete was sitting in the lounge playing with some building blocks and a ball of lightning flashed into the room from the fireplace burning a circle in the Lino floor around the terrified Thunderbolt Kid. I fully believe this family story told to me by my Uncle because it pales into insignificance against the things I subsequently witnessed unfolding in Pete's life.

The loss of a functional Ego

What a privilege for me to walk hand in hand down the corridors of Pete's mind as the years unfolded. Initially Pete was quite normal. His Ego was fully functional and could make sense of his inner and outer worlds. But later in life in his mid-fifties he lost his Ego completely through alcoholism and immense stress. Without a functional Ego around which to organise and moderate his mind, without a 'Self', he basically fell into his sea of archetypes and became psychotic projecting his inner people and voices out into the world.

Rampant Shadow, unmoderated by Ego is amazing to witness. To lose the Ego completely mixes inner and outer worlds and the balance, the Razor's Edge, is lost. Then Archetypes appear in droves, like fifty demons running amok in a market place…or in society or even in the same sentence. You see, the trick to living your Soul's mission, your gift to the world is to move the Ego slightly to one side, not to lose it completely, so it can still do a bit of lion taming on your archetypes and conduct an entire orchestra of them to create some decent music.

Pete's bipolar disorder

I wonder at the magnificence of his spiral into a world alive with archetypes. Half the time he was the happiest and most empowered person on this planet his eyes and mind aflame with visions of Heaven and Hell, of abundant money and godly power. He certainly wasn't suffering although he looked a terrible sight with his filthy, threadbare clothing, bits of tinsel tied into his hair as he begged and lived on the streets of Zambia for years.

But when he came down from his godly mania, he was immobilised with black fear, cut and crushed by endless shards of sadness and remorse. Mum would take him in from a cold and cruel world and heal him with a Mother's love. I would lie next to him in bed and hold him whilst he cried and suffered on and on into the night. At that time I didn't realise I was holding a very damaged man who would never find his way back from that journey into the underworld, the Kingdom of Hades and Persephone. Like I said, these journeys are never guaranteed of a 'safe' return – whatever safety means to you. You will most likely be forever changed. Maybe think about such risks when you embark on inner journeys, when your mind is slipping or the next time you pop some psychedelics.

Pete's Genius and the God of Destruction

Pete was three years older than me. Short, slightly chubby and bespectacled, he nonetheless inhabited a world of sheer creative genius. And he was always on the cusp of creative madness too and a conduit for supernatural experiences. Talk about opposites: on one hand, he was totally creative, ceaselessly building things from cardboard boxes, Plasticine and toothpicks, Lego Bricks, Meccano, paper, sand and water, computer graphics and Mandelbrot sets. Yet they always seemed to end in destruction and maniacal laughter.

My earliest memory is of him destroying my beautiful new pedal car – one you could sit in and pedal along the corridors of the house and out into a summer's day in the garden. Dad's fond memories of Prince Faisal's pedal car collection had provided me with my most treasured possession. It had electric headlights, a horn that worked and chrome bumpers. Pete climbed on top of our World War II concrete bunker in the back garden in London and stood there with my pedal car held aloft, rather like King Kong tossing a New York taxi down the street. The bunker had been a place of protection for families during the air raids of World War II twenty years before. But it provided no protection that day. As Pola, Thomas and I stood below his towering figure, and despite our desperate pleas, he threw it headlong off the bunker. In slow motion it tumbled and smashed on the concrete below. I still wince at that one.

As children growing up in Zambia the local TV channel was not a great source of entertainment because when it actually worked, it mostly featured villagers dressed in grass skirts pretending to be crocodiles and thumping drums. This meant we were forever outside playing in the garden. We would build cities out of sticks and stones and plastic soldiers and whatever else we could find. Pete loved to create a massive reservoir of water complete with a dam wall above his hapless city so he could release the torrent of water and a torrent of laughter to flood the doomed inhabitants below. Destruction seemed to come naturally to him as did the inevitable beatings he got from Dad.

Teddy bears were strapped to fireworks and shot into the sky or blown to smithereens whilst they sat innocently in tiny makeshift log cabins. Lego cars were built to indestructible standards. Yet every time Tom and

I zoomed down the long corridors of the rambling house in Zambia pulling the cars along behind us attached to a length of string, Pete would appear from a side room and with the roar of a lion and the screaming of little kids, his Terminator Dragster car would be upon us. He knew how to engineer lethal Lego battering rams and cars that could flip over and keep on driving. So in a plume of tiny cubes mixed with our screams and tears, his car would shatter all our Lego dreams.

He seemed to be living life as if it was an extreme sport. So he kept a few serpents as his pet animals of choice. He chose spitting cobras no less. He first encountered one when entering the chicken house to investigate why the chickens were making such a racket. As he peered into one of the nesting boxes in the gloomy darkness, he received a faceful of snake venom which usually fries the eyeballs instantaneously. But thanks to Pete's solar eclipse experience of some years previously- burning his retina whilst staring at the sun - he now wore glasses permanently and was spared the excruciating agony of boiled eyeballs and a lifetime of blindness.

Pete's ultimate Nemesis: The God of Fire

Pete was obsessed with floating flowers on the garden fish pond, and then blowing them to bits with the stinging lashes of a rubber band. Although he specialised in bizarre forms of destruction, he had to become really good at construction too. And he took things to a new level when he teamed up with his lifelong buddy, the God of Fire. Shortly after his induction by lightning as the Thunderbolt Kid, he tested this new-found playmate of fire by dipping his nappy and his soft baby bottom into the burning hot coals of the fireplace in London. And it seemed to affect his ability to sit still from that burning moment onwards. This was the start of a lifetime of relentless injuries to himself and to others. His skin hoisted the white flag of surrender on many occasions when the smoke and screaming had cleared.

Injury number two involved slipping off the top of our shiny piano onto the upright of a splintered chair which nearly removed his bicep and inaugurated a lifetime of quilting by the surgeons who were called time and again over the years to put him back together. When he permanently burned a hole in his retina looking directly at a solar eclipse, the rest of us school kids in the playground were dutifully looking through x-ray film or at the image of the sun projected through a pinhole in a piece of card onto the ground.

One day, in Zambia, he jumped into an ash pit where the gardener had burned sticks and leaves a day or two before. I watched Pete waist deep in that hot grey ash roll his eyes to Heaven and erupt in a war dance of howling pain. As the burning hot coals filled his shoes, he stomped and leaped and shrieked around the fire pit better than any Hiawatha. The smell of pork crackling flavoured the air attracting our three hungry dogs. They came running thinking it was a barbecue. For weeks he crawled around the house on his hands and knees. I was boggled by the blisters on the soles of his feet which resembled water-filled coconuts.

Oh, the accidents never ended. Picture him at boarding school in the Chemistry lab. Everyone else was testing the pH of a solution with Litmus paper. Meanwhile Pete, transcending such mundane activities, was mesmerised by convection currents of silver spangles from boot polish he had dissolved in a beaker of Turpentine. Earlier on he had sneaked it into the laboratory past the priest taking the class. Now he was slowly stirring this over the flame of a Bunsen burner having forgotten how inflammable Turpentine is. In a customary boom and a flash, to which I can assure you I was no stranger, Pete and the entire lab turned to flame, screams,

TRANSFORMATION AND THE GOLDEN KEYS

flying schoolboys in white lab coats, and a wild-eyed Jesuit priest like Rambo gunning the flames down with a fire extinguisher which belched white smoke and powder everywhere. I imagine the priest awash with sweat, jugular veins like anacondas, shaking with the blasts of the fire extinguisher and muttering through gritted teeth, "…….Fuck you….. Peter Ravensdale…aaaaargghh!!..!" Ka! Ka! Ka! Ka! Ka! Pete, white with powder, rather crisp and with no hair, was bundled from the smoke and mayhem of the laboratory into an ambulance. He then had his extensive third degree burns treated for many months at the local hospital in Harare.

The doctors were experienced in treating burns victims because the entire country of Rhodesia was hosting the God of War in the form of a liberation struggle at that time and this God of War loves heat in so many forms. Like for example the use of white phosphorous grenades on the grass huts of villagers and Frantam bombs - a form of Napalm - which the air force could mix up in a bucket using polystyrene, petrol and simply add a detonator. Genius, this God of War, this pure and authentic archetype of destruction.

Pete was to fire as a moth is to light bulbs. I have scars on my feet from when he walked by drizzling fire drops of molten plastic over me from a burning model airplane. He bought a tub of solid sodium metal – cubes of pure sodium that must be kept away from moisture because it causes a violent chemical reaction. So they are sold submerged in paraffin oil. And during the monsoon rains, he would throw lumps of sodium into puddles in the garden to watch it fizzle and sizzle releasing hydrogen from the water and glowing steadily with its particular amber frequency of light – the same amber that the sodium vapour street lights create. The hydrogen would ignite and explode into sizzling globules of molten metal.

They flew through the air leaving white vapour trails of caustic soda that choked our lungs, burned our skin and caused a wave of panic amongst the fleas clinging to our dogs as they fled to safety.

As scars relentlessly appeared on Pete's physical body, we failed to see all the scars within. And we took mental health for granted then. But as within, so without….the scars we could see told of an inner story. Today, I thank God with every breath for the tiny measure of sanity I have and wherever I find it in the world. And I observe with great sadness and compassion the devils and the threatening storms of mental illness roaming our communities in plague proportions because I know the suffering they bring, the chaos, the destruction of lives and collateral damage. Cherish your sanity, it is a rather fleeting treasure, and you yourself will probably be unaware when you lose it. Such is the nature of mental illness, of Shadow and of personality disorders.

Boys and weapons making

So how did Pete cover the veranda in his own blood, you ask? Well in life you will always come across under-fathered boys who spend their time building weapons. Pete was one, and he passed his skills and his under-fathering forwards into the next generation. There is genius here in weapons making. The Magician within may be symbolically trying to equip the internal Warrior with the tools needed to face the external adventures and challenges, to go on quests and tame dragons. It is a time of pulling back the bowstring to fling the arrow that is the young adventurer himself, launching him bravely into an uncertain future… and usually with a backpack full of Shadow to deal with. It is the baggage that needs sorting out which is unconsciously projected outwards appearing as the dragons and dramas we face.

Pete's son, Jeremy, was given some playdough one day to create a few teddy bears, bunny rabbits... the usual Pokemon-like things that materialise out of playdough. But Pete had been away for years in Saudi Arabia working for British Aerospace as a project manager on various military construction sites. So he left his family in Cyprus under-fathered by his absence but safely out of reach of Middle Eastern carnage. That day, Jeremy turned the playdough into lethal sun-baked sea urchin projectiles with which to impale the street kids in Cyprus who had declared war on him. Under-fathered yet he is such a loving dad today... and an ex-weapons manufacturer I hope.

I remember Pete using an avocado pear to terrorise me on his big black bicycle. Looking back over my shoulder I saw a black jet fighter closing in for the kill with a payload of air-to-air missiles. I was never going to escape because I was on Pola's bicycle. Instead, I did a front flip over the handlebars, like a fighter pilot's desperate loop-the-loop, when my front tyre hit a furrow in the lawn. I landed with a perfect dissected view of my quadriceps muscle revealed through a sizeable and deep hole in my leg... until it all filled with blood. The nursing staff held me down that day and a doctor, one of Pete's quilting brigade, plied my leg with local anaesthetic and lengths of suture. The next day I discovered how the hole happened... a long piece of my skin was dangling, dry and crispy from the brake handle of Pola's bike.

We often survive thanks to good men and women

But back to the veranda story: One day, whilst Mum and Dad were away at work for the day, Pete built a great bow and arrow. Needing a target, he proceeded to focus a death wish on me and let a few arrows fly in my direction. I made haste across the garden and came across Pola sunning herself near the front door. She, ever the rescuer, berated Peter to put down the weapon but that just multiplied his death wish by two. So Pola fled indoors with Pete in hot pursuit. He slid on the doormat just as Pola in full sprint pulled the glass French Doors closed behind her. It was a defensive move only James Bond could repeat. Pete didn't cut a thing as his right arm exploded through the glass. But he nearly cut that arm clean off at the wrist as he pulled it backwards in fright. I watched the white veranda turn red from ceiling to floor and then Pola appeared dragging our African cook from the kitchen and they bandaged his wrist in tea towels made of mutton cloth. I had the sense to call our doctor and then sat by the phone frantically reading a Bible and praying in English, Polish and the howls of a child who has seen too much. The surgeon, a certain Dr McNab at the hospital decided to amputate Pete's hand but with a couple of hours to spare before lunch he changed his mind and quilted Pete's arteries, veins, tendons and skin back together.

Pete's ability to cause collateral mayhem

Even during his recovery from this, Pete nearly got me and Tom killed. He was still bandaged and in a cast when he took us down a railway track to balance a sequence of rocks on the metal tracks for considerable distance down the line. At a corner in the track we found steep embankments on each side and a huge train belching smoke and steam coming straight at us. It was sounding an ear-piercing whistle set to full volume. From the side of the locomotive, I could see the sweaty soot-covered driver and his fireman shouting and waving their fists at us and gunning the engine intent on running us down. In front of the speeding train ran the three of us trying to make it to a cutting in the embankment up ahead. Behind us the locomotive made rapid ground with the stones on the track exploding into white puffs of powder under the tons of steel and metal wheels. Yes, we made it, diving headlong into the elephant grass at the cutting with the hot, grinding steel at our heels. Above us, black faces, white eyes and teeth and clenched fists passed by in a swirling cloud of smoke and rumbles like an earthquake. Lying there in the grass with ripples of mortal fear running like waves through my body and my eyes fixed on Heaven, I think I uttered my first blasphemous swear word.

Pete's search for empowerment

And Pete loved the supernatural. He used us as guinea pigs for telepathy experiments, attempts at levitation and communication with the spirit world using a Ouija board of Scrabble letters and a wine glass...once the lights were out and a candle lit, it was sheer terror that electrified the atmosphere of those séances.

He found his inspiration in the love of his life: Salwa – a half Egyptian, half English beauty with all the stunning treasures of Egypt in her eyes, her looks and her flowing black hair. Her voice, her ability to keep pitch perfect harmonies and melodies, her laughter and kind heart. She was a rare treasure indeed. And she had that magic ingredient: two 'X' chromosomes. Until she found her self-love and self-acceptance, her beauty came at a price: three hours of putting on make-up in the morning and sleeping with her hair soaked in fragrant olive oil.

Sal and Pete formed a rock band together with two Zambian guitarists, Rouge and Sam, and Pete as the drummer. The band was called Medusa. One night Pete asked Sam why one of the Zambians dancing in front of them had a calabash of beer and had cleared people off the dance floor. "He's a witchdoctor," said Sam, "and he's putting some kind of spell on us." Looking back, I think it was just one of many spells that came against Pete's honest attempts at life.

Turning all of this destructive yet creative mad genius to good, there was only one place Pete could go: the Born Again movement. His thirst for power and empowerment became empowerment by the Holy Spirit in a world of miracles, bristling with messages from God and Holy Wars of Good against Evil. He exchanged his Ouija board for the Bible and had no need for lesser spirits because he could now dial up God 24/7. For all its goodness, and underlying messages of brotherly and divine love, the Born Again movement also had a divine ink pad from which they could stamp various things they didn't like as 'Demonic', 'Satanic', 'Unbiblical', 'Blasphemy', 'Pagan', 'Unclean in the Sight of the Lord', 'Cult-ish' and a host of other things. Pete stamped away to create his own brand of super-spirituality in service to the Lord all with the purest of intentions and the care and compassion of a saint towards the Zambian people.

But in the background the power of Shadow was building. It does in all of us unless we process it on the run throughout our lives. Ultimately we have the potential to transcend all story and become almost mute with the advent of a loving self-acceptance, a healthy cynicism of all knowledge, all story, and the healing that forgiveness brings. This is the advent of the freedom of Wisdom: knowing that what most people call life is just a game, a story, a fabrication, a fiction that can be changed and enjoyed. You are the life within, not the game without – the game that people are so invested in to the point of delusion and blindness.

Nine years working in the hot sands of Saudi Arabia on secret military installations as an architect and project manager, stepping in the very footsteps of Jesus, Pete returned to Zambia as an altruistic Christian. He had a vision of establishing Tele-centres for the African people and empowering them with access to the internet, printing facilities, advice and training. He and Salwa established an orphanage, a school and a charity and forever took people in need into their home. But all was lost. It crumbled in his hands. Zambia is a very beautiful country and I love her people, but I reckon she has sunk every altruistic investment ever made. That's a 100% success rate. Despite his praying in tongues to an almighty god, Pete was fleeced of every penny just like everyone else who has invested in Africa. His altruistic investment went up in smoke like an offering at Solomon's Temple.

Archetypal anarchy

In my heart a voice calls out to one who can no longer reply with a human voice. Oh Pete, why did you steadily spiral into alcoholism, depression and fear? Why did you enter the gateway of a Bipolar Disorder and throw away the key? I know that Pete put his heart and soul and money and thinking into his life's mission when he returned to Zambia with his altruistic ideas. And then he found that his God didn't come to the party, that his God had failed him. He lost everything and eventually lost his mind seeking a dialogue with God about these matters, seeking peace, or an explanation.

His method of last resort was not the euphoric ecstasy of a charismatic Christian service but through Dionysus, the god of alcoholic ecstasy - through the liminoid gateway to the Gods. His alcoholic consumption became legendary and must have boosted the Zambian economy. Much of it was alcohol brewed on the streets of Ndola using everything from maize meal to old shoes, rats and snakes. It is then distilled into various spirit fractions which range from methylated spirits and aviation fuel to actual evil spirits - all of which I imagine are poisonous to humans.

In an alcoholic stupor, you can talk to fifty gods in one night if you want to - I have done it plenty of times. It's really a realm best left to the shaman skilled in such journeys, and a journey best not taken alone, whiskey bottle in hand on a moonlit night under a Zambian sky. There are so many chemicals, drugs and practices that powerfully affect the mind and take it far away to another place. So we find ourselves paying the anaesthetist and the shaman not only to make us unconscious for surgery or psychotic with visions but also to bring us back from the underworld alive and whole. In mythical terms you are asking an unusual request of Charon, ferryman to Hades, for a return ticket, safe passage, a free lunch and to cheat Death. The price is therefore usually quite high and the results can be variable.

And I suppose that only two psychiatrists in a country of 15 million Zambians didn't help Pete much. Lusaka's streets are littered with the countless boxes of pills Dad bought Pete. He just threw them all away because they impeded his euphoria. In this way I imagine he addicted a generation of stray dogs and street kids to anti-psychotics.

You see, the euphoria of his manic phases gave him a chance to live his dreams and experience his true godly power in its raw and untempered form. Why would he want the medication to take this away from him when he would then experience the reality of a living hell in a third world psychiatric ward and the Zambian prison system? His euphoria gave him reason and permission to get a measure of justice... to want to kill his family members, setting fire to his farm and home, and fights with his son and with our Dad. Raw, immature archetypes can be like this: arrogant, self-serving and full of self-opinions and grandiose ideas. He would climb onto the roof at night like a Ninja and secretly listen in to his family's conversations then burst in on them full of manic superpowers. This scared the crap out of everyone just as if Satan himself had suddenly manifested in the dining room whilst they were eating dinner.

Anyway, I have the luxury to ponder these things over cups of tea now. We all can in retrospect because as the saying goes: when the waters are still, the mud will settle. We can reflect and see things a little clearer whereas at the time the rules and the understandings were so very different and steeped in fear.

The Cinema Screen

> There is a cinema screen in my mind which creates the most bizarre movies. And I call this reality and sit and watch as if in a cinema eating from a giant box of popcorn. My Ego watches thinking it is real when behind it is the true observer, consciousness itself, the Witness. How can our five – or more – faulty senses ever come up with anything approximating reality? We are in fact like blind people groping in the dark when it comes to what is truly real. Even when you watch a TV screen or a video clip on your computer, the image that you become conscious of on your mental screen is different to whatever video or movie is being shown.
>
> This cinema screen comes alive with images constantly. Every word you read in a book throws up images on your screen, every song you hear, everything you taste and smell. If someone speaks to you, the screen comes alive because words represent symbols that can be spoken and written and seen. A sentence is just a stream of symbols. They magically modify each other as we select them and juxtapose them to define and convey meaning. The symbols of each spoken and written word are just like ribbons of film for your internal cinema.
>
> If psychosis is a serious deviation from generally acceptable interpretations of reality, then it could be argued that we are all psy-

chotic most of the time. Every student engrossed in a book or listening to a lecture has a mind alive with images and stories that are not really happening at the time. And a gifted story teller can hook the imagination and turn the listeners' minds into worlds alive with fantasy and magic.

I used to watch my bipolar brother Peter flip through a hundred mental TV channels in one sentence... like some laboratory rat high on cocaine pressing the remote button for another fix.

He would wake up and put on a pair of glasses that filtered the world into either manically happy or suicidally sad. We all pick up glasses each morning as we get out of bed to peep at the world and create focus. I sometimes forget to pick up the happy ones and my day evolves into a train wreck simply due to a pair of imaginary specs... free ones at that.

Then Pete would focus on something, like trying to kill Dad or make a million dollars or maybe about the Apocalypse. Well life in a third world country can be diabolical for anyone at times. Just try and get through the average police checkpoint and you'll appear on the other side often without your car, money, or your sense of humour. Focus is great, but whatever we focus on becomes highly significant and we become blind to the periphery. It's basically tunnel vision. That's why we need an eagle inside us to fly high and see the bigger picture too, and preferably an eagle with its own pair of golden glasses.

Pete's five faulty senses would give him faulty information depending on how he was feeling that day. Some days he was immune to pain or fear and became kind of superhuman especially when leaping off the roof of the psyche ward on another of his many escapes to freedom running through the bush to the local shabeens.

Pete's brain processed all of these inputs in a different way to you and me. We all have unique and faulty brains. The formatting of our brains has many a glitch, computer viruses and segments of corrupted code. 'I must eat chocolate' is a common corruption because the body has different and simple needs when compared to the intangible and insatiable mind eye-balling a chocolate cake. And we have different apps running all the time depending on what's ticking up there. Pete's brain was rather fried on cheap alcohol, lack of sleep and a smorgasbord of anti-psychotic medication taken at random.

His Pattern Gathering Apparatus would scan for patterns in his perceived world and join the dots in bizarre ways. We all look for patterns. It is a faulty exercise but it helps for making quick decisions when we may have experienced something like this before. We also live by a set of beliefs that we hold about reality. And they are reinforced by an Evidence Gathering Machine that looks for evidence in order to strengthen and prove our beliefs over and over again because it makes us feel safe. Seek whatever type of evidence you want and ye shall indeed find.

Well when Pete was depressed, devils, demons and angels were everywhere... they sat on his shoulders and whispered into his ear helping him make choices.

I know that everything I perceive through my physical senses falls short of an ultimate truth. So in this sense all human-based *knowledge is false and at best a poor approximation to any absolute truth. And all data I receive is corrupted and tainted by humanity whether in its transmission, its capture or in how I perceive it. At the same time it is all I have got to make sense of the miracle in which I live. It's like I am blind, yet I rejoice with what I can see. It's all I have with which to speak with another.*

All of our acquired knowledge and memories are faulty because they are based on human concepts. The universe doesn't really care so much about our mathematics or any of our science and it doesn't submit to them the way we would like it to. All of our inner concepts and schemas have associations that colour or taint what we are trying to perceive. To make matters worse, our memories become severely distorted with time. So we live in an approximation of reality, best referred to as a dream.

We project some garbled image onto the cinema screen and call it reality. Then we judge it against our values and weigh it on an Inner Weighing Machine that balances the cost of Pleasure versus Pain, of our two basic fears of Rejection and Failure.

Now just imagine that like a mad painter you throw buckets of colourful emotion over the screen, wobble it with your physiology and hormonal chemistry of the day and soak it in all the drugs you've been taking including coffee or alcohol or sugar or whatever you're addicted to, and then let your inner archetypes and Shadow loose as actors in the show and conductors of the orchestra and the very composers of the script and soundtrack.

Well it's like anarchy in a zoo really. The chimps have run off with all the bananas. We domesticate our children to keep this pande-

> monium in check to an acceptable degree. But it is the best we can do to come up with a concept called 'Reality'. Just don't ever take it too seriously. And if you don't like the movie, simply change it by positively modifying all those filters and inputs. They affect your choices. And your choices add up to become your destiny. How about creating a great destiny by tweaking a few things? How about creating your own myth to live by if it's all just a story?

Ndola Central Hospital

There is a huge regional hospital in the middle of Ndola. When we first came to Zambia all the local architects and builders were involved in its construction which started back in the 1960's. Mum and Dad were therefore involved from the outset but it seemed that this hospital was constantly in our lives from that time on for an endless array of reasons.

The mortuary of this sprawling hospital was situated near to the psyche ward which thereby grouped the psyche ward and the mortuary into similar regions of horror. In either facility things were very unlikely to ever end well. Pete, in a manic state of archetypal anarchy was treated by the local police to a truncheon-fest - basically beating the shit out of him with their batons - before throwing him into the Ndola Central Hospital's psyche ward. Chefs all over the world tenderise steak in a similar way before frying it. There, Pete would find himself incarcerated on many occasions, the Minotaur in the psyche ward's Labyrinth.

Mistakenly our local Keystone Cops thought he would never escape but somehow Pete became possessed by the very spirit of Harry Houdini. He probably inspired a generation of Zambian escape artists as a result - and many a James Bond sequel - by escaping from all sorts of places and situations. I mean, you have to be given the opportunity to practice and hone such skills…how else is say an accountant or a café barista supposed to perfect the skill of police evasion and maximum security building escape techniques?

Freedom, Rights and Responsibility

Pete loved escaping from the maximum security psyche ward in Lusaka. He delighted in it because the prize for doing so was sweet freedom… and we all crave our freedom. Archetypes hate being restricted because they love the absolute, they love becoming inflated and bigger than Ben Hur. Western society allows us some freedom, as long as we do it responsibly. Otherwise they lock us up to ponder these issues for a while. Freedom without a seasoning of responsibility can become a self-serving, self-indulgent form of Sigmund Freud's concept of the 'Id' … that demanding little rascal within who wants, and believes it deserves immediate gratification. The learning is: have your freedom, but be responsible with it. It has consequences. It impacts on others. So moderate it with a bit of Ego control and a bit of conscience, a bit of humility.

Being responsible seems to go hand in hand with mental health. The healthier my thinking, the healthier my behaviour, my ability to respond in a constructive fashion, the care I can give to issues. We need to cherish responsibility because to give it to someone else, to pay someone else to care for it or to elect a government and give away my personal responsibility is to give away my power, my freedom and my control to others. All I have left to shout about and demand are my rights and then I wait for someone else to do the work or fix the issue. And I will then be speaking from my 'Id' that is totally demanding about its rights just as raw archetypes are. As a general principle, that seems mentally retrogressive and like asking Mummy to make it better.

Anyway, I reckon Pete's archetypes could have taken on Alcatraz and Colditz. His untimely and spectacular end happened when his Escape Artist archetype chose to escape this very world and its system of being. Inflation does this. The archetype gets too big for its boots then appears to shoot itself in the foot. And in this way he discovered the freedom of being in Heaven. Stick with me, I will tell you what happened soon enough.

The Mortuary: seeing things that young eyes should not see

Well I must digress but when we were eighteen year olds, Scooby and I used to go to the hospital's mortuary every week to watch post mortems there. The resident pathologist was an Irish doctor, a really wonderful man who, true to the Irish stereotype, and like some medieval Irish Alchemist he had discovered the Leprechaun's Gold. It was an endless amber coloured liquid served in shot glasses down at the local golf club bar at 10 am every morning. And this pathologist had spent years purchasing a vast fortune of this amber liquid using a vast fortune of his own money. The Leprechaun's Gold magically helped him transcend the hell of working in a third world hospital, And he drank it all up to the point of destroying most of his nervous system and shrinking his brain into something like a well basted alcoholic prune before he eventually popped his clogs. His last 'one for the road' resulted in him being inadvertently dropped off at the Pearly Gates by a celestial Uber Taxi losing its way.

So his hands shook worse than Parkinson's disease, worse than a man possessed by St Vita's Dance, worse than if he were working a petrol-driven sand compactor. He could no longer be trusted to maintain any adequate grip on a sharp scalpel as he sliced and diced his way through the day's cadavers. This made it dangerous for his two Zambian staff and anyone in the room including the cadavers. Consequently the hospital gave him a Russian pathologist as his assistant. Despite the fact that the Russian could speak no English, he had steady hands with which to wield a scalpel. He also had a spectacular full set of gold teeth and I always imagined the golden beams of light from the operating lamps reflecting off these glistening teeth in spangles around the dissecting room like a disco ball. He used to serenade my mother on his Russian Guitar at our farm on the weekends whilst she slugged back another vodka and swished her skirts to his lively Polish Mazurkas. All the while he flashed his wealth and life savings to her with every smile making himself almost as irresistible as the golden mask of Tutankhamen.

Music seems to heal everything... even Mum's wartime animosity to the Russians when Russians will forever be sworn enemies to her part of Poland. There is a saying in Africa which relates to the mythical story of Nadzikambe, the Singing Chameleon. Zambians superstitiously believe that chameleons are just mini-demons in a lizard's disguise and readily flog them to death with sticks whenever they come across one. But a Zambian chameleon is totally harmless and quickly settles in your hand to become your very best friend. Nadzikambe could charm all of nature with his silken voice and the music of his harp just like this Russian charming Mama. You see, the myth says, "If your face is ugly, learn to sing."

Scooby and I would dress up in white lab coats pretending to be students from the capital city's university and under the protection of our two pathologist mates, one shaking, the other shining, we would find ourselves in the morgue each week watching things that no 18-year old eyeballs should ever be watching. I remember helping to empty the contents of a dirty hessian sack onto the dissecting table. Out bounced a shriveled old man who had gassed himself making charcoal out in the forest. He was very dead, cold and stiff and covered in maggots. The Zambian assistant sprang into action. He was no stranger to the tussle of maggot versus man and began gunning down the maggots with liberal doses of insecticide from an aerosol appropriately labelled: "Sudden Death Insect Killer". Nothing was going to get out of that morgue alive.

We saw two Zambian soldiers brought in from a vehicle accident. They had ploughed into a lamp post at high speed and by the looks of surprise on their dismembered faces I reckon the lamp post won. Death by misadventure seemed to be commonplace: we will never forget the smell of alcohol on the human brain from a man who had died of blood loss from a tiny wound on his wrist. He had fallen asleep in a ditch very drunk on New Year's Eve after trying to break in to a house through a window. On the broken glass he had suffered a very tiny cut to a small but, in his case, an eternally significant artery. Some tiny things we do definitely have eternal consequences. It's a macabre form of the Butterfly Effect.

Scooby and I saw lots of things at the morgue, most of which we would rather forget. But I guess the message we got was: Yes, definitely, the party does not go on forever. The Angel of Death had taught us to live fully, to forgive and to grab the present with both hands. She tempered our reckless adolescent behaviour and humbled our former beliefs in adolescent immortality. So send your teenage sons to India. Stepping off the plane, they will be confronted with a very cost effective, harsh and instant enlightenment as their eyes search in vain past the diseased, dead and dying for the quaint facades of western society. They will come back home and embrace all that they have as they step off the plane to kiss the ground with gratitude.

Lem the Rescuer and Mission Impossible

Tom paid for my ticket to fly to Zambia to try and make sense of what was going on with the Pete fiasco. I arrived in the afternoon at Ndola airport – a relic from the 1950's whose Nissan huts built by the British Colonial administration are still very much the entire airport building. It's just full of Chinese people now as is much of Africa. I met Mum and Dad there and at once I could see that things were abysmal because they both looked so jaded. After their divorce, they hadn't spoken to each other in years and would even avoid each other on the high street, yet here they were sitting in the airport cafe being most civil. So I felt twenty years of relief pass through my child within.

In the face of a gathering monsoon storm which in Zambia gathers enough lightning to power the storms of Jupiter and with raindrops the size of watermelons, I drove with Mum to the psyche unit in Ndola Central Hospital to see Pete. Knowing the deluge of a Zambian storm I wished I had brought some water wings and a wet suit. It was like approaching a haunted building on a stormy night because the place has no real windows, just bars and has not been cleaned since it was built fifty years ago. I am sure the construction dust is still there waiting for a broom that will never come because it was stolen long ago.

Peering in through the bars of a window I could see Pete, totally unkempt and barefoot, stumbling alongside a wall absolutely shitfaced on medication. He saw me and with a glimmer of recognition collapsed onto the bars to hold himself steady and started berating me for cigarettes. Behind him an ominous black face appeared and skinny arms reached out around my neck. I felt I was being lifted off the ground by this inmate and my eyes were pleading to Pete for help whilst my voice trembled and faltered. The man soon let me go and as I fell back and felt for my larynx I realised he had kindly done up the buttons on my shirt lest I catch a chill in the gathering cold and stormy weather. In this one moment I was struck with an epiphany: prejudice died within me and I learned to love the ones I often label as 'insane'. They really are simply trying to do their best with whatever their state of mind is at the time. There is truth and goodness in all. We mustn't lose sight of it or lose sight of the fact even if we don't feel it sometimes.

Psyche ward anarchy

Two nights later we returned to the psyche ward to see Pete. We found him much as before: barefoot, unwashed, medicated and clad in filthy clothes. Not much different to a raver at a rock concert, just without the music. Mum happened to pull out a juicy chicken sandwich for his dinner. Well if you have ever watched a Kung Fu movie, this was the real thing, and fifty times better. Twenty ravenous and deranged inmates were upon us as Mum, Bringer of the Sandwich, fled to the safety of the nurses' station. I was next to Pete pinned with my back against the wall as Pete lashed out with incredible kicks and punches to what looked like an ever advancing host of Zombies trying to get a piece of his sandwich. "Try and get some, you motherfuckers!!!" he yelled peppering the throng with blows and kicks. Dull thuds punctuated the air but Pete munched on regardless. Like seagulls after a chip I saw about ten of them fly in slow motion onto a small slice of lettuce and mayonnaise. It skidded across the black and sticky floor before being ripped to even smaller shreds and devoured in relish by the hungry mob. Once the sandwich was gone and people had licked their fingers and the floor clean, it all went peaceful again.

Any commodity in short supply causes us humans to regress into a modern day lizard's brain. You will see handbags lashing out at a fellow bargain-seeker skipping a queue, campfire grabs for that last sausage using forks and knives. There are tussles over a blanket on a cold winter's night between previously loving couples, or the sound of gunfire resounding in the desert over that last sip of water. I see this on my treks all the time: when a scarcity hits, so does fear. In the psyche ward that night, peace returned when there was nothing left to fight over. The seagulls had basically run out of chips.

Life in a third world psychiatric system

But before this, for a couple of years the usual pattern was Pete running amok in Ndola and the Police tenderising him with their truncheons. He would spend a week or two in the crowded cells and then be transferred to the abysmal psychiatric wards of the central hospital or a more extensive facility 300 km south in the capital city Lusaka. Pete would get a band of inmates together and escape from the psyche wards on a regular basis running across the fields to the freedoms and illicitly brewed alcohol (probably pure methanol) of the township nearby. He told me of how he once leapt from the rooftops with a fellow inmate but his friend seriously injured his leg on impact. So Pete tried to drag him across the fields only giving up when the guards in white uniforms who had been alerted started closing in on the pair carrying sedatives: wooden table legs which they used as clubs.

Pete could amplify money by first begging for it and then gambling it at the local casino. He eventually got evicted from the casino for rolling himself a massive cone of cheap tobacco floor sweepings all rolled up in a piece of newspaper and lighting it. The staff thought the place was on fire with all the smoke billowing from behind Pete's stash of casino poker chips. At night he would sleep in the cemeteries or in the homes of prostitutes who seemed to understand men like Pete. Beaten up by street gangs, disheveled to the extreme with tinsel tied in his hair, he roamed the streets of Lusaka in threadbare clothing periodically getting re-captured. I visited him during a time when they locked him in a caged room and actually it was quite peaceful in there if it weren't for the swarms of malaria mosquitoes that gave us no rest. I was horrified at first when I heard they had put him in a cage. But once again, when I investigated the reality it was not what I expected. In fact the cage was a blessing: it kept the other inmates away from him so he could rest and find his centre and even read the magazines I brought him without being pestered.

The Truths inside Mental Illness

The most important lesson I learned along the way was the truth that Pete had tried to convey in every sentence but no one was listening. So I look for the truth hidden inside bizarre forms of behaviour and the bizarre things people say. This search for the underlying truth seems to fill me with compassion so that I can join them and be with them in what seem like crazy conversations and crazy behaviours.

For example, Pete was always hounding Dad for the money he claimed Dad had stolen from him… and I mean hounding Dad to the point of trying to kill him. No one believed Pete, but actually it was true. When Dad had been given Power of Attorney over some money in Pete's bank account, he did two brilliant things with it… he gave a large sum of it in two payments to a scammer who he only ever knew through a couple of phone calls. Of course the scammer has never been heard of since and nor has the money. He also bought some mining equipment which he hoped to make money on by re-selling it. Unfortunately, no one was interested in the equipment.

But Dad was a Born Again Christian so it took him years of shame before he finally broke down and told me the truth. I had spotted *that* rabbit running a long time back because Pete was always so insistent about the theft and so I didn't give up. I kept questioning Dad until he finally told me the truth. The truth sets you free so I did him a favour by listening to his confession like a catholic Priest in a confessional with acceptance and not with judgement. In a world without judgement there is really no need to lie or to hide things. There is hardly a need for forgiveness either. But Dad could always get forgiveness from Jesus anyway because he believed it so and probably confessed to Jesus a thousand times.

Mum phoned me once in a state saying Pete was cutting his clothing and that it was offensive to the locals because all the holes were revealing his underwear. Well I saw the clothing and it was absolutely beautifully cut with small triangles all over. So when I asked Pete WHY he did this, he said that it was simply because he was very hot in the tropical weather and needed to create a form of air conditioning and air flow. That made perfect sense. We would all do it if society permitted us to.

And when he rammed his car through the front gate of his farm he could see nothing wrong with destroying the gate because he owned it and could do with it as he wished. The logic here looks pretty sound but in the process he terrified and nearly injured the security guard who had dutifully refused to open the gate for him.

So I learned to always look for the truth in humanity no matter how bizarre the behaviour or what was being said. There was always some truth there or a message somewhere. Everyone on this planet was basically doing their best at the time with what they perceived and what choices they could come up with. Now I always try to look past the person to that part of the cosmos (order) or chaos (disorder) that is actually doing the talking. They might have forgotten how magnificent they are and what a miracle Life is, but on my half of each relationship I try not to forget such things. I try to look for the good and the truth in everyone and in everything going on in this world however offensive or bewildering things may first appear.

May your Dreams Come True

We lived for 9 years in Margaret River where I joined the most dysfunctional rugby team called the Margaret River Gropers. It comprised a full spectrum of nationalities, abilities and ages - rugby chaos at its best. The team endured 80 minutes on the field just to create a man-sized thirst. Then we could slake this thirst at the nearest bar ignoring any life-threatening injuries incurred along the way. They were safe under all the bandaging and strapping tape anyway. I broke my arm once and twice I was knocked unconscious playing for this team. But lots of us got injured and we all wore our injuries like badges of honour.

Getting knocked out is a blissful experience. The impact is like an anaesthetic, like your head hitting the softest pillow in a 5-star hotel. On the other side of the impact is your Inner World and the place of your dreams. It is the place you go every night after a cup of hot chocolate and two Tim Tams.

Once you enter the dream world, you are technically in your Inner World. It is the flip side to this Outer World we live in when we are awake. Inner World, the inner dream-like stuff, is going on all the time in the mind even when we are awake... it's all the Shadow and projections and unconscious stuff that swirls the emotions and prompts many of our conscious thoughts. But we really get to live the Inner World and experience it with sight and sound through our dreams. Here we get to wander amongst the Inner World and live amongst the archetypes with only the faintest memories of our waking world. Meanwhile the waking world tries to speak to us through our dreams but it has now flipped to become more like the unconscious. It is lovely to be conscious during a dream – a lucid dream – where the dreamer is imbued with magical powers.

People who walk the streets hearing voices and many who are incarcerated in mental health institutions have flipped their inner worlds for their outer worlds. To all of us, our inner worlds, our dream worlds, and the private thoughts they generate are simply filled with madness. I often wonder if 'mad' people have perfectly rational dreams. But the Inner World is of infinite value, just as our Outer World is. They just don't mix very well, and the tangles are usually seen as idiosyncratic quirks or handed over to Psychologists to unravel and put back in their proper place when they cause dysfunctionality.

So I see the two worlds as complementary: Inner and Outer is like wakefulness and dreaming with the subconscious and unconscious becoming the opposite world to the one we are experiencing. There is always the presence of the Witness observing whichever world we are in. And we always find ourselves trying to make sense and respond to whatever event is going on in either world.

Anyway, there is wisdom in both. There is the huge collective wisdom of the Collective Unconscious in the Inner World just as much as there is a huge amount of Wisdom in this Outer world of humans and Nature. Not only do we have to understand this Outer World as part of our personal growth and also understand our Inner World of psyche, of the mind, but also we need to understand the dream world and what it all means because it is giving us wisdom every night. What a loss it is that so many of us pay it no attention whatsoever. Dream interpretation is a skill and you get better at it with practice. Robert Johnson has a great book on this and there is much in the Jungian literature and writers like James Hillman amongst many others. So read up about dream analysis from a reputable source such as a Jungian approach, just not from some hallucinogenic guru or kitschy dream dictionary.

For me it involves firstly remembering every element of the dream, listing each element and defining some meaning or significance for every element. Each element is a symbol for something and represents something of significance. Often my Anima is there even in a cryptic form – a chicken maybe - pointing something out.

Then I define what the tension in the dream is. Most dreams have an underlying tension, something which needs to be resolved. Lastly I hold the decoded elements together in their tension to see what the dream is trying to say. Energy builds up before a change just as it does in liminal changes when we enter the cocoon phase of transformation. Here, in the tension of the dream, my inner world is speaking by showing me an energetic build up, a dilemma, a paradox, an opposite that needs resolution. It is calling me to come and take a closer look.

So this process is really about identifying and decoding of symbols. Always decode them as elements of your own mind, your own energies, your own archetypal world, your own underlying matrix.

> Even if they contain images of real people and events, these people and events have triggered the tuning forks of inner schemas, complexes and archetypes so they are resonances within your own mind, ripples within your own pond. They are saying something about you that the real people in the dream only represent.
>
> Then two things happen: either I get my insight, or I have to re-enter the dream (best done with someone asking open ended questions about what I see and hear) and allowing the dream to unfold further into some kind of resolution. This is what is referred to as 'Active Imagination' or 'Active Dreaming' and it is a form of Lucid Dreaming where the Witness is in the Inner World but in an awake state of consciousness.
>
> Its opposite is similar and you will come across it in individuals affected by liminality on transformational programs especially in Nature. The individual affected will stumble around as a kind of liminal, dreamy glowing Witness - wandering starry-eyed and looking from within at this rational Outer World as if it were all a dream, and making bizarre but golden connections.
>
> The learnings, the insights and pearls of wisdom are always profound from this process. But it is not complete here. We have to go out into this Outer World, preferably into Nature, and re-create some kind of ritual around that particular piece of dream work and dream insight. Even something simple. You will know what to do when you get there. It may involve bush art, ritual theatre, a prayer, a song, a dance, a stillness. It could be anything. Even simply talking to a tree. **Then** it becomes a **real** thing.

> *In this way, your dreams will come true in very beautiful, wonderful and real ways. We are not here for the Ego to dictate to the dream world our selfish desires. Instead, from a wellspring within the dreams resolutions arise spontaneously. They bring the joy and happiness regardless of an Ego that would have us searching for a lifetime in vain for such things. This Ego dictates all kinds of things it desires, but surely by now we are older and wise enough to know mostly this is not where true happiness and peace are to be found. It is found in a man or woman on mission, in giving your Soul's gift to the world. Your dreams are signposts, food and guidance for this blissful journey.*

Letting go of the ones we love

So as I said before, when the Ego cannot handle life anymore it becomes overwhelmed or dies and falls into the world of the Archetypes. And then these powerful and often immature entities express themselves unmodified and unrestrained by the Ego. I would be sitting in my car by the beach watching yet another golden sunset sizzle and melt like metallic sodium into the Indian Ocean and the phone would ring. It would be Pete in the form of ten archetypes all talking at the same time and very, very fast all the way across the Ocean from Zambia. Maybe that's why it is called 'pressured speech' because the entire gang of archetypes was fighting for control of Pete's phone.

These were spectacular monologues with promises of imminent wealth beyond belief and then angry demands for money. Each sentence lasted an hour on the phone. I would sit there in my car overlooking the beach at the end of the day trying to hold the conversation as the sun quickly hid itself in fear behind the distant horizon. But I failed to decode his tsunami of jumbled thoughts. It was all so draining because I just couldn't keep up with his Olympic pace of words per second. Archetypes love an audience to display in front of. They can behave like opera singers hogging centre stage making lots of noise.

I eventually blocked his number and secretly thanked God he was now locked up in a Zambian prison and not sitting on my doorstep. I blocked his emails when he tried a cyber-attack on my brother's massive accounting firm in Poland. And I could no longer bear to read his international tirades against his wife Salwa and my Dad in the public domain of social media. I basically euthanized him metaphorically by dispatching my internal warrior archetype to block him in every way and thereby protect my rattled kingdom. And when I compare my behaviour to his, I am not convinced who became the more wretched of the two. So now I sit in the forest from time to time talking to trees. And for long silent moments I stare far into the centre of the earth with those misty eyes us humans know so well wishing it had all turned out some other way.

Pete's choices and subsequent Destiny

One day Pete paced up and down outside our father's flat with a stolen carving knife smashing the windows and shouting threats laced with enough anger to sharpen the flying broken glass. Dad, the bravest man I ever knew, stepped out of the flat that day to take Pete on in mortal combat, unarmed. Dad was ever the Gladiator. Within him was an archetype of David taking on anyone he perceived as a Goliath. Pete had turned his attention to honing his new-found knife skills on the tyres of the tenants' cars parked outside each of the owners' flats. I think he had reached a world record score of about 16 tyres. Whatever the total it was more than Dad's annual income to replace and testimony to the strength of that particular make of carving knife. So he turned towards Dad with knife in hand like they do in the good old cowboy westerns at High Noon. And at that moment, the local Keystone Cop Cavalry arrived just in time to truncheon Pete once again to the ground and into two years of incarceration in a ghastly third world prison.

It was basically a life sentence because the Magistrate's Court in Ndola ruled him to be detained indefinitely 'at the President's Pleasure' for attempting to murder my Dad. I don't think countries like Zambia, renown for corruption and bureaucratic laziness, allow case files to get too big before they exceed some limit, some kilogram weight, some threshold of paper and then incur a life or indeed a death sentence. This 'President's Pleasure' resulted in a slight increase in peace on the streets of Ndola, in the psyche ward and down at the police station where our Keystone Cops could get on with counting all the money they had extorted from their fellow Zambians uninterrupted.

Dad thought the British High Commission would come to the rescue and get Pete out of jail and into England because we were British citizens. But one look at Pete I am sure they wept with thanks for the efficient Zambian judicial and prison system and possibly begged for his execution.

They kept him at a prison in Ndola. For well over a year, Mum would despatch one of our workers - Kennedy - on a bicycle with some food for him. Sometimes food is just a symbol of hope, a slender thread to hang on to. They slept the prisoners 50 to a room in shifts throughout the day because there was simply not enough space in the prison for all the inmates. With gangs controlling access to the toilets I imagined it was not dissimilar to how the seniors at boarding school controlled our access to the toilet block with mortal fear. For Pete the brutality was at another level but he was tough. I reckon he established his own power base there in some form. I hope so. I could ask Kennedy what he saw, but my mind and my heart are not yet strong enough to hear what he might say.

So our younger brother Tom got involved and I reckon he put a million Euros of his money into trying to support our family in Zambia through all of this. It was just the start of Tom's financial haemorrhage because he took on the burden of supporting all the workers on our farm and our parents in their old age. He basically ran the farm in Zambia from his office in Poland for years. Can you imagine how phobic Tom got of the phone every time it rang with requests for money and news of another disaster? In the middle of a board meeting to discuss millions of Euros going through his business, the phone would ring… another 200 chicks had been delivered and they needed chicken food urgently… oh, and last night lightning had struck the borehole pump motor and there was no water for the farm. The board members were unlikely to understand why Tom had turned a whiter shade of pale. They just could never comprehend the paradox of Zambia and Poland, the neurotic mayhem it brought to Tom's poor brain as he stood there like a rabbit caught in the headlights struggling to hold the two worlds together.

Tom paid a lawyer and lots of other people to get the President of Zambia to release Pete from life imprisonment. He got 10 Downing Street in London to accept him as a British subject under the British health system and he flew Pete across from Zambia to England heavily sedated with two burley men, South African psychiatric nurses, to accompany him on the long flight to England lest Pete insist he could fly the jumbo jet or empty the drinks trolley single handed. Tom got him settled into a psychiatric facility just south of London where they kept him for long periods in maximum security because Pete was far from ever being mentally stable.

TRANSFORMATION AND THE GOLDEN KEYS

Tom even bought Pete an apartment nearby. But Pete regularly lost his mind there and Police were often sent to bring him back to the psychiatric facility. The police would enter a filthy and unkempt apartment strewn with empty vodka bottles. On one occasion, Pete was acting totally sane, but when he excused himself, dropped his pants and proceeded to have a crap in the middle of the lounge in front of the officers, they suspected that something didn't add up and took him in to the police station which for Pete must have felt like a second home. I cannot imagine how they filled in their police reports without crying uncontrolled tears of laughter... but then again, I know they have seen much, much worse. Emergency services know that 'civilisation' is mostly just a thin veneer on humanity.

Basically, in this one action, those police officers had arrested a whole array of archetypes, members of an orchestra with no conductor, with no functional Ego, but who all answered to the Ego's name 'Pete'. They were marched off to imprisonment by medication, Risperidone and Haloperidol in the maximum security section of the local psyche facility. Well, a 'civilised' society demands social order and wants unpleasant things to simply disappear. It won't tolerate anything that resembles anarchy. Even if a mere Chihuahua bites the postman it gets euthanized. But in Zambia, Pete was accepted and cared for by the people of the street. This is how, and without resources, without a functional government, the entire Zambian community gets to co-exist as a vibrant whole. They say it takes a whole village to raise a child because a village understands its own and has a place for every one of its members. Ndola was like that, bathed in the rhythms of Zambian music that transcended the hardships of daily life well into the long, warm Zambian nights. Vibrant communities can be such a resource, such a blessing.

Anyway, those days were over for Pete because he now had to face the isolation and despair of living in a city of so many millions where mostly everyone was lonely. There was no village for him there but we had all run out of options. The cleverest man in the world would have found a solution, an Ace of Spades, but we had simply run out of cards.

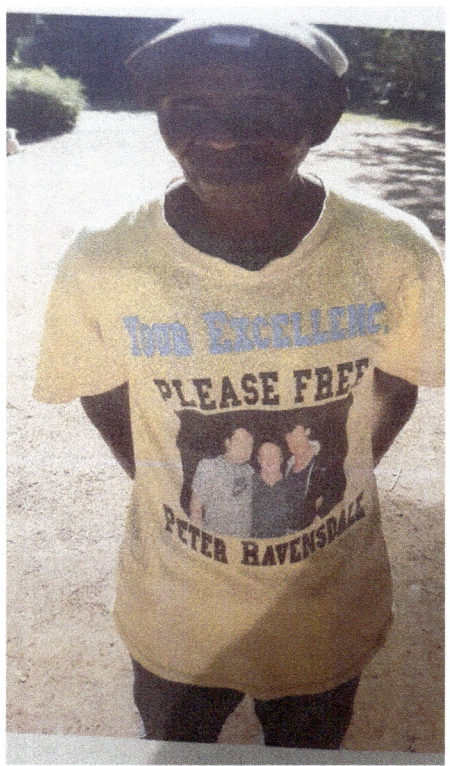

The 'Free Pete Ravensdale' campaign. Tom tried to raise public awareness in Zambia for Pete who was incarcerated in prison with a severe mental illness indefinitely 'at the president's pleasure'.

How Pete's story ended

It was towards the end of the English winter in 2018 that I got a phone call from Tom. In faltering sentences he proceeded to tell me the last chapter of Pete's life story. Pete had been living in a psychiatric hostel in London and one night his incurable insomnia led him to a local MacDonald's where he immediately established a deep friendship with a kindly police officer who was having a midnight coffee break. Just before dawn the duty squad car was called to attend an incident of a man knocking on a homeowner's door asking for a cigarette lighter. The kindly policeman and Pete met for the second time that fateful night and because it was so cold, the policeman offered to drive Pete back to the hostel. As a parting gift, he lit Pete's cigarette outside the front door and gave him his own lighter to keep. Well sitting in the hostel lounge and chain smoking conflicted slightly with the hostel's strict no smoking policy and fire regulations. The psyche nurse tried to get Pete to stop as he sat there through the remains of the night. She eventually went into her room to type up an incident report.

Pete gave her door a customary thumping and then it went quiet save for the staccato tapping of the nurse typing a report... too quiet. It was then that she noticed the smoke coming in under her door and opened it to find the stairwell engulfed in flames and Pete standing defiantly amongst them. She grabbed a fire extinguisher and tried to pacify the fire, but not having the skill or the timing of the Jesuit priest from fifty years before in the Chemistry lab, she failed to bring it under control. Inmates were now fleeing from the burning building. As it was three stories high, people were jumping from windows. The psyche nurse grabbed a lady as she raced down the stairs and they both ran through the flames to the safety of the outdoors which was only metres away.

She called out to Pete again and again through the doorway and could see him through the flames, but he was determined to stick this one out. It couldn't have been long before the choking fumes laid him out unconscious and his cremation at tax payer's expense began. Probably one of the most expensive cremations in London's history. 30 firemen and 6 fire tenders battled the blaze whilst at least one inmate of the hostel was taken to hospital critically injured. Then the coronial inquest started and the real pain began for so many caught up in something that started all those years ago in the dramas of a pregnant Polish maiden and the effects of such things on the unborn.

Pete's final fire

I read all the inquest reports. The transcripts of the psyche nurse calling the emergency service centre were probably the hardest to read. The detailed post mortem report of my own brother evoked in me only love and compassion and understanding for every aspect of a body that had unconditionally served his altered mind. I felt the courage of the firemen as they battled the blaze, the bewilderment of neighbours as they looked on in fear. But for me there is a pivotal moment captured in the reports that even now fills me with tears. As the firemen retrieved Pete's body, something tumbled from his hand. It was the last bit of true kindness he experienced on this earth given to him by the kindest of men, a police officer just trying to get someone home, safe and loved on a cold winter's night. It was the cigarette lighter. It was Pete's lifelong companion, the God of Fire.

None of us went to his funeral. Any of us brave enough to mount the podium to say a few words at the service would have been confronted with a mental blank, a mental mindfuck of opposites only somewhat reconciled in death. The cost of going to London and watching some distracted priest mumble his way through yet another funeral service was just too much for us siblings. Our Catholic boarding school had cured us of any such mystique. You see, as kids we would sit at the back of the chapel in mass secretly listening to the local radio station through an earphone that snaked its way up the sleeve of a blazer and hidden in the palm of the hand held against one ear. Or we would be playing Poker passing the playing cards between us very carefully so as not to get spotted by any of the prefects.

We let the remnants of the British Empire foot the bill for Pete's cremation. It happened at the Crown's expense and cost the British tax payer about Eu 90. They should have done it for half that price because he had already done much of the work himself burning down the hostel. And so, in a puff of smoke, Pete and the God of Fire helped tip the world one warm step closer to an inevitable environmental abyss of global warming.

But because Pete truly loved me, because of his sense of wonder, his awesome skill at playing the drums, his absolute genius of creativity and construction, his legendary survival skills and his artistic talent, he will forever be my very greatest inspiration, my hero. And in so many ways, he was definitely the making of me by teaching me to always delight in shiny things and to always have some faith in the supernatural.

Mum and my cousin Sylvia as Polish refugees in London.
Mum was stunningly beautiful despite her severe scoliosis.

6

Love

A mother's love

Mum's greatest need as a child was probably the diverse array of needs every refugee child would have. Everything from food and shelter to love and happiness. She was so poor as a child that one of her greatest gifts in later years was charity: she gave away truckloads of money to whoever asked for it. Maybe she should have got a Nobel Prize for doing so but she would have given the prize away too. Because she had no money as an adult, she developed a gift for giving away everyone else's money instead. It became an incurable disease. The problems this created were endless. She even threw money at beggars in the street in anger when their begging overwhelmed her crying out in hysterical tears,"...Go on! Take it! Take my blood!..." The little urchins would run around in circles with glee catching money falling out of the sky. But it was other people's money most of the time.

She gave herself to the African people much as Mother Teresa gave herself to the poor of Calcutta. I always want to know how close a person can be to another before the need to pull away becomes overwhelming. Some people can't even pass each other in the street and say 'Hello". For others the conversation gets too deep just talking about the weather. But Mum had no distance between herself and humanity…be they young or old, dying of AIDS or actually dead.

It is a Mother's love. And you can feel this love again if you watch a gathering of women looking in oxytocin-bathed wonder upon a baby asleep in a pram. Or if you let yourself be truly held by a woman. They hug for what feels like an eternity, heart to heart, long enough for a hug to work its warm magic. Us men can never do it quite like this, not through our masculine side. We don't seem to be able to hug the same as women do when women just naturally melt into it. It's a profound feeling to be truly held by a woman. They have the warm hands of a gecko's embrace, a primal understanding of skin to oestrogenic skin. They are the first holders of the newborn child so they can claim ownership to something that I as a man have little understanding of. Still I buy scented skin moisturising lotion, skin toners and scented soaps for their birthday presents even though I may never really understand why they have such a magical effect on women. But women tear them savagely from the gift wrapping, drink in their scented fragrance with misty eyes and clutch them to their breast with all the instinctive wildness of a she-wolf holding a cub on a full moon's night. Then they place them lovingly into that special drawer that contains countless others each with a unique and enduring story.

And women can hold the sick ones when us men would distance ourselves and really struggle with it all. Men would prefer the newborn child washed and wearing a nappy before this first embrace. But women accept it all in the moment and wouldn't have it any other way because they are embracing their aspect of authentic and instinctive humanity that is so beautifully in the realm of the feminine.

Men generally prefer the rocket building, brick laying and lumberjack duties and saving damsels in distress or awakening sleeping beauties when they decide to need us. As men and women, we all bring along our unique skills and natures arriving from different directions into an enchanted relationship that is you and me. We are equal but from what I have seen in life, psychology and biology, we are not the same.

There was a time when things were simpler. Men's roles and women's roles and the rules were all scripted in society. But things are different now. The Masculine and the Feminine is on the shift shepherded along by voyeuristic TV shows, social media and advertising. These are not great teachers, so it is no wonder we find deception and confusion everywhere. The entire world culture is changing so rapidly you could swear it is in a blender. What is this modern spectrum of love and what it means to be me, and what it means to be you and what it means to be us? We need to study these things, educating ourselves such that we understand the mechanisms, potentials and the consequences and find our own way again with concepts that serve us. Then we can dance skilfully with another instead of being ignorant of the dance or swayed by its simplistic portrayals.

I reckon to find that one person, and go the distance, that is a rare treasure not only because of who you found, but also because of who you became and what you created along the way. It is not always about whom you marry - an easy or a difficult personality - but about what you make of this marriage or relationship that counts. Both of you need to grow so that one does not leave the other behind. If you were tough like Shackleton you would never leave anyone behind.

Our history, the journey, the subtle gold that was once part of 'Us'- this is what you are preserving as a bedrock for the future. It's too easy to throw it all away and cut people loose when really those people, and their hooks and chords serve our ascendancy if we stick around long enough to grow a bit. How else are we going to stand by each other to investigate the fear and pain of our core wounds. A sprinkling of self- brutality and self-discipline to weather the storms can create learning at the highest level. And when you have learned enough lessons and if you really want to move on, transcend it well. Step gently and with kindness into your power before you move forward so as not to be simply running away or harming someone you have travelled with on sacred journeys however brief.

Sophie's story

Sophie was a little girl of about 5 years of age when her parents died of AIDS. Her parents contributed to the endless landscape of graves outside our nearby township. Actually, the graves extend the length and breadth of Africa but I have stood in the ones near Ndola and the earth mounds just seem to go on forever, to the horizon, like waves on an ocean, a stairway to Heaven. So Mum would take Sophie and her friend Mambwa into our home each morning and prepared their sandwiches and orange juice for school. She would carry little Sophie around our kitchen on her hip whilst feeding her breakfast cereal and endless bowlfuls of a Mother's loving conversation.

I wondered at all of this because although Sophie had the most beautiful big eyes and braided hair, she was covered in infected sores both outside and in. Her skin, tongue, mouth, lips – everywhere. I wondered at how the AIDS virus HIV and its associated bacterial friends do their deadly tango with our human cells. As a teenager I saw our neighbour mysteriously shrivel up and die as the bewildering disease first appeared and became rampant throughout Zambia and the whole of Africa. I so wanted things to work out well for Sophie but it was an impossible tangle. Yet Mum had no distance between her and little Sophie who was dying of AIDS. I see this same love in how Fiona cares for children on the hospital ward as a paediatric nurse. She has had a few children die in her arms as she walked the corridors of the sleeping hospital comforting them into an eternal night. And I know this is what I saw in Imogen caring for Amy.

One day, I flew in to Ndola for a rare visit to my childhood home. The streets of the farm were lined with our African workers drumming and singing as me and Tom strode down the long driveway to the house. They were rejoicing, not so much that I was there, but that Thomas had arrived because they knew he bankrolled everything that happened in their lives. To them, his wallet was like the oxygen a scuba diver relies on, and they sucked on it hard at every opportunity, as does everyone else who knows Tom. We understand… we were raised amongst poverty and its inevitable twin which is begging and a longing for what others have which manifests as stealing. I have trained my son and daughter to always be the first ones to buy Tom a beer in a pub… for Tom it is such a rare occurrence that he weeps into the glass full of amber liquid when it happens.

Anyway, because of all the noise and commotion of our arrival, the dogs attacked Sophie that day and I spent an hour cleaning her infected skin in a laundry sink thinking that the wounds would kill either her or me. In the pantry I found a tub of antibiotics and popped a couple in her mouth. A few days later she came up to me in the garden and thanked me and thanked me. She showed me her mouth, her skin, her tongue… all completely healed of the sores. And oh, her smile that day… I will never forget. Standing in the garden, we didn't even need the sunshine, we were glowing enough. And the tenderness in her little hug as I crouched down to hold her… if only she had lived longer to share more of that love with the world. So I will always try to do it for her by giving some love and prayers and blessing to the people I pass in the street. Why should we ever need a rational reason to love and to give of ourselves to the world?

Mum and Dad. They certainly did have their good times together.

Mum and Beauty

And I have to do it for Mum too. She is the reason I discovered beauty as my Mission of Service to the Divine Feminine on that training in San Francisco with the Shift Network. Mum knew all about manifesting beauty in this world. Her artistry each morning painting on her eyeliner, mascara and Oil of Olay facial moisturiser rivalled that of Nefertiti – honestly, she could have been the pharaoh Queen's makeup artist.

Mum created beauty in this world constantly from morning to night and in everything she did or said. It was all around in the flower arrangements, her collections of polished rocks, her art works, in her the food banquets she made. We would go camping and while Dad set up the tent, Mum would set up the beauty - a treasure trove of bush art with driftwood and flowers, stones and feathers gathered in her liminal wanderings... a chicken scratching in the sand lost to the world around her. Unbeknownst to her, without the dialogue and the words, the vocabulary to express it so, she was an element of the Divine Feminine. And to this place of women is the custodianship of beauty. Us kids knew it so well, she was our mother. But we never understood it at the time, the bigger picture, nor the magnitude of what she was doing. I do it now all the time, like with the school children during a bush art exercise. I get lost in the artistry, the creativity, the expression of an inner voice that speaks its words through the medium of wood and stone. It wants to be understood, to be heard, to be held. And I share my authentic work with the children because all of us in the exercise share our insights. I magnify everything they say so that they can see, and hear and witness and feel and experience Life flowing. In that river of energy and story we are just the salmon.

For Mum at this time of life, the huge house had become so empty save for the ghosts of a once exuberant family and her doomed marriage. Mum and Dad had divorced many years before and so they each separately came to embrace the Zambian people more and more to gain a sense of family and belonging. Meanwhile on the farm, the ghost of my great-grandmother - Granny Goût (pronounced 'goo') - still walked the corridors of that house at night, false teeth chattering like a pair of castanets. When Granny slept in her bed, in her room that I knew so well, her teeth slept in a glass of Steradent solution on her bedside table. It was like a spa bath of effervescent tablets that occurred every night as Granny's sacred ritual to the memory of her teeth long since extracted. And maybe the ritual looked even further back to the magic of her Tooth

Fairy and to great-great grandparents who may have left a penny or two under her pillow in exchange for her baby teeth and the delight and giggles of a magical childhood. Our ancestors are the unbroken flow of godly energy in human form from somewhere over the horizon and from an ancient history that now becomes you and me. We are never alone unless we misunderstand or forget what we are energetically.

Toby's equivalent of Sand Play: a psychology tool for processing issues

Every tropical dawn, our cook, Toby would shuffle through the morning shades of the corridor with Mum's pot of tea and wake her gently from the mysteries of her dreams. He worked for Mum for 30 years. And when he made her bed each day, he would arrange a series of dolls on the duvet… there were about six or seven dolls, and each day the arrangement told a different story of what was happening on the farm. It was psychology 101 and absolutely brilliant. It was ritual theatre, allowing his heart and soul to arrange the dolls so and to express a story from the heart. He was performing ritual art, sacred ritual and deeply processing the real world within this ritual theatre. It must have flowed from some cosmic crucible of genius that tumbled forth from Shakespeare with words and from Toby with dolls.

Playing Salt and Pepper

As I have said before, Salt and Pepper is what I do when talking to people in a coffee shop, arranging the bags of sugar, the salt and pepper shakers and Tabasco Sauce to create an outer representation of whatever dynamic they are describing as they talk to me. In this way, they can step out of the story to be their own Facilitator. This is what is referred to as 'Triangulating Out'. The magic question to ask, once the constellation of the dynamic has been set out, the sugar bags, the sweetener, the salt and pepper, simply ask the question, "So...what needs to change?" And watch the magic manifest before your eyes. The person will immediately start to move the pieces on the table into a solution to the problem.

Toby would constellate dynamics every day like this with the dolls. A Zambian moon would set. And a Zambian sun would slowly rise on a brand new day. And over an early morning cup of tea, Mum would reflect upon the symbolism of what this man was trying to say, what the dolls were authentically trying to portray. Make of it what you will, but here it was in black and white: a message written in doll language every day from our very own shamanic Zambian cook.

The Lamp of Insight

> *In the myth of Psyche and Cupid, Psyche, the most beautiful maiden in all the land had fallen in love with Cupid but he warned her to never look at him directly to see him as he truly was. And so he would only visit her under the cover of darkness. But one night, bewitched by her wicked step sisters, and with the curiosity common to women the world over, she silently edged close to him shining her oil lamp to illuminate his sleeping form. Robert Johnson, in his book 'We' which is concerned with the mechanism of Romantic Love, speaks of this particular quality that so many women seem to have: it is the Lamp of Insight that would appear to be their birthright.*
>
> *I remember coming out of a hall filled with hundreds of school children and talking to my fellow facilitators about the Rite of Passage program we were about to run with these children. We men spoke about the unruly groups of boys we had just seen and how*

orderly and well behaved the girls' groups were. But the female facilitators were abuzz with what they had seen: the girls' groups were alive with Queen Bees, bitchiness, disempowered and ostracized factions, and blatant manipulations… all kinds of relational and behavioural issues that we men were completely blind to.

Women can walk into a room and immediately sense the energetics of the people there, who is single, who is taken, who to avoid, who is in which faction and who is the Queen Bee or the Alpha Male. And ofcourse the most knowledgeable humans are the quiet 'People Watchers'. They often have the quietest voice in a group, but in the end they prove to be the ones we should have listened to first.

I always ask my wife to shed her Lamp of Insight onto the situations and dilemmas I encounter in life. Her counsel is always priceless because I realised long ago that I am blind to so many things, and she is the one who seems to carry the Lamp.

When I was working on a very difficult project for nine long months, I learned my particular version of this Lamp of Insight. My friend had developed an ingenious mechanised wooden bin for displaying hundreds of kilos of fruit and vegetables for a local farmers' market. And we had to assemble many hundreds of these huge bins which comprised mechanical gearboxes, electrical motors, switches, stainless steel and plastic panels all of which came from China. And much of it needed modifying to get each bin to work properly. So each day was filled with problem solving, with blood, sweat and tears, wood shavings, metal splinters and burns from welding stainless steel.

I quickly learned that the worst thing to do was to try to fix a perceived problem without due thought... it simply created a host of secondary problems. It was better to take a few steps back, to go away and put the kettle on and by shining the Lamp of Insight try to determine exactly what the real problem was. It was usually very different to what we thought was the initial problem.

I remembered that once when I asked one of the British commanders of the Gurkha Contingent what was the first course of action he would undertake if he was suddenly under attack, he said, "Well, I would tell one of the men to put the kettle on while the rest of us started returning fire."

And as a veterinarian, I was once presented with a dog with a very sore neck. Luckily I didn't try to manipulate the neck like a chiropractor. Instead I shone the Lamp of Insight in the form of an x-ray upon the dog and discovered it had swallowed a very long stick. The stick spanned from the back of the mouth all the way to the end of the dog's stomach. He had swallowed it playing that eternal dog-favourite called 'Chase the Stick' with his owner the day before. Luckily it was easily pulled out the same way it went in much as a sword-swallower does in the circus to a thunderous applause... in this case the applause of some attendant veterinary nurses.

Next time you encounter a problem, take 4 steps back or take even just a moment and shine your Lamp of Insight upon the problem. Or use someone else's lamp. It will break the habit of moving unconsciously into situations and all the hardship which that creates. I have discovered great respect for other people's Lamps

> *even if I don't always agree with them because I can always use their light to develop my own insights.*

How Mum's story ended: The Poles take care of their own

I found the dolls there on the bed when Mum died. She never made it to the bed that night so they sat there undisturbed like children waiting for the daylight.

Over the years, Mum's scoliosis had twisted her spine into a terrible shape with collapsed discs that caused her spinal nerves to cry out for mercy. It progressively collapsed her lung and squashed her abundant loving heart.

One night, she started talking Polish nonstop behind the closed bathroom door. You see, her Mum and Dad had come from Heaven to fetch her. Her faithful African servants Kennedy and Leonard were listening outside the door half mad with anguish. And when the talking stopped, they broke in to the bathroom to pull her gasping body into the back of a car for an agonising drive through the night to a clinic. Leonard, Toby's son, held her in his arms in the back of the car as she died. She had got him a scholarship to study medicine paid for by a local mining company. How he wished he could have saved his first patient because when she died, the biggest light in Zambia went out. It went out in Zambia but truth be told, it is still emanating out into the cosmos somewhere. And years from now some aliens in their spaceship will mistakenly perceive it came from a planet of love and book their holidays here… and then get gunned down by US anti-aircraft guns as they try to land or maybe taken down by snipers as they try to book into the New York Sheraton.

TRANSFORMATION AND THE GOLDEN KEYS

How to create a great send off for those you love

I flew in from Australia immediately I heard of Mum's unexpected death. It was a surreal night, a New Year's Eve nonetheless. I was alone in the house with all the ghosts, the huge Baboon spiders big like Tarantulas, and the spitting cobras that abound in this swampy region. But the night was tempered by the wild rejoicing, music, drumming and dancing that I could hear from the villages all around me and which continued to the dawn of New Year's Day in Zambia. Tom flew in from Poland the next day and Scooby and Pola from Australia. Our outrageous humour which abounds at times of true catastrophe was the medicine we used for our broken hearts. Still, the four of us stand-up comics were unable to replace Mum's legendary sense of humour. Like Bruce Lee, Mum had died too young.

We made quite a few trips to the morgue because they had put her in a chiller set to a warm 12 degrees when all the others were on 4 degrees and Mum started to melt as if she were being kept in a bakery's pie warmer. Tom and Scooby suffer no fools so the morticians were told to fix the problem or they would soon end up in one of the chillers too. Their solution was simple... literally: they bathed Mum in a 10% formaldehyde solution. Formaldehyde is a pungent chemical strong enough to preserve the Holy Spirit himself. And it was strong enough to preserve the endless line of people who came to pay their last respects, even curing them of their tuberculosis. Filing past the casket in the funeral parlour, their eyes responded to the chemical preservative with copious tears, wailings from the ocular pain and a lingering conjunctivitis.

Tom had been so close to Mum. She was by far the most favourite woman in his life. When Tom discovered that the funeral home was going to trundle up the road to the church service with Mum's casket on the back of an open and dented Toyota Hilux belching smoke, he really hit the roof. So the funeral home miraculously produced an ornate hearse trailer that resembled a space ship and towed it behind a civilian car. We followed this out of town to a church service and then to a beautifully located Hindu cremation pyre on the top of some hills overlooking forests and a distant township. There is no mechanised method of cremation in Ndola, so this is how it is done. You ask the Hindus. And they understand and provide wood and matches and a bucket of rocket fuel called 'ghee' – rancid butter - which to a Hindu in a crematorium is a bit like petrol milked out of a sacred cow bowser. With your bucket of ghee and with your loved one awaiting a celestial journey so as to move the atoms to somewhere more convenient comes a set of instructions and enough encouragement that you could swear you were being sent off to bake a cake.

There we lifted her body lovingly from the casket and placed it on a pile of wood. We were careful with her because Pola had forgotten to pack Mum a set of knickers when she chose her funeral clothing and we didn't want to embarrass Mum in public dead or alive. We covered her in a white linen cloth and poured the bucket of ghee on her from head to toe. Then the attendants handed us burning sticks and ceremonially we faced away from the body and thrust these sticks backwards into the pyre. In seconds her body disappeared from view in the thick smoke and roaring flames which dried our tears, singed our clothes and melted our broken hearts back together.

TRANSFORMATION AND THE GOLDEN KEYS

Mum wanted to be buried on the farm but we made the executive decision for a far more authentic and spectacular send off with this Hindu cremation.

How close can you be to another before it all gets too much and you need to pull away?

The cremation was totally spectacular. And the wonder continued into the next day when we drove back to get her ashes. As we stepped from the car, a ginger kitten ran up to us and playfully attacked our legs all the while we were there. Mum loved cats. Her two constant companions were Genghis and Khan, two big fat Ginger Toms. They slept on her bed guarding a doorway that opened onto the exquisite garden outside her bedroom. The kitten was simply Mum playing with us because now her spirit was everywhere.

Pola, Scooby, Tom, Me and our brother Mwelwa whom Mum adopted. In the foreground Mum is going up in smoke in the Hindu funeral pyre.

Beneath the corrugated iron sheets of the open-air crematorium, an old African man walked towards us clutching a wrinkled yellow plastic supermarket shopping bag. He tenderly opened the bag to reveal a shovelful of Mum's ashes. There were quite sizeable chunks of bone and teeth in there and we didn't feel right spreading these bone fragments around the farm lest the insatiably hungry guard dogs got hold of them and started playing 'chasey-chasey'.

So I asked the attendant what could be done. No problems, he returned with a velvet cloth, crimson in colour – the colour of sacred reverence and blood and passion - and a brick. Together, we poured Mum's bones onto the cloth and crushed them with the brick into a more suitable powder whilst Tom ran around us losing his mind. We put her ashes into a beautiful urn that we brought with us from the farm... a Russian samovar which is like a hot water urn but very ornate and more like a world cup soccer trophy. The Russians got her in the end, but only for a moment because we had decided to sprinkle her around the farm in the evening and she could thus make her symbolic escape from this Russian prison just like her Dad had done years before.

Mum getting crushed because the bone fragments we were handed in a plastic shopping bag were all too big and recognisable. Despite the photo it was done with great love and reverence. It's just not something you do very often so we all kind of went mental for a moment.

Pola's healing

Later that night, in a most heartfelt ceremony, Pola was the one to sprinkle those ashes the length and breadth of the farm that Mum loved so much and that Thomas had bankrolled. We got covered in the dust and inhaled it because we were rather pissed by that stage and Pola was throwing it everywhere. It was a surreal procession, beers in hand, drifting in the night past places on the farm which will always be sacred to us because of the memories: the dilapidated piggery, the servants' quarters, the temperamental borehole pump that attracted lightning.

Pola preparing for the final ceremony where she scattered Mum's ashes from the Russian Samovar over every inch of the farm in Ndola.

Pola had the last say. You see, all she ever remembers from her childhood years is the back of Mum's head. Mum, for all her beauty forgot to love her daughter. That's Polish culture for you: they adore their son's because they lost so many in wars over the years. And our Dad's history with his Bohemian mother living the high life of Turkish society gave him no idea how to love women let alone his daughter. So Pola grew up rejected in her own home and with no maternal self-image with which to construct her own save those that are archetypal and instinctive. The internalised figures of Mother and Father that were to be her masculine and feminine elements for much of her life - something we all do - were reflections of those who had simply ignored her. That's very damaging to anyone when good internal figures can be a source of such strength, wholeness and guidance in life. And, furthermore, her beloved brothers were incarcerated in a boarding school somewhere south across the Zambesi. To ignore a child in their own home like this is considered to be one of the most damaging things that could ever happen in childhood.

Pola could sit like this all day. When her brothers are around, her world is totally complete.

Pola has the most loving heart of anyone you could ever meet and a devotion to her brothers that rivals that of an Emperor penguin in the Antarctic. Her greatest need has become her greatest gift through this core wound of parental neglect. She craves love neurotically like a squirrel munching on acorns. But that night we left her to talk to Mum in the courtyard of our home with the urn in her hands and the last little crumbles left to throw. I will never know what she said, but it must have been profound. Imagine, you are holding the last fistful of dust of the most important God in your life and everything to say under the magnificent stars, a Zambian night alive with the music of insects and fireflies. Maybe she reclaimed elements of the feminine. These elements had been denied to her for a lifetime when they fell into her Shadow years before through the denial of a Mother's love and attention. Just imagine. A woman's journey can be like this: breaking from mother in her teenage years, she returns to fix it with her mother in later years or fix the split via a return to a circle of women in some form. Maybe that's why Pola now freely dances Zumba with a circle of women each week and finds her lost connection there.

Pola on the Manley ferry in Sydney. She is a really cool sister. She looks like she could take on the Sydney Opera House single handed in this photo.

Unconditional Love

I always believed that all love was conditional in some way because most forms of love have some kind of payoff. But I am humbled when I witness a mother's love for her newborn as she sacrifices of herself to care for this newborn droplet of the divine. And I always wonder at Don Miguel Ruiz's concept of how every cell of our body unselfishly serves us, serves the self, the mind, our story and the myth we live by with true unconditional love. We need to separate mind and body as different entities and to train the mind to acknowledge and love this poor body more. I have neglected mine, denied it and abused it all my life. It has been magnificent even without me knowing. It has truly been my lover and my best friend. I need to treat it so in return and it's easy because its needs are so simple. I just never knew this for most of my life.

So it's time to love it more, even just to lie still and listen to the miracle of myself breathing and feel each heartbeat for a while. In the morning before I open my eyes, I have a huge barrel of golden unconditional love that I ladle upon myself until I have upended the barrel all over me. An hour later I take this concept into the real world by way of ritual...a swim in the freezing ocean with Fiona while Scout runs up and down the beach barking madly with his own version of unconditional love.

Altar

I am standing in the pouring rain on a freezing cold morning. Twenty shivering kids have arrived to go rafting for two hours with me in a river that gives any swimmer instant brain freeze. There is beautiful music playing from my mini boom box protected from the rain in a water proof zip lock bag. And as they sit alongside each other on a log, I give them each a gumnut within which to symbolically place their hopes and dreams, or their wish for whatever they came looking for on this camp. And when they are ready, I invite them to put the little gumnuts on the top of a nice flat sawn off tree stump someone created years ago nearby. Over the three days, we assemble a hundred hopes and dreams like this from all the groups of kids who come rafting: a huge pile of gumnuts. This symbolises the gold they will bring back to their schools, to their homes, to their lives and to their community. It warms my heart as the days of the camp go by and the pile of hopes and dreams grows bigger and bigger.

And I suggest they build an altar next to their beds on a small table with a beautiful tablecloth, a candle and maybe some incense. They can assemble all their sacred objects there and need to keep it alive and clean. It doesn't seem right to hide away our sacred things in cupboards and drawers. On the wall they can put pictures of their ancestors from their mother's side and from their father's side. And this is the place for their vision boards, for their hopes and their dreams.

An altar is a place to commune with our loved ones who have gone before or may be far away. This is a place for our sacred dialogues with something bigger than us... people would call this prayer. It is a place to reflect upon our inner archetypal world. My altar contains so many things: my Mother's ashes, a Nepalese flute and a Gurkha ceremonial knife. There is my childhood teddy bear and photos of my family. There is a poem I hold sacred and a magnificent wooden whale from my uncle in Canada which symbolises wisdom. So many things. It is a reflection of my heart, my inner world, my history, my story.

And if my altar ever feels like it has lost its magic, I know that I am becoming disconnected from my healthy ways of thinking and that a mood is coming upon me. Moods disconnect. Even good ones do. I never want my altar to lose its magic. It indicates to me how alive I am because then the objects glow with life.

And in the darkest times I have knelt there and bared my soul to the gods. And in good times I have stood their absolutely beaming my joy and gratitude upon it for such a fortunate life.

So in the mornings, I light a candle on my altar. I let my eyes wander over all my sacred things and my pictures. And I talk to them all, to all my gods, big and small, asking for what I need in the day as if from a loving friend. Sometimes I pick up my guitar and strum a samba beat and look at the woman with wings and beautiful hair in the picture I painted, as she coyly stoops to pick the flowers one by one and seduces my beating heart.

An altar. A sacred place of Transformation. Everybody should have one.

My altar. Everybody needs a place to commune with the gods and keep their sacred things. I change this altar constantly depending on what is happening in my life.

Sorting out the loose ends

For 30 years Mum kept small antelopes called 'duikers' in the courtyard and this sanctuary for those tiny deer really was her sacred place. But don't be fooled: those duikers can move like lightning. Some years ago, one of them whose name was Charu tried to leap right up onto the roof of our house. He almost made it but tumbling off the roof sheets he broke his leg instead and we had it amputated. Even with just three legs, Charu would impale anyone who dared walk across the courtyard. The wounds would fester for months because duikers make an irritant secretion which coats their sharp little horns. So Tom and I would only cross the courtyard carrying a sizeable pillow each and with the courage of Manolete, the Spanish Bullfighter, we could then fend off the mighty Charu.

With Mum gone, I had to plunder her sacred space the next day in a game capture operation to translocate the duikers and some magnificent tortoises and a parrot to another property. We caught the duikers in nets and I filled them up with tranquiliser to stop their unbearable cries which sounded like the heartbreaking cries of children being murdered. Then Mum's beloved animals were trucked away as we started dismantling everything of our lives in Zambia. Trust in your Warrior to get you through these times. He can be as strong or as brutal as you need him to be. It's the Lover that falls into the red earth and dust in the moonlight with an empty bottle at hand. And sometimes this suffering takes a hold of the Lover's songs so that they become tainted with the ebbs and flows of loss and may resemble whalesong.

Sacrifice: Burning of beautiful things so they could return to the gods

Tom, Pola and I could not take more than a mere handful of tokens from Mum's personal possessions to remember her by or to keep her close. We had no luggage space and lived at opposite ends on the world in tiny houses. The workmen on the farm were given all the clothes and anything of value. The strangest celebration occurred as they picked through her things in the garage. The men began to dress in all her clothing from head to toe. Hats, scarves dresses and shoes all still vibrant with her presence and energy came alive again. A similar scene is described when Napoleon's army left Moscow in a Bohemian fashion after plundering the treasures of Russia and its aristocracy. But we loved our workers and if dressing up in drag brought them some happiness in such a dark time then it was a good thing. The rest of her possessions, including boxes and boxes of photographs and Polish books, our school reports, letters from boarding and even Toby's little dolls and teddy bears from Morning Psychology 101 we simply burned. There was no middle ground for this stuff… the choices were take it, give it away or burn it. That's brutal. That's Warrior stuff. In fact that's 'God of War'-type stuff.

I so understand the metaphor of blood and water flowing from the chest of Jesus when the Roman soldier stabbed him with a spear on the cross. An ultimate sacrifice just breaks the heart and mixes our blood, our humanity with tears. We will miss Mum forever. She was just the sweetest thing and generated life, laughter and drama in abundance. I am visibly crushed when unexpected clouds of longing for her cross my mind. But the clouds thankfully drift away when they have shed their raindrops even just to make way for all the others yet to come.

Our beloved farm on Misundu Road: a longing and connection to land and story

The twelve people employed on our small 10 acre farm were like lost sheep. For them it was the end of the world. Where would they go? Most landowners would have just kicked them off the land with a month's pay. But Tom kept them employed doing gardening for two years on full pay. Eventually the scales of his internal weighing machine started to tip when the cost of running the farm exceeded the joy of golden memories and he set about selling the farm. The men got such massive payouts at the end that two of them bought a taxi and started their own business having paid off their houses on Tom's generous magic wallet. Unbelievable.

But we all lost the farm eventually, our connection to land and local legend and it hurt badly. The stories will die with us when they cease to be told and the land will never live the same…it won't be spoken into being like it used to be as its history becomes progressively lost. We used to walk there among the Elephant grass which towered over our heads retelling our stories. But no longer. It's just like when our ancestors lost Poland, what became of the stories, the lifeblood of the land? I am reminded again why the first line of the Polish National Anthem is simply brilliant and so true. The story and the myth both live and die with the storyteller.

As the farm sale went through, I was visiting Zambia and I came across two of our workers carrying a huge fridge out of the house at sunset. They were setting off with it to a house 8 kms away over a distant hill through a most beautiful moonlit night. I wish I could have done the journey with them.

And, hey, this is Africa... the fridge was probably filled to the brim with stolen stuff from the house, or maybe 5 chickens or a sackful of turkeys. You just never know, but you have to love Zambians and indeed all of humanity for its ingenuity, especially in theft. My friend had a clothing factory and noticed that his manager always left work at the end of the day with a fresh loaf of bread under his arm. So he stopped the manager one day to take a closer look at the bread. On inspecting the hollowed out loaf it was found to contain a nice new shirt hot off the production line – meat in the sandwich so to speak - and this had been carrying on for many, many years. 365 shirts a year is enough to fill a clothing store with the added bonus of 365 crusty loaves to feed the family.

The farm sold to a very special man who fell in love with our 10 acre farm wonderland when he first visited it as a boy years before. It must have been his dream to own it one day and it seems that for him dreams really do come true. For Tom, Pola and I, things were going in the other direction: our truth and reality was fast turning into just dreams and memories. Time and life slowly slipped by as our childhood world changed through these events. Change is inevitable and insidious when you think that even the mighty Pharaohs of Egypt lost their pyramids, temples, statues and tombs to the shifting desert sands.

Tribute to Mum

I gave Mum's funeral speech. There are occasions in life when you only get one chance to do things right, to shoot from the hip. I hope I sang her tribute from my deepest, most soulful place. I told everyone that if they ever wanted to be with her again to hear her voice and her laughter they should look for her in the forest, in the wind. They could sit by a stream and hear her laughter in the life and voice of the river and the babbling brook.

But as I sit by the stream and listen for her voice, and especially if I forget to listen from my heart, I must admit I feel like someone has stolen the most beautiful Moon away from me forever.

She was born Halina Regina Kokoszko.
Our beautiful Mum.

7

Fathers and Sons

A Father's love

As the years went by, Mum and Dad became more estranged because of their differing values, financial pressures and lack of relationship skills. Dinnertime became epic battles of logic versus the irrational and I am not sure exactly who won. I do remember Dad wandering up the corridor to beg Mum to come to bed whilst she sat there with us boys watching TV, angry as a cut snake and sipping yet another glass of beer to cool her anger and cool the spitting cobra within. So I can understand Dad having various flings along the way as Mum withdrew. Testosterone and Dopamine can do that to a man despite his best intentions because they also help a man cope with stress.

Dad found his salvation at a night of spiritual mayhem when a passing evangelist, Reinhard Bonnke, walking the length of Africa, and dragging a huge cross behind him, held a revival at a venue near the mighty Victoria Falls. There were faith healings by the thousands with crutches and wheel chairs piling up each night outside the evangelical tent. By moonlight, a torrent of formerly lame people danced their way back to their homes over the hills and into religious empowerment by finding soap boxes of their own. I saw a video post of a kid in Zambia preaching, Bible in hand, to a sizeable mob with all the fervour and 'Ka-pow!'s of a Southern Baptist minister. Surely at age ten he had barely had a peep at life and would have been more authentic as a maverick singer in a rock band.

Zambians mobbed Reinhardt's altar calls with the zeal of shoppers at a Boxing Day Supermarket sale. Demons were cast from the possessed in the same way as wrestlers throw their vanquished from the ring into the crowd. Dad could not resist the altar call. With Zambians falling down to the left and to the right and writhing in the ecstatic fibrillations of the Holy Spirit, here Dad met his saviour and returned to Ndola totally transformed. Such is the power of liminality, of liminal space to create new neural pathways and circumvent the old. In a shower of holy sparks, Dad short-circuited his Dark Side and became a Born Again Christian.

Mum was having none of this 'Get out of the Jail Free' kind of Christian stuff and roasted him more than any of the chickens that she regularly cooked in our old gas oven. From then on she roasted chickens like she was working the gas ovens at a crematorium. Hell hath no fury like my mother when she was basically asked to forgive years and years of fighting with Dad and his unfaithful ways. Her passion never found a loving home in his world of British Empire and logic. By a mechanism of 'as within, so without' she channeled the energies of Chernobyl, Mount Vesuvius and the Fukushima Power Plant disaster into one long ten-year eruption. I just dived for cover as Mum, at the very mention of my father, regularly became the embodiment of the Goddess Kali, the Goddess of Destruction.

Dad, hitherto an avowed racist in that he regularly lamented the ways and work ethic of the Zambian people, could now be seen feeding the street children and destitute at dawn as they camped in the shop doorways all over town. He even slept overnight with the street kids in a ditch to experience their life and the life of swarms of night-time mosquitoes and of course to spoon out copious amounts of scripture to feed the childrens' hunger pangs. For a time on the farm we had a cook called Philemon – a jovial short Zairean. Without a suitable set of oven gloves to hold my Mum in her emotions, Dad went on to marry Ruth, Philemon's step-daughter. She was very young when he married her but he saved her from the ravages of Zambia, its diseases and tough existence. I love her dearly as my step-mother and she really is such a sweetheart. She still is my Dad's greatest supporter.

Josh and his step-grandmother Ruth.
Ruth is my delightful stepmother and is full of Zambian humour, love and a similar mischief to Fiona.

Together with Dad and her twin brother Charles, they built up a honey business totaling 400 hives using just a civilian car with the seats removed to cart all the hives around. I have no idea how you get a carload of bees down the highway with potholes that dismantle vehicles in the twinkling and shriek of a spilt beer. And how about the numerous army and police road blocks regularly extorting anything they can from ordinary motorists like bush ticks sucking on blood. They must have had some surprises and accidental discharges from their rusty AK47's as they lent into the window of the humming vehicle to demand money and realised too late why Charles was dressed head to toe in a bee keeping suit.

Trying to connect with Dad

We are supposed to try to makes things right with our parents in some way before they, or we, die. This will release golden energy which is locked up in the neurotic tangles back into our lives. Basically you are supposed to have a mega-talk about everything and maybe hear your parents' side of things before you arrived and became centre of the universe. You'll probably find you projected years of unresolved parent issues all over the place as time went by: onto the government, your spouse, your schoolteachers, the local copper and your footy coach. And if a parent is no longer around you can do much of this talking sitting in a church or talking to a tree in the forest or an attentive support group so as to shift the underlying energy. That's what my altar is for and why people go to churches and temples or draw mandalas in the sand.

Anyway, all my heartfelt emails from Australia to Zambia seemed to stir up the Evangelist in Dad. So all I got back was biblical quotations, judgements, damnations to Hell, and endless bizarre discussions about Creationism. Well he was right in the sense that modern man is the godly creationist that has altered and modified and exterminated nature beyond anything it used to be. It was as painful as sitting in a dentist's chair because honestly all I wanted was to speak to a real man, my Dad, a man of flesh and blood, not to a convoluted system of belief. I had spent 30 years in the churches, so I was no stranger to the language and the arguments that filled every email Dad sent. And yes I could see some truths and lots of love and wisdom there too in the Christian message. Dad's obsession was to convert me, to accept his myth as my own myth to live by. For him nothing else mattered much. For me, lots of other things mattered. Especially when it came to fathers and sons.

We stand on the shoulders of our ancestors. My earliest memory is of myself as a child in a London park sitting on Dad's shoulders and looking at the deep creases in the skin on the back of his neck. He must have cooked his skin as a kid always outdoors playing under the hot Egyptian sun without a white pith helmet. I have seen similar creases on the thick skin of elephants. But really, so much of Dad is out of my reach somewhere deep in my subconscious lost in Shadow. He didn't gift his finer points to us with much visible love and so there is not much more when it comes to those shoulders, to the really close moments, to being mentored into the mature masculine of my gender... not from Dad. Not really.

Dad's final weeks

Well in 2018, two years after Mum's death and six months after Pete's spectacular exit, I received a phone call from my stepmother Ruth who told me Dad was dying and unlikely to survive the night. I got on the midnight flight to Africa and arrived at Ndola's huge district hospital which Mum and Dad had helped build fifty years before. For me, my journey to Zambia was for the sole purpose to be the one to light Dad's funeral pyre and to conduct his funeral service but as you will see, events turned out quite differently. I hugged him as he lay there in bed, white as a sheet and high on medicinal marijuana oil. It was hard to believe that this was how his story was ending... on the third floor of a government hospital where the window was propped open by a sizeable chunk of concrete above a busy walkway 30 metres below. The bar of soap in the sink was nice and unused because there was no water in the taps.

I slept in the hospital overnight in a broken chair by Dad's bedside and listened to the howls and tears of the people next door whose son didn't make it till dawn. He was a teenager with liver failure and would come over and pray for Dad each day. Charles and I would laugh and joke with him but that's just memories now. He had such happy, beautiful eyes, bright and stunningly yellow with jaundice. He lived on an impossible promise that an international charity was going to fly him to Switzerland for a liver transplant. When the stress of an unresolved paradox is too much we sometimes exchange a neurotic fearful state for one of faith, hope or delusion.

Faith Healing

Christians from the local Baptist church would wander in all day to see Dad. He was famous at their church because he used to love to stand up in the Sunday sermon and berate the Pastor for being non-Biblical. The Pastor would stagger about at the pulpit speechless and clutching his heart before a stunned congregation. Now with Dad in hospital it became a free for all with Christians practicing their faith healing on Dad. They would drag me into the circle, roll their eyes to Heaven and start a passionate exorcism directed like radiation therapy at Dad's cancer. You could hear the rising crescendo of voices beating and slapping the cancer to death in the name of Jesus. Our hands were locked together as if in some death grasp and shaking the bejesus out of Dad and the rickety hospital bed nearly dislodging the chunk of concrete in the window onto the human Chicken Lickens below. But the cancer demon obviously didn't believe in Jesus and it carried on multiplying regardless, chuckling, twiddling its thumbs and biding its time.

On one occasion, a pastor was trying his skills on Dad berating the demons and crying out to the Lord. The demons were getting whipped into a Pavlova of exorcism and I had been dragged into the circle with the pastor clutching my hands and sending electricity through my body that would have better served the abysmal Zambian electricity grid. With shouts and "Pow!"s and "Jesus!"s, he gunned down the cancer demon and gave me a chiropractic workout at the same time. But this demon was clever and in a terrifying moment Dad's bowels let rip with enough gas to kill half the soldiers in World War I. I hastily pulled my T-shirt over my nose like a bank robber in order to survive the smell but the Pastor was now in full swing and didn't take evasive action in time. Poor thing. He eventually wilted like a rose without water and conceded defeat to the Fart Demon. With shaking hands he left the room muttering and with a newfound respect for demonic forces, wondering forever what went wrong.

Transformation: from Pastors to witch doctors

Zambian Christianity is seriously powerful stuff. When I asked Toby where all the witch doctors had gone, he said they were now preachers and pastors in the churches. Here they made a living mixing the sacred blood of Jesus and the Holy Spirit with wild shamanic leapings, a rampant gospel of prosperity, and miraculous cures from all diseases and situations. A cosmic revolution of spiritually had gripped the Zambian people. I have no doubt eventually the government will curb this religious frenzy with the usual combination of truncheons and arrests, but for now this new Christianity gives the people hope, not salvation, in the form of a bizarre, liminoid cocktail of Dionysian madness every Sunday. Meanwhile there are adverts all over Zambia from witch doctors claiming to heal everything from erectile dysfunction to boyfriend problems. Such is the power of belief in Zambia that I am sure they are 100% successful. The placebo effect can be 100% successful. So is it real medicine?... I would say yes because Reader's Digest claims that laughter is the very best medicine of all. Once again, there is some truth in any madness if we look for it and abundant power in our beliefs.

Modern witchdoctors. These guys can fix anything because they have incorporated Christianity into their shamanic practices and now wield a very wide spectrum of godly power.

The power of belief in action

Zambians are very interesting people, and it is a delight and never boring to live amongst them. Hydon Banda worked for us for about 20 years. He was our night watchman but also did a lot of interesting carpentry, building and maintenance for us on the farm... interesting because his tools were like relics from the Stone Age: ancient, broken, blunt or non-existent. The only power tools he had were his biceps – also relics from the Stone Age because he was very old. The drill was an old hand-cranked thing with only 3 rusty drill bits: small, medium and large, and he always put all the wood screws into timber using sweat and a screwdriver. But he is best remembered by the brilliant croquet sets he made. Mum and Dad designed them and set him up with wood and he produced hundreds of beautiful sets which we boxed up and sold to England. Somehow, by hand Hydon carved all the round croquet balls out of blocks of wood. I will never know how he did it. He was loved and respected by all and he moved with a certain grace and dignity. So it is ironical how his funeral ended in total mayhem. But it is also typical of Zambia where you could write a book about each 24-hour block of bewildering chaos... it unfolds relentlessly every day and the daily newspaper – the Times of Zambia – is an absolute hilarious delight to read.

Hydon got paid out a small fortune by Tom as his severance pay when he left our farm. It was more money than any profit our tiny farm made in its entire existence. A few months later he got very sick, then recovered, and then died. Now Zambians are extremely jealous people. And they are fiercely superstitious. Some of them went to a witch doctor and got some kind of juju paste and smeared it all over the coffin. This causes the coffin to 'travel'... and carried by the etranced pallbearers it goes to find the one who caused the death. This could be fifty miles away, but hey, don't let distance get between you and a good old bit of witch hunting and revenge. So, whipped into a frenzy by the divine paste, the pallbearers lost their grip on reality and on the coffin and managed to destroy it when it fell into the 6 x 6 foot hole in the cemetery. You see, this was a budget coffin and light on construction materials. It was largely being held together by the prayers of the faithful.

They pulled out the planks of the makeshift coffin from the grave and then pulled out Hydon. He was also rather plank-like from rigor mortis. Then they somehow did an IKEA bodge job and lashed bits of coffin and Hydon back together. Well, it was "Game On!" now because the coffin had all the supernatural ability of a man-sized Ouija board. It took off looking for the perpetrator of Hydon's death… and it made straight for Hydon Banda's son's house. The moment the white-eyed pallbearers and coffin collided with the house, guilt was divinely established and punishment was exacted in the form of a Help-Yourself-Looting of the son's residence.

Once the house was emptied, frustrated Followers of the Divine Juju Paste took it to the next level and started demolishing the house by helping themselves to the bricks. But the Gods have a sense of humour here, and while dust and sweat and the destructive looting continued, the Gods unleashed the Dogs of War, namely the arrival of Riot Police with truncheons. And with custom brutality they kicked the living shit out of everyone in the area. People ran screaming left and right whilst in the background Hydon's son's house burned to the ground. Hydon now rests in pieces as does his son's house which had become an impromptu souvenir shop and building supplies centre whilst the riot happened and with the unleashing of the Berserker Mind - that pure archetypal madness common to all humanity and all recorded history. We as children did it all the time - fighting and snatching that last biscuit off a plate at tea time.

But to dance with Hecate, the goddess of witchcraft, is a dangerous thing. It ended sadly for everyone: the sons were convicted to years of imprisonment for poisoning their father with witchcraft.

And somewhere, under a Zambian night sky, a witch doctor chuckles counting a stash of cash. He is mixing up another tub of good old Juju Paste, fattening his sacrificial chickens and stoking the muse of fire, the fire of belief and the imagination that are the greatest tools of his trade.

My Mission Impossible

So after two weeks in Zambia, Dad was still alive. Two pints of blood and all the faith healing had bought him a little time, but somewhere in the fourth dimension you could still hear, the ticking of a divine chariot's taxi meter waiting to take him back home. It was the Grim Reaper at the wheel. The fun of life and living was about to be denied him much like when years before Dad had kidnapped me for that crazy boat race around the dam and the fun and laughter was everywhere else except on our boat. Outside his bedroom window life simply carried on.

I feel such guilt and shame whenever the voices in my head tell me that my trip to Zambia was all a waste of time and money. You see, I still had a full box of matches and a magnificent funeral speech in my pocket - both waiting impatiently for Dad's big send off. It felt like I had failed a James Bond mission and I absolutely love being sent on special missions. Normally I am the man who goes where angels fear to tread and never stops until he succeeds. But truth be told, the anticlimax of Dad defying the Angel of Death really sucked because I felt I hadn't achieved very much.

Still, I was not the Producer and Director of Dad's story, only of my own. So I spent my time in Ndola having the most profound connection with Zambia that my heart, soul, mind and body could ever wish for. My older self, unafraid of dying, lived it fully. I knew it might be my last visit to the country of my childhood. I walked throughout the town and out to the surrounding farms and bushland near the Zaire border, out along the old railway tracks that meander through the sprawling townships alive with runaway chickens, bare bottomed pickanins and feral cats. The children still wave like they did fifty years ago when we first arrived as if they were greeting God himself. Beside them walk the smiling women, young, old and mostly pregnant, colourfully dressed with the fabrics of dignity. Each one is balancing a clay urn of water on her head, barefoot and without complaint. By the roadside, the oldest women – paragons of patience - sit breaking stones with hammers all day in the hot sun to create piles of various grades to sell for building homes or fixing potholes. All the while, water wells up from the ground on the Misundu Road next to the Chipulukusu Township from holes dug into the earth by the villagers to access the municipal water supply. These memories are as vibrant within me now as when I was there experiencing the perceptions with all my senses, filled with love and with nothing denying their passage through me. The cinema screen within me is the same.

A son's need for his father's blessing: the need to hear: "Well done."

Eventually it came time for me to return to Australia. On my way to the airport, my nephews drove me through the dusty streets of Ndola to say goodbye to Dad. He was lying on the bed in his flat. He had been bedridden for months. I broke down into uncontrollable sobs as I hugged him and honoured him for his strength and courage. He honoured me for my adventure work and then berated me for being a total financial disaster.

Then he started discussing medical bills and requesting money. Mum's inability to accumulate money had long since impoverished my own financial world so he was right about me being a financial disaster but asking the wrong person for money.

His last words to me were, "For God's sake, Lem... write your book! You are a writer! Write your book." Those words grabbed me and shook me. They shook me awake even as I closed the front door of his flat for the last time with the heaviest heart.

I accepted this as the best version of a Father's Blessing he could come up with. You see, all his life he had the tact and people skills of a brick. Now he was doing it through the haze of homemade marijuana oil - the palliative medicine that eventually got him through the portal of Hades to the Pearly Gates and hopefully to his beloved saviour Jesus.

Dionysus: Barman to the gods, Pharmacist to us humans

Given as a free gift from a local Australian and sourced from the sparse pickings of a Zambian marijuana field on the Zaire border, the marijuana leaves were first heated up in a simple dehydrator to activate the magical cannabinoids within. They were then crushed with a pestle and mortar and suspended in olive oil, strained and bottled. Each batch varied considerably but they all had the strength, power and potency of your first bottle of whiskey, and I am talking about just three drops of the oil. I am sure Getafix, the Druid, made such stuff for Asterix once upon a time so that he could take on the entire Roman army single-handed. Every drunk believes he's as tough as Asterix on a Saturday night blind to his own weakness, incoordination and slow motion. He then gets dazzled by the surprising speed of the bouncer's fists, and the rest he usually can't remember.

So when his time came, Dad entered the world of Anubis, the Egyptian guardian of the afterlife, pain free on a 5-star marijuana ticket riding the celestial chariot to Sirius. The ancient Egyptians believed the Soul Train terminated near Sirius at the foot of Orion. When I personally get there, I just want a job as a celestial painter taking care of the beauty of the constellations. It will be my eternal gift, my Mission to the Divine Feminine. But, being a veterinarian, I can also care for the constellations of Orion's hunting dogs, for some rabbits, a nearby dove and my pirates can care for the constellation of the Argo, the mythical galleon sailing the ocean of the Milky Way near the Southern Cross. Jason sailed across the ancient Mediterranean world with his band of Greek heroes, the Argonauts to recover the Golden Fleece in the Argo. These very heroes live on as long as their stories are told. Now through the winter, spring and summer nights I watch and wonder as these magnificent constellations plough their way through the starlit southern skies. They are magnified through the lens of my telescope and coloured by my imagination and the knowledge of their mythical origins, their stories, their lifeblood.

Blessings from beyond the grave

But a very curious thing happened that day in Dad's flat as I rose to say my final goodbye and leave for the airport. It took me many months to understand. As I was sobbing and telling Dad he was the bravest man I ever knew, I stooped to give him a hug yet he seemed very distracted and composed, very British. Then he suddenly seemed to have a bright idea, kissed his fingers and put them on my forehead. To my surprise I was overcome with an unexpected feeling of repulsion. It felt like a golden disc of plastic had fallen from my forehead where his fingers had been. Then his face melted into that of my Great Grandmother's whom I have always loved dearly. And I felt her presence, love and blessing coming through him from an ancient past. I felt somehow anointed by my great grandmother and the repulsion left me. We both loved her so much and somehow in that moment, in that gesture, her love shone through a generation onto me.

Whereas Mum had been speaking Polish to her Mum and Dad when they came to take her to Heaven, Dad was being taken there in the loving arms of his Grandmother, my Great Grandmother, the only woman to give him pure and unconditional love.

You see, when Dad was born, he was her redemption. Some people would argue that there is no greater love than a grandparent's love for a grandchild. And Dad rekindled a fire in her broken heart which had been broken so brutally through the rejection she suffered from her husband a hundred years ago on her wedding night. When Dad was born, Granny Goût came alive again with this little boy to love – a masculine element to complete the matrix of her mind and of her world which her own three daughters could not do. Now, as a gentle aspect of the Angel of Death, she was taking him home after a lifetime of their mutual devotion.

I only realised this love, Granny's love, and the love and affirmation of my ancient ones, my ancestors, when I could see past my repulsion and cognitive dissonance due to Dad's symbolic and rather feminine gesture which fell away from my forehead as a token of plastic. Then I could see another token - a disc of pure gold -stamped upon my forehead, the place of Insight and Intuition, by Granny Goût. In that moment Granny re-established the access to my ancestors which otherwise might have been blocked. From that moment on I would never have to navigate this world alone.

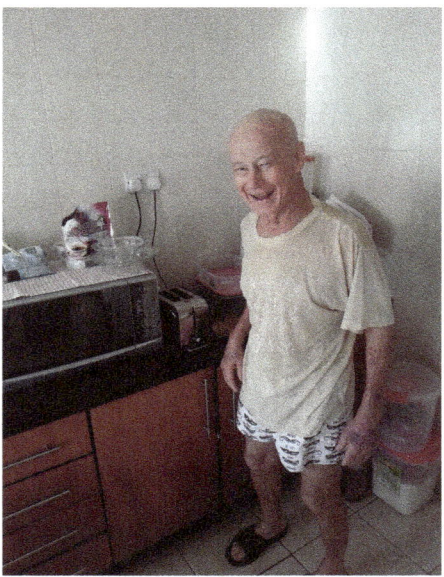

Dad at 82 . Almost blind with macular degeneration, he bravely jogged 4km each day stumbling in and out of traffic and fell into ditches a couple of times.

But because Dad never let anyone beat him in sport, discussion or negotiations, he certainly wasn't going to let us be at his funeral either. I returned to Australia, my original mission unaccomplished but so many things of my childhood were now in their proper place. Fiona collected me at Perth airport and from there took me on a diabolically epic 4000 km road trip up north so I only actually got home 9 days later living out of a suitcase and a 4-wheel drive vehicle. Dad meanwhile died peacefully in bed… one minute he was there, next minute there was just a humanoid collection of atoms and molecules and the Universe quiet and still and somehow electric around his peaceful form.

TRANSFORMATION AND THE GOLDEN KEYS

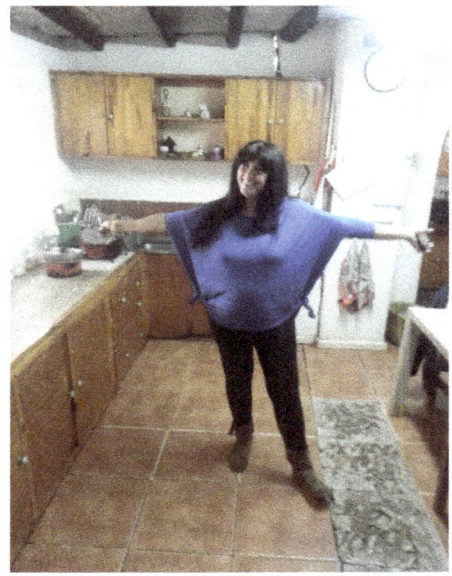

My beautiful vivacious sister-in-law Salwa.

At the funeral, Salwa, Pete's widow, and the family were delayed for an hour and a half between the church service and the cremation atop the Hindu hill. So basically there wasn't much family there at all as his body was consumed by the buttery flames and smoke in all that ghee-laden wood. He was so steeped in palliative Marijuana oil that all the smoke must have given the onlookers a mysterious outbreak of the giggles.

Whereas Anubis was the Egyptian keeper of the eternal afterlife, the underworld, and thus the remote future, Granny Goût seemed to be my gatekeeper to an ancient world of my ancestors, to my remote past, to the beginning of time when everything was One. Dad was actually the fourth of my family to go up in a conflagration of fire and smoke. The first one was indeed my great grandmother, Granny Goût.

Granny Goût at 103 years of age. She told us about the Ottoman empire. We told her about Jimmy Hendrix.

8

Ancestors: The shoulders on which we stand

Our great grandmother

We called her Granny Goût, not because she suffered from actual gout but because it was her French surname and pronounced "goo". Her name was really Honorine. She was born in Smyrna, Turkey, in 1883 and could tell me stories that her grandmother told her about life in the 1700's. That's pretty cool. We loved Granny Goût and her stories of Turkey where she mostly lived for over fifty years.

Smyrna has been described as an absolute cultural haven with hundreds of trouble-free years graced with the wealth and splendour of a diverse mix of nationalities and religions. Everyone spoke five languages or more. Granny Goût could speak fluently in English, French, Turkish, Italian and Classical Greek.

Grandmother Audrey. Audrey sewed all her dresses for the endless parties and gatherings of social life in Turkey.

Our local Greeks in Ndola would stand there transfixed when she spoke as if they were standing before the Oracle of Delphi. She would say anything in classical Greek and by the power in the magic of language they would fall into a trance of wonder. She was speaking with a music that enchanted their ancient Greek hearts, sonnets of Calypso written in their DNA, the same ones that held Odysseus spellbound for seven years on Calypso's Island. When hearing their true native language spoken after a period of absence from their Greek motherland, their hearts cried out with open arms like children pleading for ice creams. They yearned for more of the language, more melodies for their Greek souls, their connection to an ancient humanity and a time when they were the kings ruling an ancient empire. Theirs was a vast civilisation that brought so much to our modern world. Language was a bridge to their mythology and wisdom. And all myths like our nightly dreams give us insights for this real pragmatic world, insights for our psychology, insights into the spirit realm of Oneness and insights to the inner world of Soul.

The Loss and Gain in a Marriage

The British Consul of Smyrna proposed to Honorine and she accepted. He was almost twice her age. At the nuptial bed his only gift to her was a typically British upper class rejection when he berated her for dressing up like a slut. How naïve and vulnerable she must have been. She choked back the tears that night locking the pieces of her romantic dreams and her stillborn joy away in her heart forever. Then she threw away the key. Subsequently she stoically bore him three daughters always entering the bedchambers dressed to the hilt and in a nightdress buttoned to the neck.

Tuberculosis took one of their daughters, Lorna at the age of 33. But my vivacious grandmother Audrey lived Lorna's life relentlessly through the Bohemian ways of Smyrna with its endless coffee shops, bars and soirées. The wealth in Smyrna meant that entertainment and soirées never ended. Audrey would wake up at midday and with a cigarette by her side and a glass of wine never empty, she would sew the most exquisite ball gowns of the Gatsby era and wear them to the flirtatious gatherings of the rich and famous every evening.

Consequently she married my grandfather Thomas Ravensdale who rose up through the British Diplomatic Corps to become a British Ambassador to Libya, Mali and West Africa before a retirement posting as

British Consul to the Balearic Islands of which Ibiza seems to be the most famous today. Grandpa Tom loved us grandchildren but he never gave his two sons any love or conversation whatsoever. This left Dad and my uncle forever bewildered and forever robbed of a sacred treasure: the golden cloak and medals of a father's affirmation and blessing. We used to visit Grandpa Tom where he retired in France in a small village at the foot of hills on which a castle built by Richard the Lionheart stood. It was called the Chateau Gaillard in the town of Les Andelys. We kids spent many summer days rolling down the grassy embankments and sword fighting across its spacious courtyards goaded on by the ghosts of knights in armour.

But Audrey was onto her third husband by then and never stopped being the life and soul of the party. That's why Dad had such a painful relationship with her because despite his pleadings she had no idea how to be a mother. And his Dad was too busy governing that part of the British Empire to be a father. So my father's core wound - irresponsible parenting - became his greatest gift to the Zambian people. Dad held everyone in authority to account even if they were soldiers at road blocks wielding assault rifles. He told everyone to lift their game.

Uncles are ready made Heroes for Nephews

Dad's younger brother Henry - who we called Uncle Winks - tried to escape these heartbreaks of childhood by losing himself in the wilds of Northern Canada. He became a driller underground in the mines and then an explosives technician. For a time he set about demolishing half of Canada. Uncle Winks is the father I wish I had... like we could easily finish each other's sentences because we have such similar personalities. He is a wild adventurer, has the biggest and kindest heart, and spent years working with kids as a teacher of French, History and Phys Ed.

Maybe Dad never really learned how to love well. But Winks met his sweetheart Darlene when he went to University to get a teaching degree and he always says that it is Darlene who taught him how to love. His love is so immense that I often wonder where all that energy would have gone if it were not allowed to express itself in one of the most beautiful of men. I guess he would simply have blown up. But with all this love, he has time for everyone and all of Nature. Uncle Winks simply says "Yes!" to Life and he goes to the archetype of Mother Nature in the wild forested beauty of British Columbia when he wants to experience the parenting he never got from his earthly parents.

So Dad and Granny Goût became devoted to each other and in some measure soothed each other's inner longings and core wounds. In her old age, she came to live with us for 30 years in Zambia. I have to thank her eyes for developing cataracts and robbing me of hours of football practice with Tom in the front garden. Instead, I would sit at the foot of her bed reading letters from her two daughters which they sent her every week. And then sentence by heartfelt sentence I would write the replies for her. Who was I, a mere teenager, sitting as a scribe in the sacred space between mother and daughter as they reminisced over days of the Ottoman Empire and the times in which they had lived... two witnesses to an empire that only ended its thousand years of turbulent history in the 1920's and time forgot. What a privilege that was for me. I have loved the old people, their wisdom and their stories ever since.

The unpredictable God of War takes down the Greeks, the Armenians and the Ottomans

In 1922, shortly before Dad was born, a very powerful Greek army invaded Turkey and pushed the Turkish army into retreat to the other side of the country. The Turkish General, Kemal Ataturk, tried through diplomatic means to get the British and the Americans to intervene and to lobby against this invasion of his country but to no avail.

As the invasion progressed, fuelled by the intoxicating memories of Alexander the Great and his vast empire, the Greek army over-stretched its supply lines and then got beaten severely in hill country on the other side of Turkey. Now the Turks were on the offensive and butchered their way with ethnic cleansing back to Smyrna. Here, the blissfully unaware Bohemian party was in full swing as always when nearly a million refugees poured into Smyrna upsetting the soirées and idyllic vista with tales of horror. Behind it came an unhinged Turkish Army progressively led not so much by its officers, but by an unmoderated, pure, authentic archetype: the God of War. By possessing soldiers with this god's Berserker mind – the mentality named after the ancient bearskin-clad fighting-mad Viking coke heads - one of the greatest genocides of this planet's history unfolded.

A closer look at this God of War

The earth is no stranger to genocides: the God of War excels in such things. James Hillman in his book 'A Terrible Love of War' ponders the possibility that a people never really feel they own the land under their feet unless they have spilled enough of their own blood into its soil. And he makes the sobering observation that once this God of War has been summoned and unleashed, the outcomes become far from predictable.

TRANSFORMATION AND THE GOLDEN KEYS

Military commanders secretly realise they are not really in control of the beast. The rules of war are basically to win, not to be nice, so things get more and more brutal. Both sides want to be the ones to ascend the podium and get the gold medal and trophy but events and collateral damage in war keep unfolding sideways like a slippery bar of soap terrifying both the commanders and the politicians who started it all.

Adam Zamoyski wrote a bestselling book called '1812' about Napoleon's fatal march on Moscow. It is one of the most brilliant and mind-boggling accounts of the God of War you could ever read. Page after page reveals how events turn by cruel chance against one of history's greatest armies and then simply consume it. And in Thomas Packenham's masterful account of how Africa became partitioned into so many countries ('The Scramble for Africa') he describes the antics of some 10 000 Congolese cannibals lead by a very victorious Belgian commander Dhanis as they eat their way through their victories, smoking and stewing the human flesh for dinner at the end of a day's fighting. Dhanis inquired of the fate of one of his Arab rivals called Mohara in a skirmish: "We ate him yesterday" said his troops.

I have known many Turks and Turks are a most beautiful people. But the God of War possessed their Army in 1922 as it possesses soldiers to this day all over the world. It has done this throughout history. At such times, command and control is so easily lost and humanity's thin veneer of civilisation is overwhelmed by a brutal archetypal energy present within us all. It's a very authentic remnant of our forefather: the Tyrannosaur rex. It is our so called Lizard Brain in pure, raw and authentic archetypal form. So the soldiers run amok and feel fully justified in their behaviour because they have demonised the enemy so as to rationalise and make sense of what they are doing. The rules are different in the thick smoke of war.

But then time moves on and the rules change in peacetime. A lifetime of regret and emotional torment sets in as people find the time to discuss and judge these things over tea and biscuits.

I love to look for opposites. And I love languages. For example, Cosmos is Greek for 'order' whereas 'Chaos' is Greek for 'disorder'. Athena was a goddess, a female, and a brilliant hunter, tactician and a wise military leader living completely in harmony with nature. Her mother was Metis, famous for her wise counsel and tactics. Her father was Zeus who also sired Ares but to his jealous wife Hera. Ares by contrast was a god, masculine, brutal and cruel with his Berserker mentality. We probably need a bit of Ares to season our armed forces with to win a war or to win a soccer match. But Ares needs to be tempered by Athena otherwise his authentic expression creates genocides and crimes against humanity, pitch invasions and flares released in the soccer grandstands.

All of us men need to temper our masculine with a touch of our feminine, and the right type of feminine. The rampant masculinity of the Minotaur within the labyrinth of the psyche devouring the beauty of youth waits for transcendence by the hero Theseus – the Minotaur slayer. In transcending evil during his career as the greatest of the Greek heroes, Theseus probably killed just as many individuals even if he didn't devour them afterwards. Yet Ariadne, an aspect of the feminine, tempered the killing of the Minotaur by asking Theseus to dispatch her half-brother swiftly, with a measure of kindness that there be the minimum of suffering.

When the shit hits the fan in war, and a soldier's ego loses control, it's just Inner World appearing in this Outer World unmodified. Then the sergeant sheepishly announces, "…General… the officers have lost control. I regret to report that cannibalism has broken out amongst the troops…"

In such things we are really just staring at an outbreak of authentic aspects of the God of War unhinged from the ego's control.

We have a full spectrum of archetypes within each one of us

Everyone on earth shares these elements in their ancestry and within their archetypal world. The Mass Murderer is alive and well behind anyone who has ever gunned down a commando of ants invading the sugar bowl on the kitchen table. The Anti-aircraft Gunner brings down another Blow Fly with one long burst of fire from the can of Sudden Death Insect Killer spray and, chuckling to himself, feels absolutely great about doing so. The Gamers are up all night clocking up an endless body count with clips of submachine gun fire whilst pixels and kilobytes create a firework display of bullets and blood splattering the computer screen. Here, if only for a moment, the Berserker mind is alive and well and high on a hormonal cocktail of dopamine and adrenaline.

The Armenian genocide

But Granny was there in human form to witness this very real genocide much of it involving the Armenian population of that land. It had all the woe and terror of a similar historical account on exactly this subject given by Giles Milton in his spell-binding book 'Paradise Lost'. The book caught Thomas's eye as he was walking past a bookstore in Warsaw and the cover bears a photograph of the burning city, of exactly the scene that Granny witnessed with her own eyes. Evacuated to the safety of a British warship anchored less than a mile off shore, Granny watched the butchering and rape of the people amassed on the docksides. Meanwhile, Turkish soldiers unloaded barrel after barrel of petroleum from the back of trucks into the Armenian quarter and rolled them gushing with fuel down the streets of that beautiful city. In service to the God of War, they sprayed the Armenian buildings everywhere with petroleum before torching the place which was already awash with the butchered dead.

The smoke and flames destroyed an ancient city that day. And the peace and harmony of 300 years of international trading went up in the burning embers. The dead were everywhere many of them bobbing in the waters off Smyrna's quays and around Granny's warship still being robbed by Turkish youths who swam amongst the rotting dead with scarves tied across their faces because of the stench of death. 'Paradise Lost' is a book you simply can't put down. And you hardly blink all the way through so keep some eye drops handy next to your box of tissues. It's a book you only read once. You can't read about such things twice because it's just too much for the mind to make a second journey through pages alive with ghosts. How close can you authentically be in the presence of the God of War before it's all too much and you have to move away and close the book, or suppress the voices of people who cry out to be heard?

Granny Goût survived all of this and two world wars. I am left to wonder at the irony of how these things worked out. Granny got a letter from the British Home Office praising and thanking her for her great effort as the supervisor in a lethal bomb-making factory in England during World War I. She must have supervised the assembly of countless thousands of bombs and bullets yet she was a most peaceful and loving soul. Basically the letter was praising my Granny for killing lots of people and helping to save England.

These unpleasant things in life, things like death or our own personal atrocities, are best processed in sacred space and sacred ceremony. If left unprocessed, repressed or denied, they will just bob up somewhere like a beach ball in the ocean and create untold mischief. How did Granny process it? Mostly she seemed to think a lot. A gentle sigh would sail across the white watery cataracts of her faraway eyes. She would sit for hours playing yet another hand of solitaire, a card game of chance and mixed fortunes yet still a game of hope. It helped to soothe her mind as she sucked thoughtfully away on boiled sweets and Macintosh toffees. And she shared the magic of our history in her dictations to her daughters who replied with magic and longings of their own.

When the gods live amongst us

Every morning Granny combed her hair with the passion and youthfulness of a young maiden, tossing it like a gamboling filly and then gently placing a hairnet over her creation. As teenagers we would return home from a night on the town drunk in the dead of night and come across Granny in the long dark corridor. It was like walking into a haggard version of Medusa with abundant white serpent-like hair escaping her hair net. Anyway, she was rather deaf so she didn't get the full brunt of our terrified screams.

Granny would sneak into the kitchen at night to raid the fridge. One day she admitted to having finished off a very large bowl of custard but it was actually a very large bowl of mayonnaise we had made for a catering. Yet she never seemed to get sick from ingesting lethal quantities of mistaken food. She never got sick from anything. Not even malaria which is the scourge of Africa and Asia. I have no idea why the mosquitoes were not attracted to her cold, paper-thin skin, or why the malaria parasites seemed to just die on being injected there. The rest of us would lie about shivering and shaking and chewing on chloroquine through much of the year, racked with the fevers of this debilitating disease.

How Granny's story ended

Eventually she got her letter from the Queen and from the Zambian president to add to the one from the British Home Office as she nimbly sped past 100 years. She must have seemed like an immortal God to the Zambians whose average life expectancy was just over 50 years at best due to every disease from HIV and TB to malaria and malnutrition, lightning strikes, bus accidents, floods and crocodiles. And then at 103, she passed away peacefully in her sleep. Her ghost continues to walk the corridors of that house but her body now orbits the atmosphere and you will no doubt contain a few of her atoms too.

She was the first of our family to be hoisted upon a wooden pyre and set fire to. But it was on a farm behind ours at Misundu Road, not the Hindu crematorium. I only saw the photos of the conflagration. It seemed to rival that of Smyrna's. Her death hit me badly because I was living far from home by then and couldn't get back for the funeral. I really sobbed as I realised the great lady was well and truly gone and in such spectacular fashion. I knew that farm so well. It was called Cherry Farm, but that is another story. I have always felt there was a rightness and brilliance in the choice of the cremation method. It seemed to add to her greatness.

Going to Mother Nature to process things of the heart and the unpleasant things in Life

So I guess Dad lost his childhood home in Turkey, as did Granny, and Mum lost her home in Poland. I too have lost mine in my travels but at least I have found ways for my frail mind to process the loss. I don't need to make sense of a calamity or to rationalise it with lies, platitudes and convenient untruths. I simply process it using the power of ceremony, ritual, myth and symbol somewhere in a grotto in the forest alive with energy and with Nature, watched over by what I regard is a conscious universe. Any issue I have with the living or with the dead, with the future, present or past, I can take to the forest or to the beach, create a ritual or symbolic piece of art and deal with it in my own way. I sit there singing songs in the tongues of foreign lands. This helps keep the magic alive, shift the energies and enables me to feel grounded and connected to a permanence that transcends this short human existence. In this way I walk my authentic journey in the care and love of a Universe that listens and understands and works miracles because it is a miracle.

Know your values - compare and contrast them with your significant other

If only Mum and Dad had these skills to cope with their relationship. Dad valued logic, reason, law, accountability and good governance. Mum valued fun and feelings, intuition, freedom, lack of accountability and chaos. I can spot six causes of paradox and ensuing neurosis right there. No wonder they fought so much. Lovely people but roasting each other on the rotisserie of unresolved paradox.

It is a great exercise for people in relationship to download a list of values off the web and determine five or ten of their core values. Then, by comparing each their own values they can understand what motivates their behaviour and choices. And it immediately gives insight into areas of paradox or conflict and areas of synergy. I value intimacy and connection so I stop and talk to the ants or to the people on the checkout at the supermarket. Fiona values shopping at a supersonic speed. So we worked it out: she shops whilst I walk around talking to bewildered people.

It's nice to have a few photos to pull out and remember when we were kings. It's like giving the Ego a nice back rub.

9

My Personal Myth

William Shakespeare is alive and well within you

When I get to Heaven, I imagine I will be standing there feeling all alone on my Judgement Day. Around me will be gathered all of humanity that was given its own measure of Precious Time in which to live. God leans forward on his creaky throne and asks me the ultimate question, " So... tell us your name and a few things about your life... and don't rush it, we have got plenty of time to listen."

Will I be left speechless and too embarrassed to give a pitiful reply about how unconsciously I walked through the miracle of Life and missed so much of it, so many opportunities? Or will I ask for forgiveness for ransacking his holy temple as a teenager at boarding school, drinking all that altar wine? Life was abundant with wonderful things and bristling with opportunity, but maybe I kind of drifted along sleeping through it all. I could have just reached out a hand from my comatose stupor and touched endless flowers and treasures which cried out to me all along the path of my slumbering journey.

At times and living unconsciously, I gave the Scriptwriter's quill and ink to my lost Lover to write a story of isolation and longing. Instead of ink he seemed to write a lot of it using alcohol mixed with tears. As for Pete, he lost his quill to his madness. It tumbled from his hand into the arms of a mob of renegade archetypes as his mind became unhinged. They got ink everywhere and eventually set fire to his quill and to his story.

So once upon a time, like a frustrated playwright, I ditched my old story by writing a suicide note from that tearful victim in me. It certainly put that archetype in its place. The new story I tell myself, the Myth I live by empowers me and infuses me with hope because it is the wings I soar upon. When I sit in circle and we each have a few moments to share our names and a few things about ourselves, I am seen to struggle and writhe a bit. I have so many names depending on my role or which organisation I am working with. And as for what I do, I struggle to explain in a few words how I am experiencing living and breathing in this miracle of Life. There is too much to say.

I now give my quill - the pen with which I write my story, the story of who I am - to my Playwright, for that is its proper place. He is the creator and keeper of a script that is panoramic and serves my life's mission. My inner Artist chooses a million colours to drape upon the images. And the soundtracks for the opera, my inner rhythms, take their tempo from the cadence of a heart possessed by the only one who could write such a score: my inner Musician – a Brazilian no doubt.

When I told my speech at Mum's funeral, it was one of those times when you only get one chance to do it right. Part of you just rises to the occasion because it has to. And there are times in life when you get just one moment to shoot from the hip and state who you are and what you stand for. This is your story. This is the Myth you live by. It is the Myth you will die by. And it is the one you will die defending however great or however shitty and small it is. So make it the most beautiful, magnificent statement you could ever make. Don't ever sell yourself short on this one because words have power. Say it like it is the last chance on earth you will ever have to state what you stand for, to plant your flag, your banner firmly in the soil and to stand without apology. For this is your greatest creation, your life's work not some advertisement for toothpaste.

As Robert Johnson reminds us, your unlived life will come back to bite you. So live it. And those parts that seem impossible to live can be lived through sacred ritual or process so that you process your life in its entirety as best you can. Be dutiful in this, and you will have the greatest story to tell your God when you inevitably get to Heaven: the Myth you Lived By.

My story

Well you probably are wondering what became of me as the years rolled by. At that time, the Zambian education system could only take us so far. My last lessons in primary school in Ndola were about building grass huts and how to till the land to grow maize plants. So like most of the expatriate kids in rural Africa we were sent to boarding school.

At a road siding outside Ndola, a coach would carry us away from the safety of Mum and her shower of tears that rained down on us from a Zambian sky above. We cried too, but only on the inside lest any of the kids on the bus spotted a chink in our body armour. I call these 'man tears'... the ones you can't show to the outside world. Men cry all the time, you just would never know it. I must admit I am totally jealous that it seems perfectly okay for girls to show their tears any time they feel like it. I wish I could externalise all this energy too. But boys and men pick on the weak because they hate their own weakness resonating within. Rather than looking into their own mirror they would rather project it all on a convenient scapegoat.

Our staunch faces in the Zambian moonlight must have haunted Mum. Like me, she understood that the most gutting and blackest of words is the word 'Goodbye'. Every mother understands 'Goodbye'. For me it is a schema infused with so many vivid memories of loss and filled with overwhelming emotion. Try never to say it to me because I respond as if I've been shot in the chest.

A border post on the Zambezi River occurred half way along the 850 km journey to school. Here the customs and immigration officers picked through all our belongings, passports and vaccination papers like vultures dismembering a fresh carcase. I remember seeing a poor girl maybe 10 years old getting the treatment in front of a hundred of us school kids. She had packed some old horse shoes in her school trunk and the officers had magnified this into a crime against humanity. But we were just kids, powerless and milling around on the tarmac with our school trunks open to the vultures like it was a jumble sale. I remember in subsequent years when the stakes of the game were higher and we had become street wise, handing over packets of cigarettes to the medical officer lest he try to inject cholera vaccine into me with his rusty used, blunt and bent hypodermic needles.

The Zambezi river crosses under a huge bridge at this point marking the border between Zambia and what is now Zimbabwe – formerly Rhodesia. As the years went by and a local liberation war intensified, hostilities broke out between Zambia and Rhodesia and no vehicles were allowed to cross the bridge. So a white line was painted half way across. We would stop in the middle and unpack all our heavy school trunks from the school bus on one side of the line then onto a bus from the other country on the other side of the line to continue our journey. Unstructured time is a dangerous thing in anyone's hands especially teenagers and the unemployed. That's why governments and economists invented work. We would balance Coca Cola bottles on the steel members of the bridge and then tip them over the edge trying to clear the steel iron girders and cross members beneath us. They would slowly tumble through the air hitting against the steel bridge and showering the bewildered crocodiles and hippos below with shards of glass.

The Rhodesian War

At the same time as we started boarding school in Rhodesia, the terrorist liberation war first broke out in that country... and by that I mean there was terror for everyone in the militarised areas outside of any city or town. The terror basically started at the outskirts of town.

But my school had its own brand of terror because of its system of seniority and corporal punishment. We thrived on trying to beat the system and subsequently wore the beatings BY the system with pride through the welts and blood of our backsides. In our communal showers everyone got to see the zebra crossings carved by a willow cane across another's butt cheeks. The steam would periodically clear to reveal what looked like the remains of the flogging of Jesus.

Tom and I were just twelve and fourteen when the journeys to and from school took on a new twist. It got too dangerous to go by road due to routine ambushes, so we would fly in by aircraft with some of the scariest aerial manoeuvres any passenger can ever experience. The pilots had to make evasive manoeuvres during landing and take-off to avoid SAM-7 missile attacks from terrorist units in the forests below. Meanwhile, the cabin staff fought to tame the wild beast of the drinks trolley. They might as well have served the in-flight dinners on the passenger windows because they were fighting a centrifugal force imposed on us all by the pilot.

My abdominal anatomy is still all mixed up because of it felt like the pilot had handed the controls over to a pet chimpanzee… kidneys in the wrong place, spleen upside down, intestines scrambled and our screams can still be heard on moonlit nights near the airport strewn with fearful flying diarrhoea.

We had to fly in via Malawi, Swaziland, and South Africa to get to school. Just me and Tom, little kids with our suitcases. And then we did some epic trips flying into Francistown in Botswana over the wilds of Africa and taking the old steam train through the Botswana bush to Bulawayo and on to Salisbury, now Harare. Six trips a year. I used to wonder why my parents were forever broke but now I know their fortunes were spent on aviation fuel and coal.

When we finished school I remained in Salisbury whilst my friends were bundled off to National Service in the Rhodesian Army. In a few short weeks, they left as boys and came back as soldiers with camouflage, muscles and machine guns. By moulding the neuroplasticity of 18-year old boys and then using the pseudo-initiation of transforming new recruits into 'real men' - soldiers - the army inserted a new disc operating system into their minds and into their worlds. The enemy was defined and demonised to become worthy of death as is done all over the world to assist anyone in pulling the trigger. Little did they know, they would never win this war, what Robert Taber called the 'war of the flea'. In his book by this name he reminds us that a war against terrorism is seldom won.

It was a bizarre time because just about everybody had machine guns. Even teenager girls on the farms were fully armed when they went out on picnics sporting sun hats, a wicker basket and 9mm submachine guns. The country pubs had gun racks for the patrons to park their weapons within easy reach whilst downing a cold ale at the bar. There was this unseen internal war of alcohol against consciousness, a liminoid numbness we couldn't resist. So as we parked one weapon in the gun rack, the barman would pour us another from a whiskey bottle at the bar. It was another bottle of liminoid instead of lemonade to help us forget the war and numb that particular time in our life journeys. And everyone smoked... tobacco was the country's major export. At boarding school, the Jesuit priests sold us our cigarettes when we turned 17 because we were allowed to smoke as senior students for the last two years of High School.

I spent an idyllic year hitch-hiking around the country with my old school friends - now eighteen and licenced to kill because they were in the army. I carried an automatic FN rifle when we hitch hiked. For a teenage boy I don't know if anything beats the feeling of holding such a weapon, filling 20-round magazines with .762 mm bullets and that sound of steel and springs cocking the mechanism so as to feel invincible. My mates would sign their rifles out of the armoury each weekend plus one extra for their mate from Zambia. The God of War has a sense of humour because I was a Zambian, from across the border and therefore technically the enemy. The only thing that qualified me to hold those rifles was the colour of my skin. That is not such a bad thing actually, although it sounds so racist. Mostly white people didn't put bullets into white people at that time, and mostly they didn't want to put bullets into black people either. We were all just shit scared and trying to get on with life and love and mostly with having fun drinking.

Wearing the projections of others

I found the automatic rifle was a very empowering fashion accessory - a bit like a magic wand. In many of the coffee shops along our journeys I would be approached by the elderly women staff who would pamper me and serve me free tea and cake. They would tell me all about what they did to help the war effort and of how much gratitude they felt for us young men. And they would tell me of their stories of loves lost. If only they had known I was a Zambian from across the border the exchange may have not been so free or so friendly. In fact the peaceful coffee shop of love may have erupted in small arms fire from behind the cake display fridge shattering the crockery and turning the menus into confetti whilst I dived below the tables.

I spent much of that year keeping my Zambian identity somewhat secret from those who might not quite accept the brotherhood of mankind. In those days you couldn't just walk into a crowded bar and announce to everyone that you were a Zambian and shout a round of drinks because it would have been a fatal error to become the focus of some of the energies in the crowd. Many had emotional wounds from the war that hurt like hell and like all humans they used alcohol as an emotional anaesthetic. So things could get unhinged pretty quickly which meant I further developed my super powers of invisibility first honed at boarding school and always crept up to the bar counter undetected.

My Personal Myth

A long time ago there lived a King who was destined to become great and bring blessing and abundance and good governance to a very special kingdom. But he was not yet ready to govern with the power and wisdom that it would require. When bad kings invaded from the north, his bravest warrior hid the King in a cellar and, in many a brave battle, with blood and bruises, in his fear and his courage, the Warrior stood there fighting, shielding the cellar door. He was often beaten down to one knee but he kept that knee on the cellar door as he held his shield in place lest anyone bring harm to his king.

As time went on a great magician appeared to help counsel the Warrior and help him engage the battles and invaders with far more tact and power. All along, a poet, a man whose heart was made of pure love, sang their songs, wrote the poems of their longings, recorded the story in loving tones and created a majestic tapestry that would be a legacy to the world. Because of this, they called him the Lover. A little boy and his dog often sat by the Lover, filled with longing for a golden childhood that was lost and for a loving kingdom and home he thought he would never see again.

One night the Magician told the Warrior to move them all to a new camp in an enchanted forest where great men were in training to fight their own battles for their own kingdoms. And here in just three days they were shown new ways and new skills that transformed their lives with magic and light. Thus prepared, The Warrior, with the Magician's prompting, led the way further into the enchanted forest where it was darkest and where there was no path because no one had gone that particular way ever before. The path they made twisted and turned through adventures infused with uncertainty but always full of magic. And all along the way they lovingly carried their king on a stretcher hidden under a cloak of invisibility so thick that even the men had forgotten what he looked like. With love and patience, they did their best waiting for their king to be healed and for the prophesy to come true.

Years went by and one day they came across an empty but majestic Spanish Galleon amongst the creepers and bushes of the dark forest. Possessed by eternal curiosity and wonder, they de-

cided to explore it. The Warrior was drawn to stand at the helm because he felt he was a man of action and was born to be first to lead the others on any journey. The Magician stood to the left and immediately started to create an endless series of light shows, of spectacular and colourful phenomena that enthralled the crew by day and by night and brought the entire ship to life. On the right, the Lover infused with the new skills of a Playwright sat down to write a new story, the greatest story ever written. It took the crew many years to realise the beautiful gift he was creating right under their noses. The Little Boy took his pet dog and climbed into the Crow's nest where he could laugh and play and watch the antics of the men below.

Below the deck they discovered a very old man with hair and beard the colour of rust. He had been living in the Spanish Galleon in the enchanted forest since the beginning of time. This Wild Man had more power and muscle than any man who had ever lived. It was he who would power up the ship from within. And if ever the men were fearful, they could hide there under the decks where he would protect them. They would soon become infused with his abundant power because his presence was so strong, and yet strangely calm and wild.

But the King was still not well. So they lay him at the back of the deck and covered him with blankets. They always knew that one day he would fulfill the prophecy of the coming of a great king. They projected his image on the sails, a Warrior King holding a fierce Lion by the throat with his bare hand, and an ancient hand axe in the other ready to strike. There was balance in this image, an image of wildness and ferocity tempered with good governance where neither the Lion nor the King needed to die if they simply kept their balance and didn't panic under pressure.

So they set sail each day through calm seas and stormy oceans and past tropical islands. They explored the entire known world always heading towards adventure and any shining things that attracted their attention. One day they came across their sister ship with much the same crew as they had except they were all women. Their elegant ebony Queen symbolised the dark and mysterious energies of the feminine, so many aspects of the feminine the men still needed to learn about and understand. They would meet together for parties and dancing and heartfelt discussions because they knew each other so well and delighted in each other's company. The women even held the men captive for a while on Calypso Island until the men managed to escape and get back to their Spanish Galleon and their life's passion, their Mission of being adventurers.

There was a time when the men got fed up with the Lover's songs because the songs were filled with sadness and too much longing for the kingdom they had lost and a kingdom they had not yet found. They put him on the deck in a golden cage for many years until he finally wrote them a note saying he had put those songs to death. The Magician, who had so helped the Warrior, opened the cage with a golden key and took the Lover aside. He threw all the old quills and paintbrushes overboard and gave the Lover new ones with new inks and new paints with which to write and colour their world. And he wisely stood by to help dictate the script, the Myths they chose to live by so that the Lover would not lose his way again.

One day, the Lover released a huge magic butterfly. With the power of his immense wings, the Butterfly of Romantic Love brought back a great Wizardess, a Spirit Guide from the sister ship. She had wings and a garland of flowers illuminated by her gentle halo - her Lamp of Insight. And her presence was the source of all inspiration, enough for an entire Kingdom. She came on board and healed the King. And she arranged his Divine and Sacred Marriage to the Queen of the sister ship. The King and Queen had a child, a little girl who they called Happiness. The King could often be seen strolling in the forests with an elegant winged woman next to him carrying a garland of flowers. Alongside them walked a strangely contrite butterfly and a halo of happiness surrounded the three of them as they walked in endless conversation. They walked upon wooden walkways that united all the islands of his great kingdom. In this way, understanding, love and wisdom was carried back and forth between all the peoples.

One night, seated around a fire to keep warm on the deck, the men heard the wild howling of wolves on a moonlit night. And because of the peace, love and wisdom on the Galleon, thousands of wolves came and made their home on the decks. The Galleon sailed without fear of the wolves or of any creatures of the oceans or the dragons of foreign lands because these creatures all guarded treasure which they would freely share with any man who could tame and befriend them. And the men on the Galleon were more than enough to befriend the creatures they may once have feared. The men loved to look out to the distant horizons. And they loved to look into the deep ocean because alongside the ship swam an enormous whale, the great Whale of Ancient Wisdom, and dear friend and companion of the King.

TRANSFORMATION AND THE GOLDEN KEYS

> *In time, peace and happiness settled upon the kingdom with a contentment that endured forever, even to the telling of this myth to the God in Heaven.....*

Max's farm

I remember going out for a weekend to my friend Max's farm situated in one of the most severe terrorist hot spots in the country. We patrolled his farm one night and searched the workers' compound going hut by hut to check for anything suspicious. Luckily we didn't meet any suspicious AK-47 automatic fire on entering the workers' huts. On the way home we watched from a hill as below us as tracers and flares erupted from the bush into the night sky. Another drunken curfew breaker had just suffered the misfortune of cycling into an army ambush. Here the Angel of Death invited him to park his body and bike and join her for an eternal drink in Heaven.

On top of a hill in the middle of Max's farm lived an old man. He had no friends besides the night time stars and his solitude. Like most shamans he lived on the fringes of society. In that interface between community and Nature, between Inner World and Outer World, the shaman is there to explain, prevent and treat the imbalances that arise and cause calamity. One night he had simply arrived from nowhere on Max's farm claiming that spirits had flown him there from across the horizon. He was harmless but far from sane. And when he ran from his grass hut one day to scare away an approaching Rhodesian Army patrol he was given a free flight to Heaven and the keys to the Pearly Gates by a startled rifleman emptying a magazine into his shamanic world.

Max and I climbed the hill some weeks later and entered his deserted hut with great respect. It was one of the most touching moments of my life to see the simple intimate details of how this man had lived. The ash and charcoal in his little fireplace and the dry corn cob he had been cooking for dinner charred and uneaten on the dirt floor. His blanket still holding aspects of his bodily form - a ghost in the fabric - just as the treasured pair of my grandfather's gloves still hold the shape of an ambassador's hands to this day. There was not much else in the hut. He didn't need much else in life... maybe just a little bit more understanding.

Max and I climbed another hill that day to hunt the wild pigs that thrived on Max's maize crops. I crept over a sizeable granite boulder and found myself within point blank range of a huge boar with tusks like a set of razor sharp scythes. It was the Angel of Death dressed up as a wild pig. We had this Mexican standoff for what seemed like eternity and I knew if I didn't pull the trigger he would turn me into mincemeat with his set of blender blades. But I simply couldn't do it. You see I really am not a hunter. Once I picked a flower and on bringing it home I had to walk all the way back to where I found it in order to return an ant that had been hiding among the petals. Such is the twist of Fate that years later I would find myself presiding over the death of literally millions of animals in the abattoirs of Western Australia.

So there was an honourable moment between me and the pig when we both kept our balance despite blinking a bit. We didn't panic, and we both got to live. Balance under pressure is a skill I only appreciated when I played the Samurai Game in San Francisco years later. The pig turned and fled. I turned and faced a cussing from Max so severe that I wished I had left with the pig. But neither the pig nor I needed to die in this encounter. The Samurai Game teaches you to be respectful and balanced, keeping your half of all relationships clean. This includes business relationships which can experience severe stress at times. Be an honourable man and you will get through. You never know when we will encounter one another again and need each other in some way. The ones who would panic in relationship or lose their balance in business and make a grab for the assets are the first to die in the Samurai Game.

Max and I walked down from the hill empty handed. To cheer us up, Max pulled out a hand grenade from his backpack which he had acquired from a terrorist on one of his bush patrols. He tossed it into his dam to blow up a couple of very surprised fish. This ability to sow destruction is common to all young men and similar explosions occurred through our teenage years and well into our mid-twenties as we pushed back the boundaries of life.

A few months later, Max's elderly parents came under attack on the farm whilst watching TV at night. Bullets flew in to the room shattering the windows and carving up the furniture. But Max's parents were a very stoic old couple because Max's Dad was of Belgian stock. They were convinced the TV had blown up and so they set about adjusting the channels instead of returning fire. The firing stopped soon after maybe because the TV was now tuned to a more agreeable channel worth watching through the shattered windows. Max's mum got on the UHF radio to report that their TV mysteriously smelt like gunpowder and one of the farmers on the radio network suggested they had been attacked. So Max's Dad grabbed his rifle and ran outside to guard his most precious possession... not his wife, his new Mercedes Benz.

Me and Max. Max became a quantity surveyor, project manager and a loyal drinking buddy.

TRANSFORMATION AND THE GOLDEN KEYS

Scooby and Pola.

Scooby's story

Scooby ended up as a medic with the SAS and therefore I would raid Scooby's medical treatment room at the SAS barracks at every opportunity. I would drive in Max's car, a VW Beetle, to the barracks and storm the medic's room armed not with an assault rifle but with a cardboard box. I would fill it with whatever I could find: vitamins, Valium tablets, caffeine pills, electrolytes and then drive out saluting the sentry at the gate. On weekends, suffering some of the worst hangovers of our lives, my friends and I would wake up back at my flat with Scooby putting saline drips into our arms so we could recover in time for breakfast: the 10 am free bar snacks at the local pub. These were bowls of salted peanuts. They were infused with the lingering vapours of last night's alcohol and cigarette smoke and gave us enough strength to continue another day's drinking.

When the Rhodesian elections were on and subsequently Robert Mugabe got into power, the terrorist groups were assembled in camps around the country under the 'protection' of world scrutiny and British-supervised elections. But they were sitting ducks for the first time in the Rhodesian war because they were no longer hiding in the bush. Instead they were now sitting drinking tea in neatly organised camps set out with a surveyor's precision and ripe for an aerial bombing. It would be as easy as crop dusting a fruit plantation and killing all the bugs.

I went into one of the camps because my friend, Craig Bone – a famous painter of the Rhodesian war – wanted to capture these calamitous moments in oil paints on canvas. We drove into the camp in Craig's Jeep and came across an albino guy with bloodshot eyes holding his AK-47 aloft leading a hundred wild armed men in a chanting frenzy through the camp. It was like being inside a swarm of bees singing songs to the God of War about honey. Most likely they would be the ones doing the painting that day on our canvasses with our own blood. But in order to befriend ourselves to this bunch of radicalised madmen, we picked up a crowd of equally exuberant villagers on their way to join this macabre conga, this Dance of Death. So we found ourselves immersed in trouble both inside the car and out.

Foolishly trying to break the uneasy silence that ensued in the vehicle, I asked my friend Joe who had accompanied us where he got such sporting bush shoes from… ones that as it turns out were only issued to the Rhodesian Special Forces of the notorious Selous Scouts. If any of our native Uber buddies had heard, looked and understood, we would have been shortly sitting in a steaming cauldron of broth with carrots and onions bobbing all around us, prodded gently and lovingly by bayonets until we were done.

An excited, animated and angry commander came over to us and in sweeping arm movements gave us 'the Sign of the Cross'…..basically it meant, 'Take down your canvas and fuck off out of here…' I admired how Craig's jeep cruised out of that camp so faultlessly in reverse.

Cheating the God of War

So a contingency plan to blow the living crap out of all assembled terrorists was devised by the Rhodesian Army in case the elections proved unfavourable to Robert Mugabe. The entire army was on standby… all my school mates included. I am sure even our cook matron was standing by as a reservist in our school kitchen ready to charge the enemy with nothing more than a soup ladle in her hand.

Scooby was assigned to one of the tactical teams to annihilate various undesirables in a suburban attack with the Special Forces. This attack was expected to incur many casualties so Scooby, being a medic, was designated to be the second man into the residential home behind the leader once they had applied a 'Knock Knock' explosive to the front door. You see, although it is polite to always knock before entering, it was unlikely that a butler was going to open this door for them and offer them tea and biscuits. During his medic's course, Scooby had dodged as many of his medical training lectures as possible in order to go drinking beer with me. And so that day whilst loading his webbing belt with as much ammunition as his legs could carry and to thus create a makeshift form of body armour, he added a few extra bandages trying to remember what on earth they were actually for.

Because Robert Mugabe won the elections, the entire military strike was called off at the eleventh hour by the Rhodesian Army High Command. It left a generation of white Rhodesians reeling at the anticlimax and some reeling with relief to this day. The God of War had been cheated of another mini genocide of sorts. If it had gone ahead, Scooby would have been a hero either way dead or alive. But I reckon it's the second guy through the door who gets riddled with holes once the initial surprise peppering of bullets is over. Scooby is such a survivor that on the day he would have magnanimously stepped aside for man number three, held the door open and insisted with decorum and the manners of a gentleman, "No... please... you go first, my good man,... I insist..."

Looking for Chinks in the armour

I used to watch the passing out parades of soldiers and wonder at the precision with which they marched. Soldiers have to march this way because men are watching. And men are always looking for the chinks in another man's armour. The moment a man can see a chink in another's armour, a defect, a limitation, that man is no longer a threat to him. So military parades mustn't reveal the mere mortals beneath the uniforms and try to display a convincing mask of steel instead. Our Magicians are masters at spotting the Achilles Heel in another and can exploit these sensitivities and vulnerabilities to our own ends. Magicians can also be very nice. They can temper their response with compassion and empathy when they spot the vulnerability in another. It takes courage to be human and to expose our true vulnerability to the mercy of the Magicians in others.

In the world today I see so many Black Magicians. They shoot arrows at the Achilles Heels of any leaders, heroes and good men and women who try to ascend or govern and establish order and sense in this shifting world. It is so easy to do and it brings down the greatest of leaders. The Black Magician doesn't have to offer anything of value in return but can simply point to Achilles Heels. It is so easy to destroy a person or make them dance by asking endless questions without the questioner ever having to come up with any answers.

Scooby's meteoric rise

Scooby did well in the end. It must have been the constant floggings the priests gave him at boarding school that toughened his skin like chain mail armour for his life's journey. He became fearless of authority. One day he was called in to the headmaster's office for another beating with the willow cane. As Father Rector whipped the cane across Scooby's arse, Scooby cried out and swept all the papers off the office table and onto the floor in feigned agony. And with each cut of the cane he trashed more of the office: the noticeboard, the hanging wall calendar, the bookshelves. The headmaster took the real beating that day. He must have wept as Scooby left the demolished room.

From coming last in the 'C' stream of year 1 in senior school - technically the dumbest kid in entire school - Scooby went on to university to study Chemistry and Biochemistry and then on to manage massive sectors of the of some of the biggest water treatment companies in the world. He has managed teams and markets in Africa, England, the whole of the India, Australia and New Zealand. He married Pola, my sister, and I in turn married Fiona, Scooby's sister. It was a straight swap. He has travelled the world so many times that when I see him I have to welcome him back to planet Earth as if he were an astronaut. Scooby travels with only two passions in mind: his next Chicken Tikka Masala and the love of his life - international cricket.

DR LEM RAVENSDALE

Mountain Goat with Golden Boots Shining

In a mad moment with my nieces and nephews and assorted family, we decided to take on animal names whilst climbing a very steep high hill in northern New South Wales. Fiona was feeling exceedingly wild and took on the name Jungle Jaguar. And in my madness I took on the name Mountain Goat with Golden Boots Shining. Madness, I know, but everyone got a new name that day that matched their personas.

Well Golden Boots Shining is alive and well today. Whenever I am faced with a sticky situation where I am in perilous company, I simply become Mountain Goat with Golden Boots Shining. It has come to mean keeping out of trouble... being squeaky clean so as not to attract any conflict.

It's like a magic cloak of invisibility whereby I have the skills of a Ninja to simply disappear... or like a Get Out of Jail Free Card due to impeccable conduct whilst the sharks circle all around. I learned this skill at boarding school with grateful thanks to my bullies. And I practiced it in the veterinary clinics across the world when I would hide in the x-ray room to catch my breath. It was dark in there but flooded with a reassuring red light that glistened off the tanks of developing fluid and reflected my tortured image. No one could find me there. Often I stood there sweating with fear, praying to any god who would listen. You see, veterinary work can get a bit stressful sometimes.

As a new graduate I would take x-ray plates across an alleyway behind the veterinary clinic in Zimbabwe to use an automatic developer at a doctor's surgery nearby. It was a huge machine con-

taining 50 rollers that pulled the x-ray film through developing tanks and driers. One day the film got stuck because I inserted it at an impossible angle. So I gave it a good pull to extract it from the rollers and this set a hundred cogs out of alignment. The machine basically ate itself to death in a prolonged crackling sound as the teeth of the cogs sheared off one by one. The evidence of who caused the destruction was trapped inside amongst the fragmented plastic of the machine: a badly taken x-ray of a cat's fractured leg. Golden Boots Shining couldn't save me that day because they couldn't save me from the voices in my head that will forever torment me in the dead of night. But as the Mountain Goat with Golden Boots Shining matured and developed skills over the years he began saving me from some very tricky situations.

Ten Gurkhas and I had swum for many hundreds of meters down a very narrow gorge in the remote north of Western Australia. The water was freezing and we swam slowly, pushing our backpacks sealed inside large plastic bags along in front of us. Our progress was blocked by a waterfall that poured down upon us from upstream. With two large lizards and a snake in our midst we managed to pass the backpacks up to a large rocky ledge above and set up camp there for the night. But madness possessed me once again. When I had set up my tent I disappeared for a recce upstream on my own before sunset. I asked if anyone wanted to come along but they all preferred to sun themselves at the camp. Well, one corner turned into another and two hours later I returned to the camp to find the entire group fully dressed, packed and ready to march... to go looking for me. The commander was furious because he had no idea what had become of me believing I had just gone for a quick swim. And I guess he had a point: I was *there to get them all home safely through very unfamiliar territory. Now where the hell was their tour guide?*

My firing squad was assembled on a slope but there was no customary blindfold nor a last cigarette. I stood at their feet in my wet shorts and sandals clasping my wooden hiking stick for security and feeling very alone and contrite. But a light went on in my head as I went into Golden Boots Shining mode with a heartfelt apology. I asked the Nepalese firing squad that if I did a good magic trick for them would they let me be their friend once again. Gurkhas love magic – they are fiercely superstitious just like Zambians - so I was onto a winner here. And thank God I know one magic trick. It's a really good one involving coins and a handkerchief. Learn one great magic trick. It will transform your life and on occasions like this it will even save your life. I did the trick as if my life depended on it... because it did. Looking into their boggling eyes I knew I had succeeded and then smiles and cheers broke out. And Mountain Goat with Golden Boots Shining was their best buddy again which must have melted the commander's heart. He was a brilliant commander and knew which battles were worth fighting and those which were not. Under my breath I whispered, "Phew... That was close."

In that moment, the commander became my dear friend. I have a photo of him giving me his camouflaged Kukri knife – iconic to the Gurkhas. It sits on my altar, a symbol of strength and protection and brotherhood, like hands reaching out to each other from ancient cultures. Sometimes, whilst in awe of other cultures we can forget the magic that our own culture presents too. In the photo we are sitting under a sun drenched bush - it's the glow of an eternal friendship. And with the Gurkhas, when you are in, you are in forever. They never forget you, and you would always want those guys on your side because they are absolute champions.

Commander Krishna Saru presenting me with his kukri knife after I performed a magic trick for the soldiers. Moments before I expected to be sacrificed to the gods with this same knife for going on a 3-hour recce on my own in the Kimberley ranges and getting the team worried.

There by the grace of my Golden Boots Shining go I. They help keep me mindful... to think before I react, to stay out of trouble or to get out of it when the pressure is on. It is about Steady Sailing of my magnificent archetypal Spanish Galleon when the storms are about.

And magic: we can create it everywhere because we are the conduit of magic. In relationship, in playing with children, at the karaoke machine, at the supermarket checkout. Add value wherever you can, with every interaction with Life, and not just human life, all life. I chase this magic constantly. I see it when I interact with Scout or with the dolphins when I paddle out with Fiona on our kayaks into the Indian Ocean. In every interaction, simply add more.

When my friend Max asked me to chainsaw an endless pile of tree loppings into smaller bits and stack them all as firewood, I chainsawed my way through the lives of countless magnificent ants, bugs and termites. There was an entire ecology there and magic everywhere amongst the noise and blue smoke of the chainsaw. Lost in the world of Luke Skywalker with his Light Sabre, I came across the queen termite in a chamber sealed by a dry mix of leaves, sand and termite saliva. It was a heartbreaking, wondrous encounter. But as Joseph Campbell says, you have to fully engage with this life even as part of you observes as the Witness. It took courage to stay engaged in the destruction that I hate so much. Yet the magic of wonder was there as I looked into the natural world. And forever humbled through this experience, maybe in some measure, this will allow me to accept destructions that inevitably will impact on my own world.

It will take effort but you will get paid for your efforts in the delight of the magic you create. I feel it was the Samurai Game that taught me this. And Steven Covey in his book "The 7 Habits of Highly Effective People" speaks of that moment between Stimulus and Response when you have a choice. What you do next becomes your destiny. So take that moment. And choose to create magic because great magic, like love, only adds, only gives and never fails.

Golden Boots Shining is a metaphor of me staying out of trouble when all the sharks are about. I can transcend my vulnerabilities, insecurities, some of my Shadow and fear and step aside to watch others play their games and face their own firing squads knowing that come what may I will yet be given another day, a blank piece of paper on which to write, another chance at Life.

TRANSFORMATION AND THE GOLDEN KEYS

Josh, Rebekah, Fiona and me. This is where Fiona got the animal name 'Jungle Jaguar'.

Catering with Mum on the farm in Misundu

It was from these wild teenage years my surreal life lurched its way into history with too many stories to recount here and enough Zambian beer to sink the Titanic. Returning to Zambia, I had some of the happiest years of my life working in our piggery and helping Mum with her catering company. We set up a great commercial kitchen where we made all kinds of pickles, jams, smoked meats, bacon and sausages. Mum and I would still be butchering pig carcasses on our kitchen table with a hacksaw at two o'clock in the morning. And there were always empty bottles of Zairean beer scattered between the pork chops and the piles of freshly made sausages. We couldn't do this work sober and without the love, laughter and conversation just like many rock bands can never repeat their best performances without the drugs.

These poor little pigs that we were dismembering and packaging into plastic bags for sale were old friends from the piggery situated at the other end of the ten acre farm near the servants' quarters. The pigs were some of the best and only friends I had in Zambia. I loved those pigs so much that I knew many of them by name because I bottle-fed half of them, castrated all the males and clipped all their teeth. Then they appeared in the freezer, stunned, killed and disembowelled ready for the next phase of their existence which was to adorn the plates of the glitterati in Ndola coated in the tastiest sauces a Polish refugee, starved in the forests of Siberia, could wildly imagine.

On tasting Mum's cooking at the dinner parties and weddings we catered for, people would become enraptured by their taste buds. I would collect the cutlery the next day and get showered in abundant praise and thanks. Helping Mum in the kitchen was to share in her passion and genius, and her outbreaks of hysteria as overwhelming deadlines drew near. Then it was time to celebrate the peaceful joy of success over a glass of wine. We don't have Domino Pizza, McDonald's or Burger King in Ndola. But when you think about it, isn't every Mum's cooking better than all three Fast Foods combined because the one secret spice they are unable to put in is Love.

Comfort and the Mother Complex

Food is such a primal need and all our needs fulfilled make us happy for a while. So via the TV networks, food is given to us in the form of all the hypnotic cooking shows that liberally season each evening's TV line up. With such tasty pixels, they help to distract and settle our minds after watching the horror of the world news. Similarly, the evening tot of alcohol helps to numb the consciousness of mankind. Because the authentic experience of Life can be quite confronting, we can find ourselves drifting to the irresistible Mother Complex for comfort. She comes in many forms.

Yes, 'Mother' can appear even as a plate of food. And then the food becomes a reassuring balm to one of our childlike needs. Deep inside we are really playing the game of "Mummy Make It Better" whilst outwardly we stuff our faces.

Robert Johnson said that resting into the Mother Complex was always a retrogressive step because it is the rightful domain of the infant child not us adults. So it is a skill to stay aware of this and not indulge the Mother Complex too often or unconsciously lest it hold us back.

I certainly don't have that courage or strength to transcend all my comfort. Inevitably its twin – discomfort - will find me as I grow older anyway. Long ago my mind learned to love pain. It's an old and welcome friend. And in transcending pain I find the comforts of my endorphins, chemicals that have always served humanity in this way. I found endorphins in the hundreds of thousands of cattle pregnancy tests I did which took my poor body to the extremes. It was my mind, not my body, that needed to befriend pain and get an extreme job done. All my body wanted was a soothing massage - a bit of Mother Complex.

Life in the Third World

In Zambia nothing is guaranteed... not electricity, running water, oxygen or your next heartbeat. My great aunt came to stay with us for a while. On her first night at the farm I had to get two spitting cobras out of her bedroom. Every day in Zambia has its challenges. The bandits and the medical system like to claim your skipped heartbeats whilst the police roadblocks take your money and any smiles you may have had that day.

As a consequence, ordinary Zambians end up living on thanks, prayers and sacrificial chickens to get through each day. It's a beautiful country with so many beautiful people but you have to be street-wise to negotiate its ways. My street-wise friend Brian loves going to the Philippines. He goes there dressed as little more than a street urchin not as a wealthy tourist. So he escapes getting mugged, and if he's lucky, the locals might even throw money to him.

Mum told us about the time when four Zambians stole a very long metal ladder and carried it for 8 kilometers out of town hoping to make their escape. But somewhere along the way, they happened to march it into some 11 000 volt powerlines which vaporised much of the ladder. In a thick Polish accent Mum finished the story to describe what happened to the four men. It sounded more like a football score, "Two fucked. Two frazzled," she said taking another sip of beer.

Consider this: Mum and I would be catering for 600 people, slicing and dicing every manner of food ingredient, cucumbers and lettuce all day in the kitchen. We fended off the hungry Zambian flies and our menagerie of cats with stout blows from our carving knives and wooden gravy spoons. But we were at the mercy of a monster that ruled the night. It was the Zambian electricity grid draped in a bewildering array of wires across our town. The technical diagrams kept so meticulously by the colonial administration have long since been lost as have all the plans for the town's water supply. So Ndola's electricity and water supply regularly take on a life of their own. Mostly that means they spend a lot of time existing in the world of wishful thinking whilst your fridge defrosts and you get progressively thirsty around a mountain of dirty laundry.

Now electrons magnificently formed in the Big Bang and then whizzing around the Zambian electrical grid, find themselves in a totally confused tangle of wires and transformers. This confuses the electrons because the wires lead to many places the original engineers never intended. Understandably upset and lost, the electrons regularly erupt into life, light, sparks and of course the death of another hapless Zambian Electricity Supply Commission worker, or the frying of a surprised entrepreneur trying to circumvent a domestic electricity meter.

There are turbines supplying these electrons at the hydroelectric facility in a dam at Lake Kariba. The dam dared to defy the mythical River God Nyami Nyami when it was built to stem the flow of the mighty Zambesi River in 1959. It is a story worth reading one day. So, at random, a turbine would choke on an amp or a miss-applied spanner or a hippo and Africa 8 degrees south of the Equator (ie: all of Zambia) was suddenly in black out and living by its wits. Surgeons in the hospitals lit candles, traffic light intersections became instant death traps, and the best 21st birthday parties in living memory ended in darkness and sadly a loss of music. Even Jimmy Hendrix in a full screaming solo is beaten by the Zambian cicada song when his godly amplifier is silenced by a melting transformer on Misundu Road.

The power cuts could last for weeks. Mum and I, catering for a wedding or corporate dinner would be plunged into darkness in the busy kitchen - our silhouettes illuminated only by moonlight. We would fight for our beers in the darkness if we happened to grab the same bottle and race to the courtyard abandoning the dark kitchen to its many cockroaches. They stepped out from everywhere under the cover of darkness to gather sugar granules and breadcrumbs and to lick the kitchen clean.

But we were too busy to be sitting around swatting cockroaches. Plunging our frenzied hands into sacks of charcoal - the staple cooking fuel in Zambia - we would fill an array of 44 gallon drum bases (basically petrol drums cut in half) with the charred remains of some of Zambia's last remaining hardwood trees so we could continue the sacrificial act of chicken barbecue - it's been humanity's finger-licking good practice since time began. Amongst the smoke and fire and another amber Zambian night there was laughter and a passion that reflected from our eyes. We would keep on barbecuing amongst the swarms of malaria mosquitoes. They in turn completed their part of the unfolding food chain in the courtyard by eating us alive. Meanwhile, hungry mouths were waiting at a venue down the road and Mum's culinary enchantments were needed there. Her food helped to soothe the melancholy mood that seemed to pervade the community of expatriates in Ndola.

Dental descaling performed by the catering team

Running late as usual one night, we filled the back of a vanette with a smorgasbord of tasty dishes for the local Masonic Lodge. Mum pulled a bedsheet over the lot, tucked it in and gunned the engines down the bumpy road to town. She had the driving skills of a Kolkota taxi driver. As we came around the corner by the Chipulukusu Township she used the brakes, handbrake and reverse gear to simultaneously stall and stop the car because as usual the local train was blocking the road. This train conveyed a weekly tonnage of contraband, thieves and wayward humanity across our road and through the Badlands to the Zairean frontier. The train would sit there at Chipulukusu for as long as it wanted whilst traffic piled up on either side of the railway crossing totally ignored. Meanwhile police and paramilitary hastily made their fortunes parasitising the dubious activities and passengers of this ghost train.

Eventually it moved on and we careered down the winding hills into town with Mum cursing in Polish, clutching at the wheel and stripping the gearbox on every gear change. Was her mind lost in a Formula One Grand Prix, or was she just machine-gunning Russians with that bone shattering gearbox sound... I am still not quite sure. Mum and I had both developed adrenal glands the size of Zambian coconuts through years of stress and troubles of living in a third world country. So with all the near misses on the road that night we swore and cursed with an adrenal-fuelled vocabulary adding to the sound of sparks and gears shearing as Mum re-engineered the gearbox.

Unbeknown to us, the vanette carrying the food had been moving sand and cement all day. This gave all the food an unintended crispy coating as we bumped our way through endless potholes. We discovered the diabolical situation in the Masonic Lodge at serving time and despite staring into space for a while no options came to my mind. We served it up to the Tuxedo-clad Masonic Lodge patrons that night and I dare say many were toothless by the end of the meal. But miraculously, Mum's fame and reputation completely outstripped reality because everyone seemed to love the food and even asked for seconds. All I can remember is wincing at the piercing screech of sand against metal as I ladled out gravy onto each plate of roast and veg. The waiters scurried out to the dining room carrying plates of steaming food with Mum doing the sign of the cross over them and praying in Polish. I think she was praying that there was enough time for all the food to be eaten before the cement hardened and that we could escape before the ambulances started arriving.

When Christmas time came, the thirst of Dionysus would affect every throat in Zambia. But hard liquor was in short supply because the country had run out of foreign currency to buy the stuff. Mum had many admirers amongst the celibate priesthood and somehow she would get a message to the Holy Fathers across the border in Zaire... a country seemingly awash with alcohol. These priests were so close to God that they could get their hands on any contraband she requested including holy spirits.

A truck would arrive covered in dust and sporting a few bullet holes and we would off-load boxes and boxes and boxes of every kind of hard liquor into my bedroom. I would sleep amongst all this contraband stumbling over the chinking bottles in the early morning light. And for a whole week armed with a 9 mm revolver to fend off any bandits I was bootlegging whiskey and gin to every club and Italian family in Ndola for piles of cash. It paid the farm wages and made Mum happy.

Counting the money almost gave me blisters, but such blisters are always welcome. I expected to see all the street kids and beggars wearing suits for Christmas because as fast as I counted, Mum gave the money away to the poor like a frantic sailor bailing out a sinking ship. This Refugee archetype within her which related so strongly to the beggars on the street was a product of the Second World War. As a starving child living for many years in refugee camps, she would hold out her little hand and beg for sweets from American soldiers using the only English words she knew at the time: "Any gum, chum?"

The Bandits of Zambia

In the 1980's Zambia suffered probably all ten plagues of Egypt but certainly a plague of Bandits. Any form of weapon in Africa, and that includes any government stamp, is a licence to make money. So armed Bandits suddenly stepped into Zambian history like highwaymen from a time warp just minus the horses. There were hold ups and killings everywhere. I nearly got killed one night when I went to a distant farm to collect a pig carcase. On opening the gate to the property I got ambushed by two men brandishing a rifle. It miraculously jammed as my would-be executioners closed in on me. So with a 'High-5' to Mother Nature, I escaped in the car at 100 mph in reverse through the African bush somehow missing every tree on the way back to the main road. How different my future might have been as a mere shard of cosmic plasma if the rifle hadn't jammed.

One lunchtime, Tom was two cars away in traffic when a Zambian employee carrying the pay for a local company was shot through the head and all the money taken. Mum and Dad were stopped one night on Misundu Road and beaten to within an inch of their lives and robbed of everything. Imagine... Mum was so loving and kind, it would be like beating up Mother Theresa or attacking an ice-cream seller... why would you? The 80's were a tough time in Zambia and many of our friends didn't make it through.

Food manufacturing: food for the soul

Mum gave us such a love of cooking that the kitchen became the best room in the entire house.

It was in Mum's magic kitchen that Pete and I would experiment late at night with cooking and developing new food products. One night we stumbled on a great recipe for making mayonnaise in a blender. So we sold this mayonnaise in jars by the dozen in all the supermarkets of Ndola. Our success in making smallgoods quickly overwhelmed the domestic kitchen so that's why we eventually built a commercial kitchen on our 10 acre farm. Here we made all manner of smoked meats, bacon, sausage, jams, cheeses and farm produce.

Years later when Fiona and I had our veterinary practice in Augusta in Western Australia, I built my own equipment and designed my own label to market this mayonnaise and smoked fish and chicken products to restaurants in the wineries of the southwest of Western Australia including the famous Voyager and Leeuwin Estate vineyards. It was a bit tough running the food business and a veterinary clinic with only Fiona as my helper plus two small kids. I would get out of bed at 4 am to smoke the fish and chicken or to fillet Bronze Whaler sharks ready for brining, smoking and then distributing whilst out on some epic veterinary calls across the region.

Meanwhile back in Africa, you simply click your fingers and fifty workers come running around the corner looking for something to do besides stealing your chickens. On the farm we were experts in delegating all day from behind cups of tea in the dining room - clicking our fingers like we were doing the Macarena.

The talk of the town in Augusta was that the local cats and dogs were being euthanized and lightly smoked then packaged under my label. But really, it was not so. All euthanized animals were secretly buried by my son Josh and I in the bushland behind the clinic near the local kindergarten. I even buried a miniature pony out there one day and I sincerely hope none of the children wondered back into the class clutching a skull for 'Show and Tell'. Josh and I would sneak out by moonlight with a shovel carting another dead dog along in a wheelbarrow. We were re-enacting Uncle Janek's grave digging exploits of long ago in the Siberian forests of Russia. Once again it was an old man and a young child and so much to talk about.

Veterinary in Zimbabwe

But I digress. As a 21-year old on an obscure farm in an obscure country, energy was building within me to complete my studies and get a degree and a career. The time came for Fiona and me to leave Zambia for university. After three years of studying for my BSc in chemistry and biochemistry in Grahamstown, South Africa, and five years of veterinary studies in Zimbabwe, I finally qualified as a veterinary surgeon. In the graduation I knelt before the Chancellor of the University of Zimbabwe to receive the customary dusting of his hat on my shoulders and then my certificate.

The Chancellor just happened to be the Honourable Robert Mugabe, mass-murdering despotic ruler of Zimbabwe for some 37 long years. I remember looking up and his face bore a stunning resemblance to the average Australian Cane Toad. But he wielded immense power and a famous sense of humour because he was born with a golden tongue that seemed to captivate any audience no matter how long his speech. He rationalised his genocide against the Matabele people as avenging the death of his ancestors. It takes courage to look through another's eyes in order to understand what they see as their truth.

Ancient history and ancient scripts

You see, two hundred years before, a Matabele mutiny fled from the mighty Shaka Zulu and invaded Mashonaland to settle there. Bob was a Mashona and now ruled the country. Like so many rulers of Africa he epitomised what is meant by the phrase, "It's our turn to eat." He tucked in heartily to plunder the country's riches, the people, farmlands, and the masculine youth of the Matabele who, like the Zulus, are Africa's equivalent of Polynesia's Maori. They are strong physically and strong as a culture. A country treated in this way is no different to a child treated this way. The country got smashed and developed its own complex eating disorders. It will no doubt have to re-invent itself under a new global order where a huge energetic flow has inexorably been at work in history unifying money, empire, religion, culture and society.

Zambia was once the domain of lions and leopards and the dust and sweat of tribal dance. In Zambia there was no real script amongst the indigenous people until the advent of English. Then arrived colonialism, a distant white queen, and ultimately baseball caps worn backwards and rap music from America. Now the country is awash in Chinese script which the local Zambians have no hope of deciphering. For them it's a bit like the silent hieroglyphs that covered most of Egypt before the advent of the Rosetta stone.

Many thousands of years before, a human sprayed a pigment from his or her mouth onto a hand to create a silhouette of the hand on the rock face of a cave. Script began in the form or rock art. When complex pictorial script transcended into the simplicity of phonetic script it lost its visual connection to our first home, to nature and to her pictures. I love Nepali script because it is so honest, and regular and so close to the Indo-European fountain of language Sanskrit. But Chinese script has pictorial elements drawn from nature and the physical world. In the traditional Chinese script, symbol prevails with all of its power. In western script the power of the symbols underlying what we read and write are absolutely there, powerful forever to those who can see. But they are lost in history to the average reader who was never educated in these things. The ancient sacred symbols are now an alphabetic code for sounds that activate a voice in the mind. They used to be a visual code for our mind's cinema screen and in that respect may have been more impactful in creating sensory experiences in the real body.

In the distant future, if our simple English writing system became lost just as countless scripts have been lost before, would it not become as precious to you, the linguist, as the hieroglyphs of Egypt, the pictorial codices of the Toltecs, and the cuneiform scripts of ancient Sumer. The take home message is: symbol. Understand it. Understand its immense power. It is all around you and within you. It is in every letter you or any human in any script writes. It is in the badges you wear and in your allegiances to institutions. Learn to use it as a tool, not only for insight into those who believe their group's symbol but to understand the symbols you hold dear, why you hold them dear, why they create the very matrix and core symbol of who you are. Symbol is real and it is huge. But for some, the schizophrenics for example, it holds a dark side if they fall in to its immense world with the loss of ego.

Bob's behaviour is a great example of the game: 'Pass the Parcel of Pain'. All such conflicts are awash with revenge - Victims transformed into Perpetrators playing this game. I remember as he handed me my veterinary certificate he had a warm and hearty handshake.... probably from squeezing a few triggers during his career and I felt the bullets of each handshake in my chest.

Pass the Parcel of Pain

> We were living in Cyprus for a time and I set off one afternoon trying to find my 7-year old son who had gone to play with his cousin Jeremy. Down some dusty road I came across a local street kid with his gang holding a catapult to Josh's head. It was loaded with a sizeable rock. They accused Josh's cousin of causing trouble and were very upset and about to dish out punishment and kill Josh, denying his subsequent gift to the world as an accomplished genetics researcher and university lecturer.
>
> Well, I had to sympathise because at that time Jeremy had immense abilities to annoy people and spread chaos and mayhem. I managed to get Josh away unharmed but it was a tense moment. And as the street kids ran away, Jeremy lobbed as many stones as

he could into the fleeing mob. One of the stones broke a Mercedes Benz's wing mirror in the process. Unfortunately the owner of the Mercedes was standing on the street and got showered in glass. So he vented his feelings on Jeremy's mother as she came walking up the street. Salwa is half Egyptian and with that wonderfully caustic tongue typical of the Arab lands, she unleashed the Curse of Tutankhamen and the Seven Plagues of Egypt upon Jeremy.

In our own home we used to threaten our children with a wooden spoon whenever we tried to instill discipline or if we had simply lost our minds to their antics. Like magic, just the mention of the spoon brought about instant blissful peace. But in an overly exuberant disciplinary moment I once broke the wooden spoon upon the backside of Josh or Rebekah... I cannot remember which. And to this day, they both fight to claim the honour of whose backside it was. Modern parenting styles may be more politically correct today and so parents ground their children or take away their mobile phones or laptops – for hours, days or weeks.

This is a game I call "Pass the Parcel of Pain". And everyone is playing it. If I am walking through a crowded café for example and accidentally bump you, I will say, "Oh! Sorry..." But you have spilled your coffee into your lap and it hurts and you get angry and say, "Hey! Watch where you are going!" I don't like your tone of voice and I tell you so. You give me a shove. I pick up a chair. You fend it off and hit me with a lid from the Bain Marie. I smash you with the cash register. You fight back with an entire table and your wife joins in with her flailing handbag and sharp stilettos.

If I get hurt by someone or something, I want to give the hurt back even if it was not really that person's fault. We even lash out *at inanimate objects if we bruise a shin. I can retaliate in so many ways depending how creative my dark side is: with some nasty words, the tone of my voice, catching a mood, withdrawing love, passive/aggressive behaviour or a slap on the back of the head. My friend at boarding school gave the class bully a meat sandwich liberally filled with pickings of the scabs from his injured knee.*

We take things personally and part of us wants to even the score. But I found it really isn't necessary especially when working with kids. Kids are so wrapped up in their worlds that they are mostly unaware of the impacts of their actions. What would they know if they stood on my foot or kicked a football onto my car window? There is really little point in giving my pain back to them and alienating them from me by losing my balance and shouting at them. I leave that job to the teachers who seem to be masters of it and could easily be employed as riot police. I just get on with the magic of facilitating their hearts and minds and bonding them to nature.

If the Ego doesn't get involved you'll be able to just let it go. That's important in your intimate relationships. I see so many couples bickering and passing pain back and forth like poisoned sandwiches. And they pass that pain to their kids dumping their own poison from above. I also see it in fiercely overprotective animal owners of Chihuahuas and officious SPCA officers. They appear to have suffered their own abuse. A perceived injustice needs to be objectively dealt with by someone who doesn't play the game 'Pass the Parcel of Pain'. If you upset me, that is my Shadow, my projection because an authentic emotion and then a fabricated story is running which combine to form a feeling. If I act from Shadow, only bad things will come.

> *It is not necessary. Stop playing the game. 'Passing the Parcel of Pain' is simply a justified form of sadism... the Victim/Perpetrator scenario: '...don't hurt me otherwise I will bash you ten times worse.' And it even comes in very subtle tones: "...you'll miss me when I'm gone..."*
>
> *So what to do with those who have already hurt us along the way? Well, as they say: it is not the snake that kills you but the poison. Pour the poison from your heart into the Sacred Fire... it was made for such things. The fire could be a candle, a camp fire or somewhere in your imagination. And put those who hurt you and who you cannot trust into a 5-star reptarium for poisonous snakes, scorpions and biting creatures where you can lovingly quarantine them in your mind and shower them with forgiveness, compassion and understanding. Snakes and scorpions bite... it's what they do. When we take it personally, the poison goes into us and we play 'Pass the Parcel of Pain' by killing the snake or squishing the scorpion. It's really not necessary to suffer and cause suffering in this way or getting bitten again trying to exact some kind of transspecies justice. There are more beautiful ways of processing such things, of processing such energies.*

My first job as a veterinarian

At my first job, which happened to be in a small town in Zimbabwe, there was an ageing South African receptionist who for the purposes of this story I will call Moira. She seemed to embody all the evil qualities you can imagine in a small town gossip/busy body and survivor. Sorry for the feedback Moira, but it is true. Well it's true to me anyway. Moira is now safely quarantined in her own 5-star crocodile pen in my mental reptarium created especially for people who bite me.

TRANSFORMATION AND THE GOLDEN KEYS

Weaned on lemons, this critical, self-centred personality compounded my many woes as I laboured somewhat dysfunctionally for the old owner of the veterinary practice. I was a new graduate with no experience. He was a legend. She was a legend but for other reasons. She could make roses wilt just by glaring at them. Her desk faced an open waiting room area much as the guns of Monte Casino loomed over their own killing zone in Italy back in 1944. At the opposite end of the waiting room was a consulting table and swing doors which opened onto the kennelling room and operating theatre. Now, my dear brother-in-law, Alastair, being a fitter and turner, had made me an awesome dog catcher: a pipe of solid steel with a rod inside that pulled a wire noose tight around any ferocious dog's neck when necessary. Africa is awash with vicious security dogs. It's also awash with the threat of rabies, thieves and government officials extorting money from the weak and innocent... many of whom in turn wish they had government jobs. So the pipe could come in handy as a multi-functional tool for all the above.

On this particular day, Moira was painting her claw-like nails at the front desk... probably with a thickened version of human blood. Back in the kennelling room, a vicious Rhodesian ridgeback had escaped from its cage and was trying to eat me alive. Clad in my white lab coat and with the resolve of Spartacus, I reached frantically for my gladiatorial dog catcher. There was no room for error and after a few altercations of the stout metal weapon with the dog's teeth and head I managed to ensnare the beast. Now, with the frenzied animal captive on one end, me on the other and my treatment room totally trashed, I was faced with a very serious struggle and one which I was sure to lose. So with the help of the dog catcher I dragged the dog out of the kennelling room through some swing doors and into the reception searching for my assistant, helper and saviour, Elias.

Alas, he was want to making himself scarce mid-morning strolling downtown to chat to all the good looking girls along the high street. Moira looked up from her beautification to witness the swing doors burst open and the fracas of a huge dog breaking into a full sprint on the shiny Lino floor with a white robed figure slipping and skidding along behind. I locked my shoes into the floor as hard as I could and pulled the noose to strangulation point. This produced the most spectacular Red Bull aerobatic display you have ever seen as the dog and I spun in reciprocating circles before the startled Moira. When the dog's oxygen supply ran out, it opened its bowels in a copious circular spray of brown diarrhoea. Much of this landed on Moira's untrendy shoes and stockings under the reception table.

The battle carried on for many a revolution amidst Moira's shrieks and enough blasphemy to chill the sacred heart of Jesus. As the dog fell unconscious, I dragged it by the neck through the brown concentric rings leaving a smeared trail back into the kennelling room. Moira meantime was hopping mad and fled the scene in search of a garden tap. The clean-up job for me was not exactly unpleasant since in a small way I had got my own back by covering Moira in dog diarrhoea. And I could just shrug my shoulders and blame it all on the dog.

The boggle eyed monster

Across from the veterinary clinic in this town, there was a small patch of grassland next to a modest public toilet building. Early one morning, the local police station was awoken from its slumber by an African man in a terrified state reporting that he had seen a monster. He and a friend had been walking along at sunrise when they heard terrifying noises emanating from the local public toilets. They had crept up to investigate, and found the sounds were coming from a subterranean source, from a hole in the ground near the toilet block. There, in the misty darkness of the morning light they came face to face with the gleaming eyes of a huge boggle-eyed monster that erupted into noise and sent them scurrying in terror to the police station.

With muskets loaded, the brave constabulary surrounded the manhole cover and one hapless individual of junior rank was sent forward to peer into the hole with the aid of a torch. Why they didn't blow the thing to kingdom come in a shower of shit I will never know, such is the normal modicum of restraint in Africa. But it was soon found to be not some genetic mutation, but a large adult horse staring up into the daylight hoping to be rescued. Of course, instead of summoning an engineer, they summoned the local vet and I dutifully attended the scene.

Not having a magic wand with me I could do absolutely nothing. The horse had wandered down from a nearby stable and finding the green grass flourishing above the septic tank had stopped to graze thinking it had found paradise. As its back hooves came to rest on the manhole cover, the metal frame holding the cover gave way and the entire horse slid neatly backwards into the large septic tank below through a hole that wasn't much more than two foot by two foot square in size.

The rescue mission was conducted by some local farmers and a wonderful man, Moira's husband. Frank was one of the last of a dying breed, a great white hunter, someone you could listen to for hours and by the sounds of it he was a ragdoll play thing of lions, snakes and elephants. But not even he could tame the wild Moira. Anyway, they rustled up a forklift truck and using the hydraulic forks, lifted the reinforced concrete slab up enough to slide a heap of pipes under so as to protect the horse as the slab was lifted away. Frank bravely slid into the muck in the tank which fortunately was not deep and tried to robe the horse in a makeshift harness hastily fashioned by a local upholsterer. This failed to work so the wily old hunter resorted to using ropes as a sling and the horse was duly lifted from the cesspool.

But the entire town was standing there looking at the septic tank not the horse. Floating in the water were a thousand latex condoms because the toilet block had been used for years as a midnight brothel and now the town's little secret was up. Really, medals should have been awarded to all and sundry for preventing the spread of HIV which was reaching epidemic levels across Africa at the time. Instead, a trifecta of horse, condoms and septic tank waste just seemed to result in a mind-numbing cognitive dissonance amongst the crowd.

I set about dazzling everyone with my stethoscope and a thorough clinical examination of the horse. His only injuries were two cuts below the kneecaps suffered as he slid into the hole. Nothing that a bit of tetanus vaccine and antibiotics wouldn't fix. As for riding him, well it would be a long time before the smell of Eau de Toilette disappeared. God knows how long it took the local municipality to replace the reinforced concrete slab over the septic tank because you can never rush such things in Africa. To this day we have ongoing roadworks in Zambia that were started over fifty years ago. My story about the horse rescue may be exciting, but I cannot imagine the tales of heroism, courage, terror and hardship from the countless individuals who subsequently fell into that hole on moonless nights.

TRANSFORMATION AND THE GOLDEN KEYS

Tales of the unexpected: funny what you can find in a septic tank.

Exodus

With few possessions and no money, Fiona pregnant with Rebekah, Baby Josh and I left Africa for England. It was our only chance to escape because rampant inflation would soon have imprisoned us in Africa. We left with $200 and 80 kilograms of veterinary books. Josh wondered where the savannah plains of Africa had suddenly disappeared to as he scratched earth from the tarmac parking lot outside our veterinary clinic in Essex. Soon the parking lot was covered with a bewildering layer of white snow that turned Josh's cheeks red with the cold. I had experienced something similar when years before I lost the Polish family, the gherkin and London, and found myself in Zambia. These are all total mindfucks but thanks to the Ego - faulted as it is - somehow we make sense of it all.

Rebekah was born in Maldon, Essex in this winter of 1991. Josh faced the snow, rain and wind bravely in his pram. Meanwhile Rebekah as a newborn was warm as toast carried in a baby sling inside Fiona's warm winter jacket. Josh subsequently became a Spartan, immune to his own pain and suffering due to the sub-zero crucible of his pram. And Rebekah has great taste in jackets! After working in the UK, Portugal and Wales, we ended up in Australia: the Promised Land, first in Queensland and then in the south of Western Australia.

The tale of Terrible George

While working in Queensland, and close to a nervous breakdown, I got to work for 8 months at a clinic that advertised a 24-hour service. It was situated on an isolated bit of bushland alongside a highway. Alone, in the middle of the night, lying awake on the makeshift bed in the cramped office, I would try to ignore the eerie noises of the bush outside, expecting to be held up by some gun-toting, drug crazed maniac demanding vials of Ketamine at any moment. The gentle light of dawn was greeted with feeble thanks to God, and I would shuffle down the corridor of the clinic in my socks to switch on the kettle. It was a miserable existence. Whoever was on duty that weekend would stay at the clinic all Friday, Saturday, Sunday and Monday going home Monday night to give everyone at home a 'High-5' before returning to work Tuesday morning. Not much happened after 8 p.m. at the clinic. All the staff had abandoned the place by 6 p.m. so it was deathly quiet and deadly boring every night. Even now, if anyone gives me a glint of boring conversation at the bar I am gone in an instant, never to return.

Five animals lived permanently in the clinic: an agoraphobic Cavalier King Charles Spaniel called Sasha but should have been called Chicken Licken because she only ventured outside when she was sure the sky wasn't going to fall on her head, two baby kangaroos who lived in pillow cases, a huge female kangaroo called Jenny who had a pen outside the back door, and George, a Sulphur-crested Cockatoo and a trouble maker *par excellence*.

Kangaroos are most active at 4 am. I know this, because the two baby joeys would jump onto my bed every morning at 4 am for a bit of trampoline practice. I was so depressed at the time and severely sleep deprived so I didn't handle their antics very well. My sense of humor and my patience had both long since perished. After a couple of, "...Boing! Boings!..." bouncing on the bed, they underwent advanced parachute training as I booted them towards the ceiling and the overhead ceiling fan hoping to decapitate them in a moment of feigned misadventure. Years later, when I profiled myself using the Enneagram I learned how sweet little me amassed all my suppressed anger. I could regress under stress and become hysterical, and, if pushed even further, would become an unrelenting sadist of the highest magnitude.

I always tried to drown the little buggers on their nightly pre-bedtime feed of warm milk. When this didn't work I got them exiled to the consulting room one night by complaining to management. They took out their frustrations by totally trashing the room, gouging great holes in the plasterboard walls trying to dig an escape tunnel and knocking bottles and a computer keyboard from the consulting room tables. Worst of all, the room stank of Kangaroo pee to the point of being unusable without vet, patient and owner donning gas masks before entering. So eventually the Joey Brothers were re-homed across town taking all this stinky chaos with them.

This didn't stop the frequent invasions of the clinic by Jenny the kangaroo who would come looking for our precious lunchtime sandwiches. She was quite destructive and although my first encounters with her in the clinic corridor scared the crap out of me, I was quickly coached in the art of kangaroo eviction by the vet nurse. Ben Hur had nothing on me as I steered and skidded the kangaroo down the maze of corridors holding on to her huge tail as the means of control before we exploded together through the back door into the courtyard outside.

But I want to tell you about George the cockatoo whom I remember with a tear in my eye. He was forever out of his cage roaming free in the clinic. During surgery, he would sit on the edge of the operating table and watch me cutting and slicing up dogs and cats. Occasionally he would fiddle with the anesthetic equipment, pulse monitor or surgical instruments. Then he'd peer deep inside a dog's abdominal cavity and cock his eye up at me as if to say, "Stop fiddling about, boy, and EAT the damn thing!" He was so entertaining, but a darker side started to emerge as all of us - vets, pets and patients alike - succumbed to the stress of working in this clinic.

Another sleepless night at the clinic and I got up with the feeling that something was very wrong. But that was nothing unusual, I still have sleepless nights and wake up thinking something is very wrong. However, as I stumbled down the corridor in search of a caffeine fix I came across bits of computer keyboard at the entrance to the consulting room. George looked up at me from the debris that resembled one of my smashed Lego cars from childhood. His beak had more uses than a mechanic's toolbox and he had used it to deftly pry off each letter. He picked the last ones off as I blinked and tried to figure out if I was dreaming. At first, it looked to me like he had made a nest out of popcorn. But when he spat a letter like 'B' at me like he wanted to play Scrabble, reality made a brief appearance. In my world 'B' stands for Bruce Lee and like a scene from Enter the Dragon, I charged at the Agent of Chaos with my bare hands. George had also studied Kung Fu and disappeared in a flurry of the alphabet.

TRANSFORMATION AND THE GOLDEN KEYS

I abandoned the fruitless chase because the morning's patients were due to arrive soon. George meanwhile ducked off around the corner to continue malingering. The keyboard repair was delegated to a colleague of mine and although he did his best to replace the keys in the correct order, a touch of dyslexia crept in. This caused us merry hell during consultations when all the wrong letters came up on the screen and client, patient and vet all got embroiled in a technological nightmare. By lunchtime, we had figured out a code of letter conversions by which to work the jumbled keyboard, waiting for a lull in the busy consulting schedule to set things right. It was like a Halloween episode of Sesame Street.

Meanwhile, the arch villain had been lying low. Actually he was out of reach on a ceiling fan. During a lapse in police surveillance, he scuttled down the corridor and climbed onto the wooden trellis in the office on which the receptionist used to pin various important bits of paper. Using his Jack the Ripper beak attachment, he tore the front desk calendar into a pile of thin strips and created a paper jigsaw puzzle out of months of carefully allotted appointments, deadlines and schedules. Sally, the receptionist was the first to come across the scene of wanton destruction and she almost fainted at the realisation of what had been destroyed. Once again, the long chase up the slippery corridor occurred, and George, running as fast as his little legs could carry him, rounded the corner into our operating theatre where four of us were busy with the daily carnage of surgical cases. His nails were skittering loudly on the lino and a piece of paper trailed from his beak. Sally was close on his heels proclaiming various forms of death upon him. George knew when to run and when to stand and fight. And he was running for his life now. His particular brand of warfare: techno-terrorism and paper-shredding of documents left no winners, even if we could get some pleasure out of wringing his little neck.

I have tears of admiration when I remember the gallant last stand that Georgie made. Surrounded on all sides by green clad veterinarians, he reminded me a bit of the legendary hero Horatius standing alone on the bridge outside Rome facing an invading Etruscan army. Using his foot, George picked up a 5 cc syringe off the operating table loaded with anaesthetic, and clunked off to a corner of the room with his lance at the ready. I grabbed a towel, and dropped it over his head, but the needle of the syringe came poking through the fabric as if driven by a sewing machine. We had to back off in retreat and reconsider our strategy. A thicker blanket was found and George was finally captured and disarmed. He was placed into custody inside his large cage and after a short trial and conviction, the cage and its occupant were banished to Jenny's pen outside the backdoor of the clinic.

One summer's day, George was sitting outside his cage as he often loved to do. I think I heard him say, "Oh, bugger it." And beautiful George flew off, never to be seen again.

Little Twit

One of the sweetest animals we ever had was an ostrich I rescued called Little Twit. Ostriches have brains that are smaller than their eyeballs. And they love to copy one another. It is called allelomimetic behaviour and translated from ancient Greek into English, it means, 'to copy your twin'. So if one eats a stick, they all eat sticks and end up hungry and compulsively eating sticks until they all die. Some ostrich chicks had started eating the limestone gravel which the farmer spread in their pens each day. Their bones became as soft as carrots because of the mineral imbalance… you could slice the bones into rubbery wafers with a blunt knife. There were hundreds of lame birds in the pen for which not much could be done. Besides, they were all now addicted to eating white stones. I rescued Little Twit because the farmer gave me three birds to kill and chop up for laboratory examination to confirm my diagnosis. I couldn't kill the third bird so I just stole him.

He lived for many months as a member of our family and would sit with us eating peanuts whilst we drank beer on the veranda. If you were not paying attention, you would hear a loud slurping sound and Little Twit, with a neck as long as a drinking straw, would swallow half of your ale and then stumble around for hours completely off his face. Our lovely dog Miszo licked him to death quite literally. Little Twit caught a fatal skin infection from all the dog's loving saliva. One day I found Little Twit had joined the great aboriginal Emu constellation in the Milky Way. The stars twinkled like the sparkling tears we shed burying him that night as if he were our own (alcoholic) child.

Two nine year old veterinary nurses

A farmer called me one day to attend a cow struggling to calve. So I jumped in my car with two assistants: my daughter Rebekah and her cousin Rebecca – both 9 years old. The cow was soon tranquilised and I tied her out to a tree and to my car bumper. With the flash of my scalpel and some local anaesthetic, I had the calf's legs poking out of an incision in the cow's flank. Then I asked the farmer to help me pull the calf out and drag it away. Instead he turned a whiter shade of pale, stumbled off to his tractor and disappeared. So I had no option but to call in my two assistants who were busy playing 'pat-a-cake' on the bonnet of my car. They were a bit hesitant at first, but I told them that if they didn't help me the cow and the calf would most surely die. So they rolled up their sleeves, washed their hands in a bucket of antiseptic and started the mightiest tug of war with a calf who was very reluctant to vacate his nine month tenancy. With a final heroic tug, the calf and the Two Rebekaz fell over into the grassy paddock as I stood by calmly threading a length of suture to my surgical needle. "Clean it! Clean it!" I shouted and they used their hands to clear its airways and scratched away at its ribs to get it breathing. Soon the calf and the cousins were stumbling around the paddock covered in foetal fluids. Then the calf started searching eagerly for some milk to drink.

By this stage I was trying to sew up the hole I had made in the cow. But the calf stumbled over with the support of Rebekah and Rebecca - basically four extra human legs - and did a face plant back into the surgical wound. Then it backed into my bucket of antiseptic and surgical instruments before the three of them careered off into a nearby thicket. One of the girls was assigned to a game resembling Grid Iron where the calf was the attacking team trying to get at the milk. The other girl helped me stitch up all the cow's bits and pieces and helped fend off the calf with gentle and loving back kicks.

The two Rebekaz. Rebekah became an Occupational Therapist. Her cousin Rebecca sang in nightclubs, covered herself in tattoos and half of Western Australia in tiling, paving and concrete and then became a school teacher.

A voice from the grave

One evening Fiona and I got a call to euthanize a young bull terrier that had recently become extremely aggressive. An old couple owned the dog, and it had spent its two years of life choking on cigarette smoke and falling ash as if living in Pompey below Mount Vesuvius. Colin, a 60-a-day smoker, had tried everything to tame the wild beast within this dog. Shrouded in plumes of cigarette smoke as if living in an eerie London fog the little nipper grew into adulthood and his temperament relentlessly evolved into the Hound of the Baskervilles. In a room filled with ash trays and magazines, I found myself crawling under a snooker table to euthanize the dog. Only the wife was present, and we offered to dig the grave as is polite custom in the country. "No, no," she said, "Colin's already dug it." Having left my dirty work boots outside the front door, I picked up the limp body and in my socks, I followed the lady out to the back garden with Fiona helping me maneuver through the furniture and doorways.

And so the three of us assembled under the moonlight at the grave which was neatly dug at the foot of the neighbor's sheet metal fence. Not knowing what a ferocious digger Colin was, I dropped the dog into the black hole and it seemed to free fall momentarily before hitting the bottom. When shoveling earth into a grave there comes a time halfway through the burial process to compress the soil lest an unsightly sink hole appear with the next shower of rain. Having only my socks on, I volunteered Fiona for the irreverent job of stomping which always resembles one dancing Zumba on the pet's grave. She reluctantly agreed to do this having purchased a brand new pair of shoes the day before.

But thanks to Excavator Colin, Fiona disappeared waist deep into the dark hole and started screaming and scrambling to get out. The old lady hurried to pull her from Death's terrifying grasp and a titanic struggle ensued with the old lady very nearly joining Fiona head first down the hole. I do not know where superhuman strength comes from at moments like this but the dear old lady managed to pull the screaming Fiona out. Meanwhile I had collapsed in peals of laughter until the pain of my ribs exceeded whatever it was I found so funny. So I resumed the shoveling while behind me the two of them muttered on in anguish, "....you poor child....", "...the most frightening moment of my life....", "...there, there..."

But the night's antics were far from over. I soon heard low pitched growlings coming from the grave! "What the blazes...!" I thought. The dog was not properly dead yet, and half buried alive! Well, I really don't know what got into me that night, but realising that if not quite dead, it was at least fully anaesthetised, I made the executive decision to keep shoveling, and stomping in my socks at a great pace. This would constitute method 657 of 1000 ways to kill a dog. It was only after I had filled in the hole that I realized the growling was still loud and clear and coming from the neighbor's dog that was on the other side of the fence trying to lend moral support to his deceased friend. In the darkness and confusion it was the last thing we expected and the entire episode had me and Fiona crying with tears of laughter all the way home.

My own veterinary clinic in Augusta Western Australia

While I was working as a veterinary surgeon in Augusta, I bought an industrial property there and created the food manufacturing business which I described earlier making smoked products and mayonnaise. Just about every man is hypnotically captivated by the process of smoking meat. It is so primal to the 'Y' chromosome on our DNA. The 'Y' chromosome is tiny but it is packed with genes exclusive to us males. For example, next to the smoking meat gene is its consort: the beer drinking gene. There is a beer goggles gene for the beautification of women and which, I believe, women should give us more credit for and use to their advantage. Buy us one or two pints and the return on investment beats anything a woman could spend on enhancing her image with accessories, Botox, swinging hips or implants. There is a map reading gene that a woman doesn't have, a 'how to annoy your sister' gene, and a gene that makes a man pay out more and more rope until he hangs himself like I am doing now.

Running the food business meant getting up before daylight to make hundreds of jars of mayonnaise and to smoke chicken and fish for the local vineyards. I bootlegged the food products to restaurants and supermarkets in between my veterinary farm calls. This, as you can imagine, got quite challenging at times and entangled veterinary surgery with food production. I closed this business after Fiona slipped on a greasy patch of chicken fat on the floor and ploughed through trays of smoked chicken which were cooling ready for packaging. Karate black belts do a similar thing when they demonstrate breaking a stack of planks with their bare hands. Fiona just sat there amongst the bent trays and steaming fillets crying into the warm and very tasty chicken juice. But my heart broke for her. And I realised then that my dream was not her dream and I had inadvertently mixed the two. I had tangled things best kept untangled when I tried to demonstrate some leadership and business acumen. If a cave man had asked his wife to help bring home a dinosaur for dinner, it would also have ended in tears. How often have I found myself caught up in other peoples' dreams just as I had entrapped Fiona with dreams of my own.

So I closed my beloved business and converted the industrial property into Augusta's first veterinary clinic. And it was a brilliant design because I had grown up under the influence of three architects in my family: Dad,

Pete and Mum. I could never afford an x-ray machine, so instead I put a nice drum set in the room behind a door marked: "X-Ray: Keep Out" and never needed to hide in an X-ray room again. On weekends I added to the general noise of Augusta's industrial area with my drumming and no one suspected a thing. Pete had been my drumming mentor. Pete was good enough to play professionally in a band on the big stage -he was THAT good. So it should have been obvious to us that he was on the cusp of madness because extreme genius usually is. Like madness, it is extraordinary ie: not normal, and I wish he had channelled this emotional energy into his drumming instead of letting it energise his archetypes turning them into rock stars.

The years went by in spectacular veterinary fashion and maybe one day I will devote time to tell of all my adventures in mixed animal practice. My beautiful Warrior within led me through those years. Fiona would come with me whenever she could on the farm calls but so much of that time I did on my own because she was raising our two children whilst helping in the clinic. A home unprotected by a mother's love in some form is no home at all. So day or night, rain or shine I was out there with the animals up to my eyeballs in mud, cowshit, flies, blood and guts. I got covered in and swallowed almost every body fluid known in the animal kingdom in my attempts to restrain and treat animals, from feral cats and camels to rampaging bulls and wild brumbies. I even gave mouth-to-mouth resuscitation to a snake whilst I stitched up its torn skin.

But unfortunately I had caught a financial disease off Mum...that financial sickness where she gave all her money away. I had become a people pleaser, unable to charge properly for my services because of an inner Shadow that told me the only currency worth working for was Love. So we were forever poor. It is a perfect example of how Shadow insidiously creeps down through the generations. I passed something similar on to Josh and Bek by repeatedly telling them, "Be good and everyone will love you.' What does that even mean? It would have been far better to say, "Be authentic… speak your truth… and absolutely THRIVE on making mistakes and on failed attempts. Thrive on rejection!"

Australian Quarantine and Inspection Service

My Warrior who gave me the strength and courage for cattle work unfortunately encountered a very big and powerful cow one day as he was pregnancy testing many hundreds of her colleagues. She took offense and dislocated his knee using her hind hoof and about a hundred kilos of gluteus muscle. I was on crutches for months and so had to close my practice, sell off the property and went to join the abattoirs as a government veterinary inspector for the Australian Quarantine and Inspection Service, AQIS.

There I saw death in World War II proportions. I saw rooms filled knee-deep with blood, huge floor drains blocked with truckloads of tapeworm, hearts by the hundreds still beating in meat trays. In one abattoir alone we killed nearly two million sheep a year. But I would stand there, authentically, filled with guilt and dread to witness the animals line up for that last step into cosmic Oneness. Not a pleasant moment by the looks of it, but I often wonder why it is so unpleasant. If death is the completion of a journey, an ultimate journey I guess, well who wants the best journey ever to end. Surely not wanting to leave Life and holding on to it tooth and nail affirms Life, all of it, as simply the best journey. I will remember to give thanks tomorrow when I wake up with a sigh of relief in bed instead of in Heaven. I will give thanks for everything.

There are so many moments I will never forget in those abattoir days. Like watching two sweethearts fall in love and kiss under the floating dripping carcasses above. I stood and watched them for a respectful moment, my heart and Butterfly all aflutter. Kissing under the mistletoe of meat they stood, enraptured with the music of their own heartbeats, oblivious, alive, complete in the moment their lips met. Actually, any location will do when you are under the psychosis of Romantic Love. I often wonder if Eskimo-like children were conceived in the coldrooms - nothing is beyond the imagination of humanity or beyond an individual's need for connection. There is always a price to pay for every encounter of such kind, romantic, physical or otherwise... but hey... frostbite of the extremities... worth every second.

Cricket: responding to what Life bowls

> *I want to tell you how I put these principles into practice in strange ways. When I took up a new appointment as the government veterinary inspector at yet another remote abattoir, I found the people who sorted the cattle in the cattle pens were in a highly negative frame of mind. All their conversation was negative, their lives were in a mess, and many took drugs. They were in a state of negative synergy. And they tried to put all this negativity onto me. I recognized this immediately and decided then and there to change my name to Dr Positive.*
>
> *"Oh, no….. Here comes Dr Positive…" they would say every morning, complaining and awful-ising as we walked around the pens examining cattle. It seemed that my only connection with them would be through this haze of negativity. I was amongst the Shaolin Masters of Milking the Toxic Cow, masters of Passing the Parcel of*

Pain, Black Belts in everything negative and purveyors of Scratched Broken and Dark Glasses and seriously bad Mirrors. But who were they to complain about anything and not celebrate every aspect of life: the animals that went through their hands all died each day! They got to live, but couldn't transcend their pain onto a pathway of acceptance, Life, Love and simply saying "Yes!"

So on my second day I drew a line in the sand by publicly announcing to them that I had never heard such negative rubbish in all my life. They were so negative, I said, that they all must have been born with Rhesus negative blood types. So much so that they were in danger of transforming into anti-matter. The stunned audience looked on. I said that there was no ways Dr Positive was going to get sucked into this negative world and that instead he would transform them into Purely Positive People. I told them that life was special and that they were all wonderful human beings. This was quite an astonishing thing to say to some stressed out abattoir workers. But they could see I was genuine and were now interested to see what I would do because of course they really wanted to see me fail and confirm their world view.

So I just went with the flow of life and knew that somehow I would deliver on this promise. And shortly afterwards when one of the guys shouted out, "You're sick, Man! We're all sick here! We're all fucking useless!" I stood before him as if I were a cricketer readying myself with a bat in front of the stumps. And as he continued with his disempowering comments I pretended to block them and hit them for a six or for four runs. This showed everyone that any negative comments they made were getting knocked clean out of the field. And we started the imaginary cricket game.

I survived about 3 days at the stumps before I eventually lost my temper and was 'bowled out'. So I put the foreman in to bat and we watched him dealing with all the events and comments that came his way. He swung his bat all day long lasting a full 9 days before I caught him yelling and screaming at cattle and I climbed to the highest rail of the pens and shouted, "HOWZAAAAT!" and bowled him out.

Many of us had a turn at this imaginary game and soon it was not necessary to play the cricket anymore. People started asking each other how the batting was going or talking about how they got bowled out that day. And they could understand themselves and life better. It became so much more positive in the cattle pens. People started to look up and think about life and behavior. They came to realize that there is a better way to be, there are alternatives, we can make better choices for our behavior and our thinking. The cricket game gave them the principle of thinking better. And this could transform a life.

When it came time for me to leave the abattoir and to write my final goodbyes on some cards I'd bought, I drew a little picture of a batsman in front of his stumps for one of the workers, Damien, who had been so negative weeks before. He had become transformed into a wonderful, positive and happy young man despite his many challenges. I left the card propped up against a coffee cup on his office desk like a batsman at the stumps. Underneath the cup I left a note which said, "Damien... it's ALL about the batting!"

DR LEM RAVENSDALE

The shedding of human blood in the abattoirs

Abattoirs in Australia are generally run to the highest standards. But really, to anyone visiting an abattoir it must look like Armageddon. People dressed in white resembling chefs in a steamy kitchen, or angels in Heaven, set about dismembering things that God put together and only moments before were alive and proud and somewhat free. Everything and everyone starts to turn red as the day goes on. It's the God of War unleashed on the animal kingdom but in as nice a way as possible. If you ever want to experience a crash course in the panorama of life, go and work for a while in an abattoir.

I would watch the endless succession of animals tumbling from the stunning box onto the shackling cradle to get hoisted to the runner rail above by means of a hind leg and a roller hook. When we first started processing Wagyu beef, fattened on grain and grape skins from the vineyards, some of the hooks couldn't handle the immense weight and would bend, pop their rivets and drop over a ton of meat from ceiling height towards the workers below. How no one got killed I will never know because the metal hook alone weighs 15 kilos of solid steel and a Wagyu bull could easily exceed 1200 kg. The men were immediately issued with protective gear- hard hats - and the Safety Officer could tick another box. A thousand gold medals for their courage might have been better protection. Things have improved today but in all kinds of industries and occupations across the world people of courage and genius have to deal with unfolding situations in real time. These are the expressions of the archetypes that live within us all.

If on the rare occasion a cow or a bull wasn't stunned properly it would leap to life on the shackling cradle with a serious headache and run off to terrorise people in the chillers and boning room. I would hear their screams as the animal disappeared into the corridors of the establishment with the manager and slaughtermen chasing after it like they were chasing the Minotaur.

As for human blood, well of course it happens quite regularly seeing as the place is alive with knives and saws all over the place. I have seen one guy impaled right through the leg with a skinning knife as he tried to catch his friend falling off a gangway above. I saw one man accidentally shoot another right through the ankle with a captive bolt gun - the result of a bright idea to steady a goat's head with his foot during the stunning process. On many occasions I saw workers stumbling in to the manager's office clutching their bleeding and bruised skulls - metal roller hooks, carcase and all, had fallen off the overhead rail onto their heads because a rail gate had not been closed.

Every day was filled with adventures but maybe the stories should rest there amongst mostly great people who were simply doing their best. Despite all our precautions and with the very best of intentions in every industry, and just as with the Dark Night of the Soul, shit happens. How we deal with it, discuss it and engage with it can be the making or breaking of us all. Leaders can polish a corporate image squeaky clean with political correctness and weasel words. But Shakespeare's words seem to trump such things: 'This above all: to thine own self be true, and it must follow, as the night the day, thou canst not then be false to any man.' And Miyamoto's classic: 'Do not think dishonestly.' And the Golden Key from Jesus that seems to open every lock: 'The truth will set you free.' The leaders I admired most were the honest ones, courageously honest. They would state the truth of a situation at the outset so that all subsequent discussions centred on the truth and not on fear, shame, blame or political correctness.

Fathers and sons. Despite me being guarded by ten Gurkha soldiers Josh still manages to get in an uppercut to his Dad's chin. Josh came on two of these epic journeys with me and they were always life changing for all of us.

Becoming a Trekking Guide

I received a phone call one day from a trekking company in a bit of a panic asking me if I could get them some very large, heavy duty plastic bags which are only sold by veterinary suppliers directly to veterinarians. We use them for putting dead animals in for freezing or for transportation. So we call them Dead Dog Bags or DDB's. The trekking company used them to put backpacks in to keep dry when swimming across rivers or in lakes. And being dutiful in small things, I ordered the bags and drove them two hours up the road to Perth to the company. This one act was pivotal in my life. It was actually a consequence of the Samurai Game I played in San Francisco: focussing attention to detail and mindfulness in dealing with people and with life.

I found myself as a guest of honour at the celebration night of this successful trek three weeks later. It was my fiftieth birthday and I was surrounded by Nepalese soldiers, the camp kitchen awash with Tawny Port, Nepalese curry, and Nepalese music. It was the start of my trekking career and I did about twelve treks with them over the years taking them to the most remote places to the north of western Australia basically to fish and swim and practice some navigation. And I bonded them to nature every step of the way.

I taught them the names of plants and snakes and birds, insects and animals not because I thought they would ever remember them for long but so as to introduce them to nature as you would if introducing your friends at a social gathering. Once you know a plant's name or an animal's or a fish's name it becomes your friend. You are not so fearful or alone when you come across these things in the wild because you recognise one other. It is very settling. Even better to know the story and the usefulness or significance associated with the named thing. But I was careful not to burden them with endless detail. And much of the medicinal and nutritious uses of native species that I heard other guides talking about were more likely to get my friends killed than be of much benefit because we were really all strangers in that land. There is a big difference in life between those who really know, and those who just think they know. So I chose my words carefully and let Mother Nature put on most of the show and do most of the talking.

Cross-cultural magic

These journeys were life-changing because of the intimate friendships we created along the way, the experiences in nature and the magic when two cultures meet to delight in each other's ways of being. I learned their language, their customs and their songs through intense study over many years. And to top it all, I was amongst all the gods: Buddhists, Hindus, Animistic ancestral worshippers, Atheists and even a few Christians who were so sheepish in their faith because they were such a minority. It wasn't too safe for the Christians but I have worshipped with Muslims too so I loved sneaking off with the Christian Nepalese if they asked me to for a quick prayer and to call on the Holy Spirit to join us in the smoke of the evening's campfire.

I also worked with Singaporean Chinese and Malays. The Malays were devout Muslims, the Chinese were maybe Taoists, Christians or Buddhists, I was never quite sure. It was at mealtimes that the Muslim element was evident because they had different coloured cutlery so as not to contaminate their food with anything unclean. They were senior intelligence officers from the Singaporean Police who come to Australia for leadership training and some of the most bizarre scenarios I have ever witnessed or been part of. I used to play cameo roles in these scenarios where a terrorist was running amok in the region and the police officers had to send out personnel to catch him. So I might be a reporter harassing them in the middle of the night in a remote location, a cave guide taking them through limestone cave systems and dropping clues for them along the way, or the actual terrorist which ended up in water balloon gun battles through a series of chalets and down at a local seaside caravan park with bewildered tourists looking on.

It was immediately apparent that the Chinese operated completely differently to the Gurkha soldiers because they were more used to working from behind a desk and a bank of CCTV screens in an ops room. Theirs is a collectivist culture and if a team of Chinese were asked to climb a hill it would turn into a cerebral brain storming exercise of over-analysis with the team leader disappearing in the democratic discussion that ensued. An hour or two later the entire group would wobble itself to its feet like a hesitant flying saucer and haphazardly climb the hill trailing their belongings behind them. With the Gurkhas, and their Command and Control structure, the entire group would have their packs on in minutes, climbing the hill in an orderly formation without any discussion needed whilst I chased after them trailing all of my own belongings behind me.

On one occasion, the Gurkhas set off quickly after a break and vanished over a treacherous hill just as I stood up to follow them and the button on my shorts broke. This dropped my shorts into an embarrassing position around my knees and I could easily have overtaken the soldiers head first on the descent if I had stepped over the cliff. They quickly disappeared as I fumbled with my shorts. I was lost and immobile, stuck way behind the group on a mountain and wondering about the games and tricks of Mother Nature. But She only tries to teach us through these things to become older, bigger, kinder, wiser. I was at risk of floundering into negativity because panic is a choice. We have a very definite moment to say "Yes!" to life and choose not to panic. Quickly, I worked my mind out, fixed the fashion drama with a length of string and descended the hill with the courage and dexterity of a parachuting kangaroo.

The Gurkhas have a love for the village life and organic things. They would eat hornets, drink oil which they rendered from any plump fish we caught and they would pass around endless containers of chewing tobacco. In their villages, a pregnant woman will get the best food and will eat first. Their food is laced with vitamin C from all the lemon juice and abundant chillies. This is how through the mother's milk, the infant becomes pre-conditioned to the adult's diet. Meat and fish is cooked with smashed splinters of bones for the added minerals. Walking side by side on the hot treks through the Kimberley ranges, sipping water constantly from our Camelbaks, my Nepalese friends would tell me of the wonders of their triple distilled whiskey and the health benefits of their

Yarsagumba caterpillars which are found in the soils of their mountain passes.

One day I was walking with Fiona and Scout to the forest in the early morning, and because the Gurkhas had opened my eyes to such things, Fiona and I shook the nectar from all the flowering bushes we encountered on our walk that morning to taste and compare their sweet flavours of burnt sugar and honey. Disaster struck when Fiona asked me what a particularly low-lying blossom tasted like. To her surprise, I spat it out moments later and replied, "Don't tell anyone but it seriously tastes like dog piss…"

Ujal and the wallaby. We found this wallaby trying to swim across the crocodile infested Ord river. Ujal caught the wallaby and I towed his canoe to the riverbank where we let the poor thing go.

The Nepalese Gurkhas: A band of brothers

The DDB's – 'Dead Dog Bags' - were really quite cool and we always had adventures and dramas because of them. On one occasion I arrived at a designated river crossing with my ten men only to find that the river crossing was now 100 metres of black stinking mud and none of us was prepared to get that stuff all over us and into the pores of our skins. So I hatched another of my brilliant plans: a large boat was due to pick us up in two hours and transport us up the lake to a spot where all three teams of soldiers convene at the end of the trek to celebrate. My plan was simple: we would all change into our swimming shorts and tie up our backpacks securely in the DDB's so we could swim triumphantly from the boat to the celebration in full view of all the soldiers already assembled there.

The boat arrived and we made a nice neat pile of black plastic DDB's containing our backpacks along the midline of the boat and set off across the lake to the celebration. Wearing just our shorts and sandals ready to swim, we arrived looking like a bunch of tourists on a leisurely cruise. However, Sasha, the boat's resident Staffordshire bull terrier had been to visit all of us for a cuddle and a stroke along the way. When we threw our DDB's into the water and plunged in to swim, the bags had been punctured by Sasha's sharp claws and they all started sinking. So it was bedlam, many of us nearly drowning to get our submerged backpacks to shore. Every single item in our back packs had to be laid out on the rocks, secured with a pebble lest the wind blow it back into the lake, and left out in the sun to dry. Everyone else was lying back on the shore watching the fiasco unfold enjoying the shade and a very welcome cool drink whilst I unravelled roll after roll of wet bandage from the medical kit and then turned to deal with the rest of my soaking belongings. From left to right in front of the camp was a panorama of clothing, socks, underpants, vests, sleeping bags, radios, cameras. The men looking on seemed quite content because it reminded them of the market places in Kathmandu.

My dear friend Salti. The name is an endearing one in Nepali. It means 'Brother-in-Law'.

Action overcomes fear

On another occasion, I was swimming across to an island and feeling rather alone when I looked behind to notice a Gurkha soldier was following, paddling along straddling a small log. But when I looked forward I came eye to eye with a very large crocodile and almost crapped my pants in fear. "What shall we do?..." I hastily asked my Nepalese friend treading water. He immediately shouted, "Attack!!" and so we swam directly at the beast with the power and resolve of Kamikaze pilots. And the crocodile disappeared never to be seen again. Such is the power of discipline and training. The Gurkhas are soldiers. In moments like this attack is far better than defence and you only have moments to win the fire fight. That's what a bouncer once told me... in a bar brawl, the one who puts in the first ten punches wins the fight. "So get punching really quickly and don't stop for a breather or a sip of beer." he said.

In that moment as we moved from indecision to committed action I learned to face my fear, face my dragons, and get my treasure. The Warrior and the Masculine is all about taking action.

I learned so much from the soldiers especially about leadership. And I would always bring loads of material from my own life experiences and all the books I've read to share with the group in discussions at night around the fire. It may not have always looked very authentic because I invariably would sit there drinking too much whiskey and coupled with fatigue from the day I was regularly carried to my tent unconscious in the moonlight by my Nepalese brothers and then plied with coffee in the morning as if I was in the hands of the Red Cross.

There is a beach in Lake Argyle, Western Australia littered with hundreds of these sticks. It is where our treks with the Gurkha soldiers end and the kayak expeditions down the Ord River begin. These sticks were truly our very best friends because they saved our lives constantly.

Balancing Sticks

When I used to take Nepalese Gurkha commandos trekking through the ranges of far north Western Australia, the soldiers always carried their famous knives with them. The knife is called a 'kukri' and it is basically a small machete shaped a bit like a boomerang. And there is a whole lot of story and history about the kukri but basically they use it for chopping things as you would with a mini axe. When we crossed the valleys and reached the foothills on our treks, they would use their kukris to cut us great walking sticks with which to climb the very hazardous ranges on our trek. Without these sticks many of us would have lost our lives along the way and I was always sad to leave the walking sticks behind when we finished our trek on the shores of Lake Argyle. There are hundreds of them discarded there at the spot where we would all convene at the end of the 8 day trek.

So after one trek I took my stick thousands of kilometres back to my home. And each morning I stand under the stars and balance this stick on the end of my finger until it stands there perfectly still. It brings back the memories of heartfelt stories around the camp fires, of the soldiers' undying loyalty once they let you in. I hear our Nepalese songs, and sway with the dances. I can taste the chewing tobacco and the tot of whiskey we would share each night.

But most of all, the balancing stick reminds me of my own leadership. It is about keeping my balance when the pressure is on. It is about quieting my heart and my mind so that I can lead by instinct and intuition, trusting the process that something greater leads us on and provides so much magic. It reminds me to keep a rock solid sense of who I am so that I keep access to all my skills when the going gets tough. No one can trust a wobbly leader. And once we forget who we are, forget to trust the process, once we become unbalanced, we lose our skills and the quality of leadership starts to plummet. If I can keep balanced and learn to lead myself well, I can lead others well also.

It also reminds me to keep all of my inner elements balanced. These are my masculine and feminine energies, my array of archetypes all in balance around what I call my 'Axis Mundi'... the axis of my inner world. Gilbert and Moore's book King Warrior Magician Lover depicts these four archetypal elements of a man as a pyramid – each one can either be expressed too strongly or too weakly at any moment, but at the apex of the pyramid, each archetype is expressed in its beautiful form. And as we ascend this pyramid, responsibility increases leaving behind the irresponsible childish behaviours. Responsibility and mental health go hand in hand.

So one day, I was taking the Gurkhas into a wonderful cave in the southwest near Margaret River. And sitting in the forest I had them meditating, doing Tai Chi and then I gave them all balancing sticks and talked about leadership. It was a magic moment because they all understood the power of this metaphor as they stood there amongst the beautiful, giant Karri trees in the forest finding their balance through the winds and the storms of Life, finding that internal sense of self and of peace.

The Nepalese Gurkhas are highly trained commandos. But inside every man is a little boy who loves to play.

10

Rites of Passage

Facilitation

Because of my work with facilitation of initiation in the Mankind Project and with the Gurkhas, I started picking up more skills for outdoor adventure work, school camps and then Rites of Passage facilitation for school kids. Many of these programs were aimed at helping 14 and 15 year old boys' and girls' transition into adulthood and so were called 'Into Adulthood Programs'.

This involved taking kids caving, camping, sea kayaking, bush walking and rafting in those huge rubber super rafts that are used in white water. The super rafts are so light that if the wind picks up on the ocean you will get swiftly blown over the horizon to China with a boatload of terrified kids. When kids get scared, they immediately become weak, useless and stop paddling and the situation gets worse. And if some of them have jumped off in the water and cannot swim fast enough to your drifting raft, there is immediately cause for major panic because as the separation distance gets bigger and bigger the sharks probably get hungrier.

But I had a lot of fun working with the kids. Fun is used to hook their attention and keep them engaged. So a good facilitator has to become something of a Games Master. And then you are the life and soul of any party. But if the kids are demanding, and you have run out of fun they will just as soon punish you because hell hath no fury like a child - especially a teenager - who is not having fun. Fun is a two-edged sword, a bit like using sweets to coach a child to eat.

Playing Rescue Teddy with kids as part of a playful challenge activity. There is a teddy in the bucket adrift in a crocodile infested ocean with a rescue helicopter suspended by ropes trying some desperate manoeuvres to save teddy.

General elements

There is an art to facilitating kids. It comes with practice but as with all new groups and especially with cross-cultural work somewhere deep down they will be asking: are you one of us and can you provide us with what we need and what we want? Hook them as soon as possible with your stories, with your playful child within, with the promises of the program or with some kind of magic that they are looking for. Then they will let you in. And as they trust you and follow you, they will come to see a new way of being in this open, honest and authentic adult. I talk to them as adult to adult or friend to friend, never as parent to child or from a place of ego. Often I come away thinking that it was simply the time spent with an authentic man that changed their lives not all the activities themselves. We become Games Masters, Storytellers, Magicians, Posers of Great Questions, and Wise Counsellors. And we listen, reflect and hold the space for transformation and insight to unfold in its due course.

I try to give them ample time to sleep because tired kids are mostly disengaged, not listening and then get themselves offside with the Facilitator when it is really no fault of their own. If they are tired, instead of flogging a dead horse, how about letting them sleep for an hour. It might be their best experience on the entire camp.

I never tell them horror stories. I am there to build up their confidence and their connection to nature not to harm this relationship. Countless millions became estranged from the oceans and from sharks themselves because of the movie 'Jaws'. Until I was about 25 years old I was possessed by the irrational fear... no, absolute *terror* of sharks in whichever swimming pool I was in. So you can imagine that I was somewhat against the tradition and practice of throwing a headless life-sized dummy from a balcony into the centre of a group of children as they listened intently to the telling of a horror story in our camps at night.

DR LEM RAVENSDALE

Mother Nature's Voice

As a Facilitator, I do my best to help people examine aspects of Soul, Spirit and Self. But mostly I bond them to nature to help them see that it is a matrix of life, alive with relationship and connection and information from deep within the earth to outer space. Relationship is all about finding our place in this living matrix because despite the veneer of our humanity, we are very much an integral part of this living matrix of life. It needs us to know this and believe this. Then we will love and respect nature more and be in a conscious relationship to her. We will not be out of the relationship nor living unconscious of the abundance that is there.

We live unconsciously when we forget these things, when we forget our first home and our first Mother. But we can always wake up one day and rediscover our place in it all, slotting in like the missing piece in a jigsaw puzzle to complete the picture and to rest into it. Relationship sets the natural world out in a 3-D map and indigenous peoples establish a sense of these relationships within the minds of their young ones. We do something similar when we teach our kids about the matrix and the soul of a city and their relationship to its natural features of traffic lights and zebra crossings. But connection is when we tug on the invisible threads that join us to another and this helps to keep relationships alive and vibrant. It takes courage. And it means doing something. Maybe that's why they say love is an action.

It is not easy to teach school kids anything meaningful when they are either freezing cold wandering around a forest in the pouring rain, or if it is too hot and swarms of biting flies have turned the Bush Survival class into a class resembling Irish Dancing. So

TRANSFORMATION AND THE GOLDEN KEYS

I decided to get the kids to sit on the huge veranda of the camp's wooden dormitory building, eat as much imaginary popcorn as they wanted, and to relax and enjoy my show: 'How to THRIVE in Nature'.

I talk to the kids about a range of survival aspects. All of them are simple and practical including how to set up a tent in 60 seconds, how to use a signal mirror, how to catch fish and how to make a stretcher. It is great, it is simple and I have loads of stories to throw in to hold their attention by hooking the cinema screen inside their heads. But indigenous communities across the globe don't spend their time trying to survive in Nature. They thrive in it.

One day trekking with the Nepalese Gurkhas I came across a perfect fishing pool with the fattest and tastiest fish sunning themselves in the cool water. "Get fishing, Boys!" I said but not a man moved. With immense shame and guilt they confessed that they had left all the fish hooks ten kilometres back at our previous camping spot. "But what if one day you forget your radio, grenades, bullets or machine gun behind..." I said. Forgetfulness may have its uses when it comes to painful memories but not when it comes to equipment.

In a flash of genius I got some safety pins from the medical kit and started to tie one on to a fishing line. With my tired and shaking hands, this was going to take a bit of time. Well, the old sergeant looked around and with a flash of Instinct, and none of my western mental genius, he tied a lump of beef jerky to a piece of line, cast it into the water and immediately reeled in the fattest fish I have ever seen. He continued pulling out fish after fish until a tortoise spotted the bait and became a major nuisance. So the old soldier captured the poor tortoise and put it on its back next to him in the shade so he could carry on fishing and he soon had the quota for a huge meal for all of us. I still hadn't finished fastening the safety pin to the line when he picked up the tortoise, gave it a kiss and let it swim away back to the place it called home. We are only ever limited by our thinking. Creativity is a skill we can learn. It means coming up with ideas that are not only new and innovative but are also practical. Basically, the sergeant's beef jerky eclipsed my safety pin by a million miles.

Transformation and renewal. It feels so good.

The most important part of my show was to get the kids to recognise what I meant by Mother Nature's Voice. It is just a profound connection with Nature because Nature is sending us signals and information and teachings all the time. We just need to be aware. If I am in tall grass and walking next to a river and I can hear water running, it is usually a sign that this is a crossing point with stepping stones across the river. If the ants are going crazy, it probably is going to rain. If there are no fish in the river, it is because there is a waterfall up ahead preventing their ascent from the valley below. Some fish species, notably the Spangled

Perch, do get above the waterfall but that is because those particular species lay eggs that are sticky and attach to the legs of birds which can then transport them to higher ground. If I can see tiny birds there must be water within a kilometre of this vicinity. And if I can find a kangaroo track I can use it to easily find my way through some very treacherous hill country because kangaroos have been using that track for hundreds of years.

Mother Nature's Voice and her presence is profound when we live by instinct. Then Nature comes alive and speaks to us. But she is also there to teach us and she suffers no fools or an excess of liminality in her surreal world. She wants us to function within set limits and set parameters otherwise we will suffer the consequences. If we walk too fast, we will get exhaustion and heat stroke. We may stumble and fall and suffer injury or death. If we move too slowly, we will never get to our camping spot by nightfall and will have to make do with wherever we find ourselves. If we drink our water too fast, we run out of water. Too slow and we've got dehydration. If we take every fish from a pond, we leave nothing for the future should we pass this way again. Whatever comfort we want, we have to carry. Like our Mother Complex, we need to leave most of our comfort needs at home where they best belong and then accept the ensuing hardships or overcome them with innovation and genius.

All animals in nature have to hit the ground running each morning. There is magnificence in being wild. So Mother Nature will constantly challenge us to lift our game and to be our best and express our genius just as in a similar way, our inner Spirit Guide will help us to negotiate and explore the inner world of Soul.

> *I found that Mother Nature would give and take at the same time: we may find water but it would be hot or dirty or there would be a dead kangaroo in it. We may find shade, but soon ants were climbing on us so we couldn't rest. We may have food, but it was the hottest curried fish on rice aflame with chillies and bristling with vicious chopped fish bones. The guest of honour - usually me - might just get a bowl of rice and a fish head for dinner. Then the fish's eyeballs were the only bis of protein in that sumptuous meal even if it had been served as if to a god with trembling hands. Most of the time our offerings to the Gods are just symbolic anyway, not the best bit, because our gods are easily appeased. The best bits we reserve for ourselves because we are much more demanding.*
>
> *Mother Nature loves us. She waits for us and prepares herself for us each morning with the mist and the dew and the dappled sunlight. She is like a woman, maybe even Aphrodite herself, sitting before her vanity mirror each morning to bring out her best into the world and present herself with all her love manifesting it in an array of colours, shades, reflections and rainbows. She has a voice and is a great teacher. Listen to her. Learn from her. She absolutely comes alive on Rites of Passage programs as linear logical thought inevitably shifts towards the diffuse and the liminal. And I thank her constantly for who she is because she enhances everything and every activity. And then us Facilitators take much of the credit and look so damn good!*
>
> *Without Mother Nature's voice the forest would not speak. And the magic would be elsewhere or maybe just in stories about once upon a time when Mother Nature walked amongst us.*

Rites of Passage Programs

I underwent Rites of Passage training to further understand the aims and design of such programs even though I had been involved in them for years. There are certain energetics around which the programs are built just as you would in designing any group event. Each activity contains a certain energetic whether it is play, discussion, adventure, rest or challenge. So we first establish the energetic flow of the program through each day. This energetic flow then becomes the underlying framework on which to pin the actual program activities and timings.

However, during a program, we have to make frequent assessments, keeping a couple of fingers on the pulse, watching group morale and meeting the group where it is at. On the day, with any particular group, the script goes out of the window the moment there is magic worth chasing or group dynamics that warrant a change of script. It's the magic we are chasing, not the program itself and the Facilitator needs to spot these rabbits running or be able to pull them out of a hat when necessary.

I just chase the magic as it unfolds. Maybe we begin with a soulful start around the fire before breakfast which unfolds into discussions and questions and then challenges and reflections as the day goes on into an enchanted night. Along the way the Rites of Passage elements of the program occur. These have already been discussed with the client - in this case the school - to align the program with what the school's focus, values and desired outcomes are. We reserve time for sitting in circle, for mealtimes, unstructured social time and rest breaks.

Different skills and information are needed for the various stages of life. They are often best imparted on a timely 'needs to know' basis. Yet I still make the mistake of giving too much too soon and too deeply. At a young age they need more ego-based skills such as body language, making a first impression, public speaking, conversation skills and deportment. Later in life comes the time to deeply discuss things like intimate relationships, wisdom, Spirit, Soul and Eldership.

So once I told them whenever I go to a mechanical workshop to get the car repaired, I dress up like a mechanic and the subsequent bill is usually a fraction of the normal price to the general public. Is this dressing up being deceitful? Well, isn't that a great discussion to have around the fire.

In all our programs there are real challenges. And here is where the Facilitator gets to be like Rambo or Bear Grylls and do some real stuff, real action in a real ocean or on a real mountain and with very real consequences. All the talk in the world is fine, but you had better be able to walk that talk. That is what real leaders do. We all have to lead ourselves well in order to lead others well or to be worthy of the gold they invest in us as their heroes or mentors in order for them to ascend. So Facilitators get qualified in various disciplines like caving, abseiling, sea kayaking and remote first aid to create real adventure.

Adventure

What does adventure look like:

- Kayaking up to a huge freshwater crocodile on Lake Argyle and the crock running towards us to plunge beneath our boats and swim to the safety of the deep.
- Getting chased by a rogue bull on a trek in the Kimberley ranges.
- Makeshift rafts falling apart mid-river spilling all the kids into the water.

- Fighting the wind and the rain to attach a tow-line from my kayak to a rubber super raft full of kids getting blown across the horizon to China in the Indian Ocean.
- Trekking with a disabled teacher and getting him safely across a waterfall and series of rapids.
- Spending solo time in a starlit forest or surviving a night time storm together.
- Being sent as a group of two or three on a reconnaissance mission.
- Abseiling into a cave system.
- Calling in a chopper for a casualty evacuation.
- Discovering a Death Adder under your backpack.

Close calls

Although we often talk about real risk vs perceived risk in designing adventure programs, I smile knowingly when I think of the times we unwittingly faced really fatal risks and for some reason the gods let us live. Adventure often involves risk and challenge. Somehow, when the shit hits the fan, the Warrior within has to have enough sense to keep balanced and live to fight another day. Events can unfold quickly often as a result of the 'Swiss Cheese Effect' – the alignment of insidious things. But with skill and experience, you will be able to spot the unfolding of the mischief which is a prelude to disaster. Maybe it's a flat battery in a UHF radio or a rope trailing from a raft in the water but each one has a red flashing warning light which is so obvious in retrospect. We need to stay awake by keeping an eye out for this kind of mischief rather like an Eagle soaring above to see the bigger picture. And then we can inform the team, "Be careful. Be vigilant. For mischief stalks us nearby." After a close call, I just smile with humility and whisper a prayer of thanks, and move on knowing I will always do my best, and even better next time. Others may process such things with fear, scapegoating, shame, blame and reams of paperwork.

Teenage Boys

We have to remind ourselves that teenagers are in the grips of something like an identity crisis. They are trying to separate things in their heads so as to find their uniqueness and identity. All the while, their brains are still forming under the powerful effects of hormones. It's a bit like a truck driver trying to navigate the busy CBD whilst on LSD. It is easy to misunderstand their attempts at fleshing out a persona. They are often acting from behind thick castle walls besieging themselves with arrows of self-consciousness and self-loathing and criticism.

Their cocoon mush doesn't compare too well to the image of perfection society demands of them. But society's perfection fails each one of us anyway because it is a phantom, a concept, a golden standard, an image in a mirror held up by others which we can never achieve or maintain in order to be acceptable. It forces us to hide behind a mask of perfection lest the crowd project the scapegoat upon us. Life isn't easy for most kids.

I am often asking the boys to do things they are mentally not capable of or which is not socially safe to do. To 'sit and listen' is a foreign language to many of them unless their physical needs are met as in food, shelter, rest and water. And I have to hook their attention with story or bizarre things like a magic trick, and all manner of facilitation props. I have to be creative otherwise I will be eaten by the crowd.

They are trying to break away from their parents and the establishment to enter their own cocoon of change so that a butterfly may emerge. The adolescent boys are often destructive, boisterous or disengaged and disruptive. Like silverback gorillas in the mist, they roar, display and shirtfront each other because their newly found archetypal masculine power is so boorish and new and needs to mature before it can be channelled into useful work. They are just testing it out in the forest. It is normal. It is all about 'I', protecting that emotional self and creating some kind of personality with which to engage or disengage with this world and protect a core wound from ever being touched or seen.

In years to come, as they create their own persona, create a myth to live by and establish a healthy ego in this busy world, they will return to the concept of 'Us', to embrace community, to be creative and to contribute when they are ready to do so. We Facilitators of this work may be stepping stones, or an inspiration or we may simply be holding sacred space for their transformation. But the kids will never forget us because they tell us so with a certain fire in their eyes when we meet them years later.

Tossing the script and running on instinct

On any program, it is important to meet people where they are at. And on Rites of Passage programs we have to be mindful to attempt to divulge and encourage knowledge and insights in appropriate measure to the appropriate time in a person's life. When I am inclined to delve too deep too soon and disclose too much, I need to remember this lest my own Shadow drive me to disaster. But overall, I just 'trust in the process', that the human minds involved will take what they need in Life and that seeds will be sown and impacts will be made at all kinds of levels of which I may not be aware.

This silences the critical voices and seeds of doubt inside my own head. Just sharing my authenticity with young people often seems to be what they value most. It means just speaking from my heart and anyone can do it when it comes from there.

Mission and Values: greatest need – greatest gift

> I am standing in a beautiful green forest. It is still but for the gentle breeze that brings the scent of a thousand flowers and the earthy tones of the forest litter. A group of adolescent boys on a Rite of Passage is seated in disarray all around me. Each one has a piece of paper printed with a long list of values and they have been given time to clarify their individual values and to share them in turn with the group.
>
> It is a great exercise to print out a list of values and capture maybe five of them that you hold most dear. And if you can compare this list with those values of your partner or significant people in your life it will reveal so much of the paradigms behind each relationship. The insights will reveal the sources of synergy and the sources of conflict.
>
> We are constantly making decisions and choices as we move forward in life. And I tell the boys that in the human mind is a set of Golden Balancing Scales where we weigh up profit and loss in worldly matters. It is the place where we determine Pleasure and Pain. And in that moment we weigh up what we value most. It is strongly influenced by our core values. So our values determine our choices. And these choices add up to become our destiny. By understanding our values, we can have more control over that moment of choice and thus enhance our destiny.

TRANSFORMATION AND THE GOLDEN KEYS

So with their hearts resonating with their values, it is time to take them on a guided visualisation to find their own unique mission and their gift to the world. Standing there amongst the group I ask them to close their eyes and listen to the gentle music coming from a small boom box on the ground. Some remain seated and some lie down comfortably and as their minds quieten they drift away into the story.

"Once upon a time, you had a dream that you were living in a tiny fishing village on a coconut Island drenched in Sun. And each day you walk barefoot through the shallow water along the shoreline feeling the sand between your toes and the warm water on your ankles. Around you are the fishing boats and you can hear the slapping of the sail ropes against the masts and the chatter of the fishermen as they sit there mending their nets. There is a warm breeze that barely disturbs the water and seagulls are slowly gliding by. Up on the hillsides you can see the village huts and the womenfolk hanging up washing and tending to the children.

You notice a dark shape on the horizon which slowly and steadily comes closer and closer. And as you shield your eyes from the sunlight you see that it is a magnificent Spanish galleon... with a pirate, bronzed and magnificent, standing on the foredeck. As the Spanish Galleon gently beaches itself in the sand before you, the pirate cries out, "People of the village, have you got an adventurer such as me to sail off over the horizon in search of adventure and to bring back treasure for the village?" And from deep within your heart a desperate voice cries out, "Take me!"

The pirate's strong arms reach down and pull you aboard the ship and with a tearful farewell to the village you set sail across the sea, across the horizon with the wind in the sails and the waves beckoning all around."

A story such as this can unfold in many ways. Maybe it takes each child to examine a magnificent world that they have created or to a place where they are being honoured for the greatest accomplishment of their lives. But it is designed to help them see more clearly their gift and their Life's Mission without any scripting from the Facilitator. As they use their imagination to resonate with what their souls want them to create and want to find, it will appear in their imagination and in this visualisation. The Facilitator takes them to a perfect place or a perfect time and asks them to see more clearly what is happening there. In the subsequent discussion and debrief, the Facilitator helps each one flesh out their unique Mission and gift. It doesn't work for all the boys, because they are still so young. But many of them get it and to these ones it gives focus and purpose and motivation. The seeds of their unique mission have been planted and will quietly grow for many many years.

My Mission is this: "I create a world of wonder, adventure and learning by connecting, encouraging, empowering and teaching." It is a sentence, almost a mantra, composed of a vision and an action that at any time I can state what I stand for. It might need refining and it may change in the course of my life. If the visualisation is done properly it will reveal a unique and profound gift that each individual can give to the world. It will never be fulfilled in its entirety during the course of a lifetime but it is a direction, a compass on the ship that will almost never fail. Life will always back a man or a woman on mission.

And yet a man or a woman can lose his or her way just as easily from time to time by becoming marooned on the Island of Calypso on some romantic quest or in chasing a career. We may become cynical or forgetful or complacent. But I have found that life is abundant when I walk the path of my mission. And for me, in the real world, it is an attitude that I bring as I engage life whether as a facilitator for transformational work and Rites of Passage or in my veterinary activities and even mundane tasks. I just have to remind myself of what I stand for and the magic unfolds in the course of the day.

When the young people are confused about their future and what kind of career they should pursue, I simply explain to them that their greatest need as a child usually becomes their greatest gift to the world. So many biographies testify to this fact.

And as we get older, eventually the Soul comes calling because it wants to give this gift to the world. And so often this gift can be seen through the window of some core wound. Psychology would want to close and heal and medicate that core wound because we find it so painful. But the wound needs to be given due consideration for its potential of abundant blessing and strength. I always think of my own core wound as a window to my Soul and a gateway through which my Soul's gift is born into this world. It is also the foundation of my unique personality.

For those who resist it or don't understand it, the Soul will brutally express itself anyway when it is unlived for too long. The danger is that their gift may be stillborn into a life in total disarray. For those who understand, the expression of their Soul with its gift to the world can be done more gently and beautifully.

The Journey continues

The kids tumble out of the school buses and into our programs in numbers varying from maybe thirty to nearly three hundred. A facilitator will have a maximum of twenty kids in a group, settle them down, do a check in and start moving into the program. I often use a rope circle to build the first circle and the feeling of connection and team work. The actual rope is the strongest tow rope I can buy because the force on the rope circle can be immense. We always start with crazy games first as ice-breakers but then the program will move through things like the telling of an insightful story, examining of values, life's mission, immature versus mature behaviour, and a contract of values this particular group wants to embrace during the program as a code of conduct.

I often have Nature cards to show them how Nature is a reflection of the Soul. Any resonance the picture evokes in me is because of something within me, some schema, some Shadow. The positive question to ask is, "What do I like about this picture and what does that say about me?" With kids I usually don't ask the opposite question, "What do I dislike about this picture and what does that say about me?" One teacher stood before the class holding a picture card of a penguin and all the kids burst out laughing because he was their water polo coach. One girl picked a card of a cow which caused a few comments before she told the group that she actually grew up on a dairy farm and her cows may have provided the milk for their breakfast cereal. Others could see their wild aloofness in the card of a wolf or their love of freedom in a soaring eagle. But once a boy was very reluctant to share about his card because he had inadvertently drawn a card displaying a skunk so I had to throw that card into the bin.

I may use story dice whereby four story tellers each roll a dice and contribute to a unique story. I may show a magic trick if morale is going down. But throughout all of this, the day is interspersed with challenging adventure activities, fun, discussion, reflection and debriefs. We may discuss topics of life and death, suicide, drugs, sex, girls…whatever they want to discuss. We may do bush art, create a mandala, we may do drumming or go swimming or kayaking or go on a challenging ropes course or on a blindfolded trust walk at night or a midnight solo. The activities are infused with storytelling, myths, ritual theatre and ceremony so that they are touched by the sacred aspect of Life. The programs will inevitably end with the honouring of each child in turn in front of his or her peers, the giving of tokens and blessing.

If you are ever at a loss with kids, simply tell them a story. In this case it seems to be the Zambian folk tale: 'If your face is ugly learn to sing'.

But at the end of the day, when all things are said and done, mostly what they want and what works best is just spending time with an open, honest, loving, courageous and authentic man or woman as their Facilitator and acceptance by their peers. If they can pick up some resonances from this, some inspiration, some great attitude, some life skills, some hope or direction…then we have done enough and they have found something to aim for and maybe they have found their own Golden Mirror and Golden Glasses. Time with an authentic human can be powerfully life changing. It is a repository of alchemical gold, of golden projections and evokes resonances for transformation.

Such programs are life changing for all the adults involved too. I once had a lady teacher weeping her way onto the bus taking them to the airport for their journey back home. She never wanted to leave this magical place of transformation. I wasn't worried because I knew the memories were all in her heart anyway. She would be taking the light and conversations of our camp fires back to her home and family as a blessing. For her, kayaking along Lake Argyle's spectacular coastline and through the gorges of the Ord river with twenty of us as her brothers must have been quite an experience. She often wondered at how me and my co-Facilitator dealt with our own gender. But the magic for her really came when I took her in a kayak to a deserted, heavenly rock pool and left her there alone and undisturbed for an hour. There she could sit in this miniature Garden of Eden by a gentle waterfall, and write, and swim and reflect on the most magical of journeys. It was the perfect place for a woman to find her centre, to still the waters of her mind and to really connect with herself probably for the first time in many years.

Inspirational Speech to the Kids

On the morning of the second day at a bush camp I stood at the front of a huge hall filled with a hundred kids and teachers. The kids had been awake half the night because kids always arrive excited on their first day at a camp. So Day 2 is always the tough day. Outside, the forest was a quagmire of rain, mud and freezing cold wind. Because we still had 10 minutes before the start of activities I cleared my throat, called for silence and gave my usual "I Have a Dream" speech to them. It is something we all need to remember every day and it goes something like this:

$E = MC^2$. This is a simple equation that tells us how much energy is present in a kilo of matter. And if I weighed any one of you, I could plug your weight into that equation and find out how much energy you are made of. It's a bit more complex than that but it works out that you are the equivalent of maybe thirty atomic bombs. Thirty times the amount of power and energy of the bombs that hit Nagasaki and Hiroshima. That is how much the Universe has invested in creating YOU. In fact it has invested a lot more than this for you to be here. And that is how much the Universe loves you. And if you asked anyone who really studied physics how old you are, they would have to answer that you are about 14 billion years old and made up of the very same energy from the beginning of time.

And inside each one of you is a huge 200-litre drum of emotional energy. It is the same energy that flows through you when you are watching a football match and your team is about to score and you stand up screaming, "Go! GO! GO!" That is emotional energy. And this energy can flow down any one of a number of channels. They are like pipes labelled, "Happy", "Sad", "Angry", "Fear" etc etc. Each one has a tap so that we can control how much of this same emotional energy from that 200-litre drum is going down an emotional channel.

And it's great to experience these emotions because they colour our world. It is great to feel any one of them... even fear and anger have their rightful place in our lives. When we learn to work these emotional taps and channels appropriately, we can channel our energy towards achieving great things even if it means channelling kindness to save a drowning bee or courage to steady the hand of a surgeon or being moved by anger to speak out against injustice. Anger used in the right way can be a great source of strength and courage and action. And if all these emotions have an element of love, you will never lose your way.

Learning to keep your balance under pressure will help you lead yourself well and help you to lead others well. Because keeping your balance under pressure means keeping access to all of your skills when the pressure is on. And becoming unbalanced under pressure means you lose access to your skills and you will lose your followers because no one likes an unbalanced leader.

We wake up every day and put on the dark and scratched glasses that only let us see life as terrible, sad and meaningless. Today the world is looking through the dark glasses and all it can see is fear and dark shapes. People only see the dark in each other, and they start to fear and hate each other. And when they look in the mirror, no wonder they don't like what they see. But you have to

TRANSFORMATION AND THE GOLDEN KEYS

learn to take off the dark glasses and put on the Golden Glasses where everything around is alive with light. The forest becomes a paradise. Your friends around you become beautiful and golden because all you can see is the goodness shining out of them. And with the Golden Glasses you will find a beautiful person staring back at yourself from the mirror. Why do we speak against ourselves and tear ourselves down by looking in the mirror with dark glasses when in reality we are golden and made of light. And so is everyone else. Why do we pull ourselves down before we even step out into the day when we could learn to love ourselves and step out into a paradise of opportunity?

When the world looks dark, and we are disconnected from everyone - when we are sitting all alone and everything seems washed up, and pointless - we are just experiencing an emotional flu....an emotional spell. We are suffering a mood that just won't go away. If someone were to come along with words of affirmation and say, "Hey... Don't look so sad... you are the happiest, funniest, most brilliant person I know! Remember when you helped us win at sport, how magnificent you were! And everyone thinks you are an incredible friend, so kind and always full of adventure and wisdom and great to be with...." Well the emotional spell will immediately be broken. Fully affirming someone in this way is the golden key to break the spell of a mood and immediately the sun starts to shine, a world of connection comes alive again, inspiration returns and happiness illuminates the heart and mind. They are suddenly looking into their Golden Mirror.

Don't wait for someone else to come along and affirm you! Give it to yourself! Learn to start each day by saying, "I am incredible! I have done great things! I am a wonderful and lovable human being! Life is a Miracle and we must live it that way! Something amazing is going to happen today, all I have to do is look around for it!"

Start saying "Yes!" to Life. Don't fear it so much or try to control it. Just say "Yes!" and let it unfold... all the good and the bad and the ugly... say "Yes!" to it all. Because Life flowing through you is God flowing through you! Life is Life! Get out there and experience it! In the rain, dance around and feel how great it is to be alive! If you scuff your knee, let the blood flow!

Because make no mistake, YOU are the one who picks up the paint brush and paints the picture of today. Each day you get a brand new page to paint whatever you like. Do you paint it all dark in black and red, or do you want to pick up the beautiful colours, of gold and silver, and all the colours of the rainbow, and paint a beautiful picture. YOU are the one who picks up the coloured threads and weaves the tapestry of your life. When you are old, you will look back and see what you created in all those years. You are the one who sits at the grand piano to play the music of your life and sing your authentic song, bringing your unique gifts to the world. Do you want to play sad, angry music, or a majestic symphony? Do you want to sit for years playing just one note - boring yourself and others to death, or do you want to master the art of playing an immense spectrum of music that fills every corner of your life?

And if someone comes along, and trashes your world... if they throw black paint on your canvas... simply colour it beautiful! Make it the shadow for a beautiful tree or flower in the picture. If your tapestry is torn, sew it back together, or cut out the parts you don't like and re-join it.

Learn to understand where your emotions, feelings and moods are coming from and how to channel and balance them. Learn that you are a beautiful creation of the Universe and to say "Yes!" to Life because it is all a miracle. Knowing this, I cannot imagine why you would choose to live Life otherwise. All you have to do is live this one day and this one moment well, and all the rest will take care of itself.

Dead Dog Bags. Because I once dutifully supplied these plastic bags to an adventure company, I became a facilitator and trekking guide working with the Gurkha soldiers for 8 years.

11

Conclusion

Our journey through these pages nears its end and so I can feel the dragons of sadness and goodbye stirring within me. But I know what to do: I will feed the dragons some coal and put them back to sleep. You and I must recap on what we have shared along the way so as to consolidate all these things we spoke about.

We have considered Romantic Love and its potential for discovering the energising principles of the Anima and Animus as guides in our inner work, guides to bringing our gift to the world. We have looked at Enduring Love in relationships where we can learn to love twice, falling in love once with an illusion and once with actual reality. We talked a lot about a Mother's Love, a Father's Love and the love of Mother Nature. We considered that most forms of love have some kind of payoff and are therefore conditional. But arguably the best example of Unconditional Love is how every cell in your body serves your mind and we need to love our bodies more and listen to their simple needs. We also discussed the Mother Complex and how disempowering and retrogressive it can be for anyone other than an infant. We discussed that when couples fight it is often because the partner is not matching up to the expectations of a projected idealised image of disowned contra-gender elements. I hope that overall, you gained a sense of what a resource love can be.

We talked about social contracts, relationships magnifying the experience of life, connection and oneness. We talked about symbols, myths, dragons, treasure and mission and how they relate to the Hero's journey. We learned the importance of the myth you choose to live by and the life story that you yourself write each day. You are the painter, the author, the singer and the weaver. You are also Keeper and Curator of the Archives. So whatever you don't like and whatever doesn't serve you in your past, go and change it, make your peace with it or let it go. In this I am saying simply change the way you interpret your life's events so that they empower you and become a blessing, not a burden.

In discussing archetypes, we considered concepts of ego, spirit and soul. We contrasted aspects of the inner and outer worlds and the thin border in between – the Razor's Edge. We discussed dream interpretation. We talked about the use of sacred processes, of ritual, theatre and art in processing life issues and as a completion of the process of dream interpretation. For whenever a dream is interpreted it should be followed by some symbolic process in this outer world to bring it here and make it real.

We talked a lot about life skills, psychological concepts, wholeness, gifts and challenges. We found our Golden Mirrors, Golden Glasses and a Comb for all the Tangles. These are symbols, dynamic transformational symbols that work their own magic even as we sleep and can be freely given to others in a sentence.

We learned about opposites, paradoxes unresolved and the source of neurotic behaviour and delusions. We talked about liminal states, drugs, mental health issues and suicide. We considered the formation of personality around the core wound concept and it's potential for being a window to your soul and your greatest gift.

TRANSFORMATION AND THE GOLDEN KEYS

We talked about the brutal aspects of war, where it appears within ourselves and in the dark side of humanity, and we learned the mechanisms of where it comes from and how to temper it. We discussed lots of Gods including the God of War, the God of Destruction, The God of Alcohol and the God that is everything, that is all of Life - a conscious universe - the god that is you. We learned about altars, prayer and attitude and how to create magic in our lives and to delight in the genius of creativity within us all.

We looked at components of Rites of Passage programs, adventure work and male and female Initiation of which there is more in the appendix. And we delighted in the magic of cross-cultural interaction and relationships.

But most of all, we shared some stories about ordinary people and Life and just wondered at it all. For this is the role of two friends sharing such things on a trek, even a trek through the crests and valleys of these pages, chattering away while the Witness, the Universe, simply looks on and listens. Hopefully the Universe smiled a few times too.

What are we to do with our Precious Time between birth and death? Whose tender voices will we hear coming to take us home to the stars one day? Why should we fear growing old when the alternative is to never grow up, or to die young or to never know the honour of living your years of wisdom? If you could truly believe that there is a greater good, or in a conscious universe, or God in some form... if you could believe that Life really wants you to get involved and experience it... if you could believe that you have some gift for the world and that it is not that hard to discover because it is going to come bursting out of your chest at some stage anyway... if you could believe that you can change the very way you perceive life and perceive yourself and perceive others: well, I believe life would simply be a miracle and you would live it that way. You would delight in even the smallest of things and be completely transformed into your authentic self.

Now, as the end of our journey through these pages approaches we can look back and see that these concepts, all contrived by the human mind, are a simple choice to create, to believe in or not. Or maybe they are concepts to simply resonate with like playing beautiful music. But choosing to believe in beautiful concepts, writing beautiful stories using the story teller of the mind, has consequences - beautiful ones - and a beautiful destiny if we believe it so. Every artist must have works of art to show. Every singer must bring forth a song. We cannot arrive at the end of our precious time empty handed. We must create a life of value despite the realisation that our perceptions of reality will always fall so very short of the truth and that all of society is a contrived fiction successive civilisations chose to create and believe in, share and even to delight in. Despite the fact that the mind is often capable of terrible things and beautiful things, we must still plunge into the River of Life to swim, to play, to struggle, to wonder and to enjoy. There is a meeting place for all of these things, the Razor's Edge, where all of these concepts, worlds and activities are in a beautiful balance.

I wish you a blessing on your journey, on your unique work of art. And I thank you for sharing this journey with me. I can never really leave you. I already told you it would tear the very fabric of my mind if I were to say goodbye. But let the candle flame between us burn bright for just one more precious moment so we can see the sacred fire in each other's eyes and simply say, "Namaste" or, "…until we meet again…" because I believe that dreams really do come true. And dreams become your truth if you choose to live them so. Xox.

Oneness and Eldership

There is a video clip of a man eating an apple. The man is called Scott Plous and he is delivering an online course about Social Psychology for Coursera. His question to you, the viewer, the Witness, is essentially, "When does this apple become Me?" He takes a bite and chews it for quite a while. Then he swallows it and stares patiently at the camera. It is your job to press a key on your keyboard to signal exactly the moment you believe this mouthful of apple becomes part of Scott Plous. The results are collected from the viewers' response times and displayed graphically as a curve.

Well, you could write a book about this one social experiment alone. It is simply brilliant. Does it matter if the atoms of the apple are in his mouth or on his hands, or in his stomach or his bloodstream? How separate are we from other things? Is it a matter of distance… because distance will always occur between all atoms? Is it about location? Relationship? Connection? Is there some invisible boundary that separates 'Me' from other things? Where do I stop and you begin? For this same reason, it is hard for astronomers to define the size of the Sun because its plasma and light shines out to infinity

For me, there was only a Oneness. Scott and the apple were made of the same fabric so there was no delay for me. Scott and the apple began as one thing at the beginning of time. They mixed energies in the tangles of an evolving Universe and contained atoms of each other before the video was filmed. And, wherever we look, especially with eyes of love, in the moment of percep-

tion there is a Oneness where distance and separation become somewhat meaningless or not such useful concepts. The resonance within perception seems to transcend such things and the Universe becomes one again, one thing. It becomes God.

And we are home again and in relationship to all that is, part of the matrix, part of the fabric, part of the Universe's myth that we simply forgot for a time during the amnesia of our busy years and the noise of the Chattering Mind which soon enough intrudes once again.

Maybe this is the form of energy that sits at the corner of the street, in your mind or when you are old – the wise old man or woman whom everyone comes to seek counsel from and to tell their stories to. Maybe this is the energy that nods and sighs at the right time with bright eyes of love. And at the end it encourages each one to go and write a new story with colour and beauty and music. It hands over the golden threads for a new tapestry because wisdom is simply knowing that you can indeed transform your story.

Lem. Just an authentic man trying to bring his gift to the world. Lake Argyle November 2014.

Appendix

Appendix 1: My working model of the Mental Array

Aspects of the Mental Array: The Ego makes its appearance

From an initial state of wholeness and oneness at conception and at early childhood, the mind moves on to a constellated state (when sub-elements appear and become clearer) usually as the result of a core wounding or a brutal domestication into the world's prevailing system. An archetype which we call "I" (the ego) arises from the mind and it sets about creating a persona, an entire personality built around protecting its core wounds and associated fears from ever being touched.

If core wounds are a natural and inevitable aspect of life, it is a sobering and maybe an impossible thought to imagine what core wound you would select for yourself or for your children knowing that through this core wound most likely will also come your gift to the world.

The Array unfolds
 the mind becomes constellated into:

- an Ego (with its Persona) to understand and moderate interactions with this outer world
- an inner concept of Self (the Ego is a small part of this)
- an Animus/Anima which is your true Soulmate and inner guide to the depths of your unique Soul
- the Unconscious ('Shadow') from which dramas flow

- the Collective Unconscious - the bedrock of all consciousness and a source of great wisdom and insights.
- Spirit. The Witness and that sense of Oneness.

The Ego first has to acquire vital skills to find its way and establish itself in this outer world, to earn an income and put food on the table. It needs these skills to maintain its mental array in some cohesive and functional form. And it also has to develop the skill to put itself back together in some functional form after major experiences have fragmented or melted the Ego.

The start of Inner Journeys and Life's Adventures: a Guided experience

Sooner or later another wounding occurs to shake us awake. The Ego and its Persona are forced to see that this two-dimensional journey is ultimately not enough and it is failing us. The inner journey begins at this point in order to discover deeper and wider aspects of the Self and of Soul. A time of self-discovery and self-awareness now unfolds. Here, elements of Shadow can be reclaimed and integrated into our conscious mind so that Shadow does not create so much drama in our lives from an unconscious aspect.

The mind is so desperate to understand, to define what it is when actually the mind is the myth I live by, the story I tell myself. And I believe my story completely. But we get another chance to re-write the story and change the script and change the destructive elements of the mind.

An inner guide arises from within. It is an archetypal figure to help negotiate the inner world of Soul. This is what Carl Jung called the Animus in women and the Anima in men. Ultimately, with a wholeness and balance of the mind established, connection to the wisdom of the Collective Unconscious progressively unfolds as we live more instinctively and pay more attention to our dreams. All of these aspects of the mind develop over time. Meanwhile the hair on our heads steadily turns to white and we become wise. As within, so without.

I think of inner world and outer world like a huge big tree. The roots go into the archetypal world, my world and into the world of all of humanity, the so called Collective Unconscious. If I need an answer to a problem, I can ask my Ego at night to go into my dreams, into the archetypal world and access the wisdom and knowledge of the Collective Unconscious to find the answer. This is where the scientist Friedrich Kekule found the structure of the hexagonal rings of carbon atoms that pervade organic chemistry and create all manner of compounds, from hormones to benzene. The donut structure of a 6- carbon ring came to him in a dream.

Archetypal Arrays

Discussing archetypes is a vast subject but for our purposes you can think of them as all the people in your head. Each has its own voice, its own story and its own function and impact in your life. They try to express themselves and get their needs met through the Ego who tries to moderate them and keep them in check. But they will push the Ego aside and speak directly if they need to. The list is endless but within you is a Good Father, a Good Mother, a Leader, Soldier, Doormat, Lion, Mouse, Dictator, Warrior, Control Freak, Best Friend, Rescuer, Judge, Victim, Whinger, Policeman, Addict, Castle, Sovereign, Winner, Loser, aspects of the Masculine, aspects of the Feminine etc etc.

From an initially raw, immature form when they are first expressed and first come to your awareness, these archetypal elements mature with time and might learn to work a bit better with the Ego. They have the potential to express both their positive and their negative potential at any moment. People often find the unmodified archetypes offensive, grandiose, self-serving, narcissistic, making proclamations and bold, extreme statements. Archetypes are prone to inflation and can rapidly expand to hog the centre stage and take over the mind. So other people often attack them or simply move away. And in their fear and anger and lack of insight, people wish upon another's archetypes destruction by **humiliation** as opposed to the tempering gentleness of **humility** that would transform such things to greatness.

To avoid pain and chaos, the Ego tries to present the archetypes in a more socially acceptable form. So masks are not all that bad really. Like a social lubricant, masks serve a purpose for those archetypal elements that are still immature and raw within us. Inner work helps in maturing these inner elements, but it will be a hard and brutal journey regardless of whether we do our inner work or not. Engaging archetypal energies is hard. Not engaging them, even denying them, is masochistic and almost suicidal. It's a bit like forever denying the existence of a tiger that is rampaging through your house: you would forever be bewildered by all the blood and carnage that mysteriously unfolds around you and within. It is mostly just the consequences of unprocessed Shadow.

Failure

In a sense many external things have to fail us in order for us to internalise the projections, recognise our Shadow and grow. A mother needs to stop carrying a child in order to allow it to learn to walk. Patriarchal and matriarchal figures have to fail us in some way so that we can transcend their restrictions. The system has to fail us so that we stop our dependency and instead become the change we want to see, and live responsibly not always simply demanding rights. The Mother Complex must fail us for us to mature. Some of us have to fail to find our humility. And lovers must fail each other so that they can find their own centre of love and bring that centre to all relationships.

Your life in a nutshell

So in summary, the journey starts in wholeness. The infant has no idea it is a separate entity to its mother but as time goes on this realisation becomes apparent. It can be done well and it can be done badly but it sets up a lesser or greater core wound as a foundation on which the unique personality is built. It is the Ego that arises and creates a persona with its associated behaviours that constitute a personality. A crisis sooner or later confronts the Ego and forces an inner journey to find greater aspects of Self. The Spirit Guide (your Inner Guide called the Animus or Anima) appears to help negotiate your inner world and bring your unique gift to humanity.

For a woman her Animus brings the rocket fuel of discernment and decisive action. A middle aged woman suddenly quits her job in the post office or a loveless marriage and with incredible courage takes off to live in India or the wilds of Africa as if she has waited for this all her life. She projected her Prince Charming out there and then found it within and maybe revisits it within her holiday romances along the way. And whilst men will revisit their feminine in their midlife crisis, women in later life will move past their masculine in order to deeply reconnect with the feminine elements they lost in their younger years when they split from their mothers.

If done successfully, the journey pushes past the constraints and blessings of a number of Mother and Father figures along the way. It eventually leads to reconciliation of the masculine and feminine elements of an individual into a wholeness within (the so called 'Divine Marriage').

It creates a greater awareness and appreciation of the Unconscious (the 'Shadow'... everything we deny, depress or don't know about), and it brings about the coming of a time of Eldership... of the Wise old Man or Woman... this being an awareness and association with the great repository of wisdom and knowledge which Carl Jung called the Collective Unconscious. It is a time when we come to realise that the mind is a dreamer, a Storymaker. We are authors of our own life's story and have the power and means to change it because it is simply a story. With this knowledge, we can make forays into transcending Shadow and projection.

All the while, the physical body progressively wears glimpses of these archetypal journeys and voices. Look to the tattoos, the piercings, the creases and wrinkles of the smiles and the frowns. In these things, in the fruits they produce and in the very aura - the energy of another - lies the story of their travels. But it is **their** story to tell, not ours. So do not assume or merely judge on appearance because that would be a story of your own making. Instead use gentle questions and people may offer up their precious story, their myth for you to cherish and hold sacred or to cuddle up to like a bedtime story.

Appendix 2: Male initiation

Introduction

Many times I have been asked to speak about initiation. Firstly, I always acknowledge the work of Gillette and Moore in their book *King Warrior Magician Lover*.

The primary male archetypes

Gillette and Moore describe four male archetypes that are so useful as a tool in this discussion. They help as a tool to understand aspects of male behaviour, the development of the male psyche and male psychology. There is ofcourse a vast array of possible archetypes that could be described for an individual but they found these four as the most useful to describe and discuss the male psyche.

I was standing in a service station which serves the traffic on a highway stretching from the deep south to Perth. A Burmese family walked into the food court carrying a tiny baby with jet black hair and a heavenly smile. Everyone in the food court, maybe a hundred people, looked upon this divine child with awe and bliss. The power of its presence was overwhelming. We always think of the newborn as weak but in another sense The Divine Child, an archetypal element which Gillette and Moore speak of, is immensely powerful. It is present in us all - young and old - and has its own journey. Initially it is cradled in the mother and the Mother Complex which is its birthright and protection from the Tyrant Kings, the Herods and the Pharaohs that would kill this baby Jesus or baby Moses. Men can feel threatened by a youth in ascendancy. Maybe they instinctively know that in time, this child will become the King, the sovereign element of an individual's life and newborns challenge a couple's relationship.

But there comes a time for the Ego to step up and transcend this infancy and the Mother Complex in case this state of infancy continues for too long. All archetypes are immortal. They live within us forever and across cultures and generations. So this child will reappear within us from time to time and so will the Mother Complex. We need to accept and transcend these things lest for example men project all this on the woman they are in relationship with.

Once, I lost my way on a trek. I was clinging to an impossible rock face that was crumbling in my hands. I felt the urge to give up and let go. It was the child within me that wanted to give up and surrender into the comforts of my Mother Complex. Years before when I was infant it was appropriate to do so but letting go of the rock face would have been fatal. An archetype never leaves us. It can either be suppressed and become troublesome, or it can be encouraged through dialogue and allowed to mature. As the years go by ,my Divine Child will eventually mature and transform into a wonderful King, the sovereign of my life and bringer of order, good governance and prosperity into my kingdom. At nearly sixty years of age I am finally feeling the King's presence.

Such are the archetypes in this life-changing book *King Warrior Magician Lover*. Read it. Find them. Knowledge of them is such a blessing.

What is male initiation?

It is the paradigm shift of taking a man from adolescent psychology into relationship with mature masculine psychology. It is typically enshrined within ritual in such a community. Whereas immature male archetypes are generally tied to Mother and tangled in mother issues, the mature male archetypes present after initiation are aligned to the Mature Masculine. For example, **the Divine Child** is replaced by the **Sovereign King**. The adolescent **Hero** - who would lose all his men in battle but return to claim his medal - now manifests as the **Warrior**, a brilliant tactician whose men will always live to fight another day. Such a warrior would regard medals with disdain as someone else's golden projection pinned upon him to wear.

In the process the man's level of responsibility to himself and his entire outer world goes up a level. He is no longer innocent of the shadow that drives his behaviour and can then own his choices consciously even if they don't look pretty to an onlooker. Because mental health and responsibility lie on the same continuum, if his psychology improves and his responsibility improves, then his mental health improves. And as he learns to think better, his entire world gets better.

Initiation has the effect of cutting adolescence down to days or weeks instead of allowing it to drag on and on for years. If we do not initiate the youths, if we do not give them mature insight and a new way of fronting up in the world, they behave irresponsibly and basically run amok to varying degrees pushing back the boundaries of experience without proper guidance. An immature adolescent is mostly allergic to taking on roles, responsibilities and self-discipline. So in many communities initiation is forced upon the youth and this is welcomed and celebrated by the community because they understand the benefits. The youthful, destructive and risk-taking behaviour typical of adolescence is there to break boundaries and discover new horizons and to explore new potentials. It has to be tempered by the mature masculine so that it can enhance the community in some way otherwise it is so destructive because it goes against social order of a structured society that others value. Basically without guidance such as initiation or mentoring, it turns into anarchy.

A long description can be cut down into a sentence if we speak in terms of an archetype or complex and hence the dynamic it creates in one's life. Examples include: Mr Rescuer, Mr Victim, Little Miss Princess, the

Petulant Child or Mr Addiction. So we can incorporate such paradigms into modern initiation and create a common forum, language and dialogue for which to quickly process and transfer concepts, valuable teachings and life skills in this new code. This is where the Jungian approach is so useful because it is so picturesque and visual.

Contrast these two images: one of the adolescent who is contributing so little to village life, distracted, fantasising about being fed and cared for by Mummy in all her forms. The other is the Warrior returning in the early evening with the day's kill ready to feed the village. His eyes are steady, he commands respect, his nobility is so present.

An uninitiated world or one which is not educated in these concepts looks upon it with fear, anger and severe unease. Just mention the word archetype or initiation to someone in the street and watch the reaction. Modern society does not like the brutality of forced separation of male youth from Mother and so suffers his **endless adolescence** in the name of political correctness. And these adolescents become tomorrow's leaders with endless shadow unprocessed. No wonder that leadership in this world is overcome with shadow. And to step up now into leadership is to invite the kiss of Death via a volley of arrows from the Shadow Magicians who seem to run amok in our global village. They know only too well every individual's Achilles Heel at which to aim. Male Initiation would have fixed this.

And of course there are other forms of initiation. Some of them are really not good. For example when youths are initiated into street gangs or destructive cults. The hunger to find their own masculinity even projected onto a father figure can draw young men to accept anything that resembles initiation, masculinity and power. And anything that involves secrets also creates a dangerous sense of specialness and bonding. I am not speaking of these initiations. They are as different as the profane is from the sacred.

What are the essential elements of an authentic initiation?

1. **It occurs in sacred space**: Hence initiates are taken away to a place of seclusion where things become dreamlike and time has little meaning. In this respect, it is also liminal space.
2. **It is presided over by a Ritual Elder**: He energetically holds the sacred and transformative space. His job is also to watch for elements of shadow that may appear in individuals or in the group and call it and process it as necessary so that shadow behaviour does not hijack the process. As we do our inner work, ever greater elements of shadow are encountered. So the Elder is especially watching the leaders because their shadow may be the greatest of all. In this sense he is like a referee, separate and above the leaders who may themselves be directly leading any number of group processes.
3. **It involves a ritual death:** The elements that die are those of adolescence, the umbilical cord to mother, loss of the Mother Complex, and the setting aside of Ego to enable a soulful existence.
4. **The process is usually kept secret**: Mysteries are the hidden truths. Here they are kept in the sacred space of mystery to resist the meddlings of the Shadow Magicians that would tear things of value down. Questioning and changing the mysteries and their practices is best left in the hands of the Elders because without some protection from the general public, shadow and immature masculinity will debase the transformative power and value of the sacred. An element of secrecy provides a freshness to the initiatory experience as the initiate fights his or her fears of the unknown. It allows for the initiates and initiated

men or women to convene at future initiations to assimilate further profound truths when their minds are ready to do so.

Before and After

The initiate usually arrives ruled by Ego and steeped in the feminine, blocked from his mature masculine. Some, often the most deeply wounded, are ducking and diving, a Shadow Magician, as slippery as a bar of soap, playing "**Catch me if you Can**' and with that wry smirk particular to this archetype. But such an archetype has nowhere to run when identified in broad daylight in front of the large group of men typical of an initiatory gathering.

The initiate will leave the initiation transformed into **service to soul and to his soul's mission**. He will have differentiated many of the components of his life for their subsequent re-integration and will see himself as a golden gift to the world, to the community, to the greater good. He returns in celebration with full rights as an adult, maybe to take a wife or to sit in the circle of men. His words now attract respect. And he has all the blessings and burdens of leadership upon him including having to fight for the tribe as necessary.

The process of Initiation

I want to now take you to the Initiatory Process. I will describe that which relates to three organisations that I have been initiated into and the differences between them. Later I will tell you of the Kimberley aboriginal paradigm which is so real and so visceral that I now try to live some of its truths every day in my own life as best I can in a modern world. It is not always easy to live it in this modern world as an initiated man or woman because people cannot help but notice you are somehow very different to others. Your conversations and vocabulary are different and the unfamiliar scares them.

Lastly I want to show you how this can be taken into the real world today using two examples:

1. Hard core special force Nepalese troops – the Gurkhas - who come from a totally different culture to mine and comprise Buddhists, Hindus, Christians and ancestral worshippers.

2. And my dog Scout - a huge, white and very hairy golden Retriever.

Initiation involves the same energetic phases of the Hero's journey

(See Joseph Campbell's books for more on this one.) The phases comprise:

1. **The call to Adventure:** are you in or are you out? When the Pirates and Adventurers try to recruit you to sail the seven seas for a while, are you in or are you out? Always say yes! They will return one day with chests of treasure, tales of adventure, and will marry the most beautiful women in all the land. Meanwhile their friends stayed behind wishing they had gone along with them but were held back by their stifling comfort zones and Mother Complexes.
2. **The Descent:** as the pirates - the adventurers - sail over the horizon there is a sense of buyer's regret, "Oh my God, what have I done?!!" and the descent phase occurs where everything familiar is stripped away including any claims or delusions of grandeur that existed before. The Ego realises it is not calling the shots anymore and must step slightly aside to allow for new insights and new experiences.
3. **The Ordeal:** here the initiate enters the **Enchanted Forest** and gets to face his dragons and demons as if facing Death itself. It's Judgement Day. It's High Noon. It's Time. Time to stop running and face the self and the big issues on which his life is

floundering. At this point there is nowhere to run. It's do or die. But the initiate is ready to die because he would rather die than go on living in hell without his masculine power - even if touching it would cost him his life. It is a primal and visceral calling. It is a time to begin a life-long dialogue with shadow.

4. **The Triumph:** He transcends the dragons and moves past the psychological block that was keeping him small and holding him back. In the process he claims back the inherent power that was locked within the old dynamic.
5. **The Homecoming and Celebration:** He returns to the community as a hero. Men even move aside for him at the bar and offer to buy him drinks because they want to listen to what he has to say like a pirate returning with treasure. The entire community feels the blessing of the ones who return to enrich and energise community life with their new learnings and ways of being.

What this looks like in the Mankind Project

We rent a suitable and private site with access to nature and enough facilities to care for 60 – 80 men. 40 or more staff men will gather together on the eve of an initiatory weekend to sit in circle and to process all the emotional charges and integrity issues that the staff men may have brought with them. We have wonderful protocols which we stick to that enable this process to occur cleanly. In so doing we get everyone grounded and form an integrated container, a clean crucible for alchemy that will accept the hearts and minds of 20 or 30 initiates who will arrive the next evening. The team includes a doctor or a medic, a psychologist/psychiatrist or experienced male mental health nurse and has a safety team in place should anything happen.

It is not really physically demanding yet it is real work: people have died on initiation and some have collapsed with shock or psychogenic amnesia. Some don't ever come in to the camp. They turn around at the gate never to return. Some arrive having contemplated suicide. Others are there at the insistence of their spouse that this is their last chance to save a marriage. But many would be considered as normal and many are professionals. Their ages range from 18 to 85. We don't take those suffering high levels of mental illness unless they are on medication, in remission or in some adequate state of mind. And we accept men from any faith, ethnic background or sexual persuasion – it is all inclusive.

A lot of preparation occurs on the Friday such that when the initiates arrive on Friday night they walk into a world beyond their dreams. By Sunday they have been put through more than 50 psychological processes and are in touch with their mature masculine energy having experienced a massive paradigm shift.

- They have generated their own Life's mission through guided visualisation processes.
- They have discovered the concept of Shadow and have touched elements of their own Shadow in profound and visceral ways.
- They have become integrated in a new and wonderful way with their principal archetypes of the male psyche.
- They have discovered their Wild Man, someone like Iron John, a huge repository of raw masculine energy that can be channelled down any number of channels to create both great and indeed terrible outcomes.
- They have touched the sacred, the symbolism of a Talisman and of reclaiming a new and empowered identity.
- They have sat naked, shoulder to shoulder in a sacred sweat lodge reverberating with singing, shouting, crying, whispers – whilst guarded by warriors outside who also tend the fire and

pass through the lodge's doorway the glowing rocks of 'the grandfathers' to the Lodge Keeper within. He creates a shamanic-like journey that constitutes 'The Sweat'. The world and the ego are burned away by the heat and this brings about transcendence, epiphany and insight.

Many times as I guarded the sweat lodge, my dearest companion called Meesho would appear and walk by my side. He was our golden Labrador retriever who died too young during our darkest days at a time we lived in Margaret River. I would return home from initiation and my wife would ask me, "Did you see Meesho? How was he?" and I would say with tears, "He was looking magnificent, he's doing fine." No wonder I took on the name Meesho as my animal name. Everybody gets an animal name in the process of initiation in MKP, and I will forever be known there as 'Meesho'.

For the Homecoming celebration we usually go to a club in Fremantle and get the initiated men on stage to tell their story to an assembly of community, family and friends. They stand there glowing, smiling from ear to ear, arms around each other's shoulders like a victorious football team. And they tell the world of the gold they have found and that initiation is one of the best things they have ever experienced in their entire lives.

Women's Initiation

Conversely, women's initiation is not like this. Their weekend allows them to go to their **emotional processing centre**, a much quieter place in their minds, and they return far more grounded and quiet, often not having made many new friendships. It is a somewhat more solitary journey, a stilling and settling of the mind and of the heart, to re-connect within. It is almost like a Vapashna to discover the woman they lost along the way. It came as a complete surprise to me that the energy of their journey was somewhat opposite to that of the men.

They form their own women's circles subsequently in the weeks ahead and here begins the friendships that will last a lifetime. My daughter Rebekah was able to process her eventful and challenging University years by sitting in a Circle of Women once a week after her initiation. This continued for many years and it was pure gold. She was by far the youngest in the circle and could share her youthful energetic paradigm with the wisdom of the ages from these women. She and Fiona went through initiation together and would forever hold dear the sacred journey they shared as mother and daughter.

Support and mentoring after the initiation

A three day initiation is not enough to sustain someone on their journey – it mostly only starts the awakening. So after the weekend, each new initiate is cared for by a mentor who phones them occasionally to make sure they are okay. Re-entry into the real world can be a brutal experience after an initiation weekend for everyone including the staff. I knew one young man who tragically took his own life six months after I had taken him on a Rite of Passage journey and I believe that if I had been in his life as a mentor things would not have ended so tragically. It is wise for fathers to actively find good mentors for their sons and not leave this role to a footy coach or some distant hero on T.V. But I was completely unaware of the dynamics that rose up in this young man's life and overwhelmed him. Every adolescent needs a 'go to' person to check in with as life unfolds because so many parents are blissfully unaware of the real day to day lives of their adolescents.

After initiation, the new initiate is encouraged to attend a ten-week integration group where he can discuss the experiences of the weekend and his re-entry into this world as a man forever changed. Each week he sits in circle, and the circle checks in emotionally processing any emotional charge and integrity or accountability issues before doing a learning piece. It finishes with a blessing round. It is not primarily there as a forum for victims to magnify their pain or for social chit chat although naturally fellowship occurs before and after the meeting. No one is there to give a man platitudes or well-intentioned advice unless it's specifically asked for. And even in the giving of advice it is done through a carefully controlled process so that an individual can take or leave the advice given because the advice is just a projection of the speaker.

Any time a man wants to leave MKP he is welcome to. It's not some kind of cult; no scripting of belief is forced on anyone in liminal space. In this respect, the initiatory process and outcomes are self-guided and originate from self whilst shadow in the organisation is kept in check by the oversight of elders. MKP is a place for men to do their inner work.

By contrast, **The Crucible weekend** in Perth is run by Christians, who initially were members of MKP and wanted to bring this process of initiation to the Christian world. It welcomes all faiths even in its leadership, and is done absolutely beautifully. I have the highest regard for these men. They do not push their religion on the initiates. They are tough but gentle at the same time. To witness their outrageous authenticity in the face of their religion was pure magic to see, confronting, refreshing and funny.

And **the Shift Network** ran an amazing male initiation into service to **the Divine Feminine** in Petaluma near San Francisco some years ago which for me set the stage for integration with my **Anima** and a deep connection to her feminine world. It helped establish my foundations as a man both empowering and tempering me. The 40 initiates attending this came from diverse and accomplished backgrounds in Personal Development. I was so honoured to experience this pivotal event with them. We learned techniques of Voice Dialogue, meditation, yoga, storytelling and interpretation of myth, projections, giving and receiving of blessing, and the learnings of the Samurai Game. We also learned of the harm men and women have done to each other as we interfaced with a woman's group on their own journey for an afternoon. On and on the learnings went for nearly a week - all wonderful stuff. At night time we would float outside in a steaming Jacuzzi trading stories under the northern stars that were so foreign to me.

Examples off Initiation in my personal world

1: Trekking with the Nepalese Soldiers:

Fiercely brave Nepalese soldiers known as Gurkhas have served in the British army for 200 years. Currently there are Gurkhas in the British Army, in the Singapore Gurkha Contingent, in Brunei and there are about 40 000 or so in the Indian army. Three times a year, 30 Gurkhas from Singapore used to come to Western Australia for leadership training and adventure training in the remote Kimberley region. Many had waited 15 or more years for this privilege and opportunity.

As one of three facilitators working for an adventure company, I would take a group of ten of these men trekking for two weeks in the Kimberly and one week of caving, kayaking and abseiling near Margaret River and Augusta. The Kimberley phase involved three days of briefing before setting off on an eight day trek and three days kayaking down the Ord River back to Kununurra.

With my group of ten men, I was given the freedom to take what is an awesome trek to another level, to one in many respects like an initiation or a Rite of Passage. We could have just gotten off our bus at the drop off point and headed into the bush and three weeks later put them back on a plane to Singapore. They would probably have been quite happy with that. But instead this is what I did:

Over the course of seven years I have taught myself their language in order to create a solid connection to them. I learned it using flip cards, CD's, a study guide, a dictionary and their local radio stations which I listen to each morning. I take my group into the forest a day before we leave to honour their group commander with a ceremonial Tibetan scarf to wish him welcome to Australia and a safe journey though the Kimberley. And I give the commander a boomerang signed with my best wishes as a memento of our Australian journey together. In this way I honour their own cultural practices of giving scarves and gifts when they travel because in Nepal it is custom to enter a village with a gift – a 'koseli'.

I teach them about attitude, that the most important word they can ever learn is the word "Yes!"… yes to life and to all that happens on the trek. That their spirit and energy is welcome on this journey. That the glass is always half full. I speak of the miracle of life and of the passing of time, a concept that is culturally close to their hearts. I teach the entire group of 30 men all about the indigenous culture, their connection to all things and how we are going to move ever so gently through the Kimberley. I paint the picture, a metaphor, of the Kimberley as a beautiful woman who loves us. But she loves to play with our minds. Whenever she gives us something with one hand, she will take something with the other, and we must be mindful of this and stay vigilant.

It is her way to say there are no free lunches in this world. We may stop to rest, but it will be in the sharp needle-like spinifex grass that kisses us from our first step to the last. We may sleep at night but our tents will be steaming hot, and the outside air alive with insects and mosquitoes. On a cool night we will be sleeping blissfully only to find there is a spider running wild in the tent impossible to catch. I teach them to accept all this. Do not fight it. Give your blood freely to the mosquitoes. Gently pull the blood-sucking tick from your skin and let it go on a piece of grass with your blessing to find a kangaroo as if the tick were your brother...because, actually, it is.

As the bus drops us off at the side of an endless lonely highway on our first day of the trek, I get them to walk into the forest a little and we sit and have a time of prayer to their myriad of gods, a prayer for their safety and their family's safety whilst they are away from home, a time of centering. One of the men scoops up a handful of red dust and places a red dot, a 'Tikka' on our foreheads - a reminder to keep the gods and the sacred at the centre of one's thoughts whilst the eyes are looking outwards. Then, divinely anointed, we head to the ranges singing their heartfelt Nepali songs - all about life - to the Kimberley Queen and to the forest.

We enter the land rubbing the sand in the palms of our hands and throwing sweat covered rocks into pools as we approach in obeyance to local indigenous custom. Thus we enter the soulful land of the Kimberly with great respect and humility and the land in turn loves us back. We are never allowed to kill anything except the fish we catch along the way. I speak of the scrub bulls as our brothers, the crocodiles we swim with are our cousins. The stars are our heaven as we sing to the silver moon as if to a maiden each night over a small tot of whiskey around the camp fire.

Each night I facilitate a check-in and a debrief of the day to build the unfolding soulful connection. We reflect on the day as an experiential learning process about leadership and life. The night's discussion finishes with a learning piece so as to encourage their entry into a lifetime of personal development and a fascination for psychological concepts. It was only a few years ago that the older officers whose country only experienced widespread school education in the 1980's seemed almost fearful of psychology whenever I mentioned it. To the older Nepalese it had the taboo of witchcraft that someone could have insight into another's mind. But now I am free to discuss with them emotional intelligence, archetypes and archetype balance and aspects of leadership. The chatter and songs and sharing never stops along the enchanted and liminal journey as we make our adventurous and totally hazardous way across the treacherous ranges.

Near the end of the trek, I tell them that tomorrow night the One we have searched for on our journey, the Kimberley King himself, is magically coming to our fire because we will be staying at his home on the last night. And that night it comes to the grand moment when they so want to meet this magical figure who has followed us every step of the way, whose voice we heard and whose reflection we saw as we stooped to drink from the rock pools, his voice echoing in the narrow gorges as we swam pushing our floating packs before us.

It is time to show each man that he himself is the Kimberley King, the king of his own life, of his own kingdom. And with shouts of affirmation and surprise, they affirm this fact into their minds and somehow a massive peace settles over the group. The hierarchy seems to melt away. They are all affirmed and wonderful and liminal – a true band of brothers.

The Kimberley Queen

One night a huge snake with a jet black pointy head came slowly right amongst us. She was not scared, she was curious and yet somewhat aloof. She crawled near us as we were fishing and caused a commotion because it was almost nightfall and she was amongst our tents. She slowly crossed the pool and settled in a crack in the rocks for the night. The sergeant and I had a serious discussion about what to do because she looked like one of the most dangerous snakes in all the Kimberley. I said we must leave her, not kill her. Everyone must be extra careful that night, but I could not bring myself to kill such a beautiful snake even if it meant the death of one of us. Then I looked in my snake book and found out she was **a black headed python**, harmless and she even ate poisonous snakes. Far from harming us, she was actually keeping us safe! So, overjoyed, we called her our Kimberley Queen, doubled the ration of whiskey that night and sang songs of love to her late into the evening. What a learning - when we meet people for the first time we so quickly make up stories about them. But it's just a story, if we ask questions, maybe we will learn how truly wonderful they are.

The celebration and homecoming from these journeys is immense and 33 men take to the dance floor at a local tavern in Kununurra when we return from the bush. Twice we took over the karaoke microphones and sung to hundreds of tourists there in celebration. This journey which is called **Crock Rock** - it is truly a journey of the heart. And I believe it carries all the elements of an authentic initiation that I listed before including liminality, the Ritual Elders (me and the commander), the sacred space (the Kimberley), and a ritual Death (we face death every step of those ridges... one false step and you fall 200 meters to your death - there are no second chances and it is absolutely terrifying). Swimming with the freshwater crocks for them is also facing death and on two of my treks, the last man has very nearly drowned as we swam out to the islands of Lake Argyle and during a river crossing. We have had men struck by lightning, men convulsing with heat stroke, helicopter evacuations and been chased up trees by scrub bulls.

2. Good Boy Scout

The second example of initiation involves my dog Scout, a white retriever. He was absolutely crazy as a puppy so his training was something of an initiation, a massive paradigm shift, taking him from puppy psychology to noble dog psychology. It involved sacred space, my back garden, a ritual elder (me), and Scout's imminent death if he didn't do what he was told. His craziness was so deeply ingrained that he had to be woken up from it and taught his nobility and inner peace and all about transformation. From 'Mad Scout' to 'Noble Scout'. Just like from adolescence to mature masculinity.

I believe every man should train at least one animal in a lifetime. The experience was life changing for me. When Fiona and Rebekah first brought Scout home to live with us I stared aghast into Scout's eyes and saw my own craziness staring back at me. The word 'pupil' comes from the Latin meaning a 'small boy' or a 'small girl'. It refers to the miniature reflection of yourself seen in another's eye. Maybe this was the projection I was driven to exorcise out of Scout. So I trained him to into a projection I preferred. But now I breathe a sigh of relief: I can see my own nobility there reflected in his ageing eyes.

Good Boy Scout. So unlovable as an adolescent developing his personality and so wonderful as a noble dog: living testimony to The Power of Transformation.

Appendix 3: Aboriginal cultural practices

The Aboriginal paradigm is one of connection and relationship to all things

Ancient cultures had an approach to life that lends itself so intimately to the Jungian language to describe a symbolic, mythological and archetypal worldview. To illustrate this I will be referring to a particular Kimberley aboriginal community of North Western Australia by way of example. When I studied the Kimberley aboriginal paradigm, it seemed so profoundly Jungian because of the resonances it evoked within me. They lived and breathed in parallel to my Jungian truths. So here in this forum I will discuss it in these terms.

Here is a brief description of the culture and story of the Ngarinyin peoples - Aborigines of the Kimberley region of norther Western Australia with special thanks to Hannah Rachael Bell. She sat with me and twenty other men some years ago to explain these things to us. Sadly, Hannah passed away shortly after but the legacy lives on in her marvellous book *'Men's Business, Women's Business, The Spiritual Role of Gender in the World's Oldest Culture'*.

The Ngarinyin's paradigm has many parallels with the metaphors of Jungian psychology. Nature becomes the interface between world of spirit and the real world, between the inner world of the sacred, the divine, and the outer world of what we perceive as reality, between the inner subconscious world and their outer conscious world. Nature becomes a tool for psychological processing and the transference of knowledge.

This is why removing the indigenous people from free access to their land has been so damaging because it took away their contact with nature. Nature was their instrument through which they processed their conscious and subconscious worlds and resolved the paradoxes that always abound in life. An unresolved paradox charged with emotion is the basis for most neuroses. The elements of the Shadow, which is such an important component of the subconscious mind - the elements of our personality that we repress, deny or don't know about and consequently project onto others and the outer world- need to be resolved and dialogued with otherwise sooner or later these chickens come home to roost.

For so many indigenous communities, this instrument has been denied or damaged and their ability to relate so profoundly to all the elements of the physical world has been largely lost. They have lost their upbringing within nature which was the equivalent of losing access to a library of knowledge. Nature provided a means of experiential learning – debriefs after an event - and provided an instrument of psychological processing. Their cultural system was about their relationship to all things. And it is a system much of the rest of humanity once subscribed to but with the advent and growth of knowledge and urbanisation, this ancient wisdom has been forgotten by so many peoples. The elders of the Ngarinyin tribe asked that this knowledge be recorded and widely taught to remind even the western world what it had forgotten.

Consciousness, once it has broken out and expanded does not want to regress and be put back in the box. In ancient times it was not right to put new wine into old wine skins. To rediscover our Paradise Lost – our wholeness - means returning to it with a new consciousness in some form. It is not a case of simple regression - it is a shifting of the paradigm to new insights.

The Indigenous culture

The aboriginal people had a lot of ceremony and ritual. They worshipped their gods and their ancestors, nature and the animals. They knew who they were. They were connected to all things. They were never lonely, never alone. This knowledge also held gender-specific knowledge called: "Men's Business" and "Women's Business".

They saw that everything in life came as two things like Yin and Yang, masculine/feminine, good/bad. Always two. Never one. **Everything came in pairs**. Everything had paradox. They didn't seem to like tangling things that shouldn't be tangled.

And what was important was to have a relationship between both things. They formed some kind of synthesis between the two. We must have a relationship between men and women, between the stars and the earth, with life and with the spirits. Men and women can survive alone but together they can thrive. And thus the paradox is resolved.

All of these stages in life had their own songs and stories and ritual and law. Men and women had equal responsibility, respect, authority and power.

The woman's job was to **grow** things, ideas and conceptual development. She grows life; she is keeper of the home, of nourishment, medicine and wellbeing. She keeps the language and the law, the fire, the joy and the sorrow. The man is the warrior and the teacher to the young boys. He is all about **action**, about doing.

The **seasons** told them when things in nature would change and likewise the body growing older would tell them when a boy or a girl must change and be taught new things. So men's business and women's business was all because of nature and biology and because of changes in time, because of changes in the body - hair on the arms meant a boy must become a warrior, white hair meant wisdom and respect, breasts meant pregnancy and marriage. They understood the biological clock so well.

How aboriginals teach the young ones

They use stories and songs and ceremonies and nature just as we do with the children on Rite of Passage and Into Adulthood programs. The story goes inside the mind and informs the listener because it is irresistibly projected onto the internal cinema screen of the imagination. The story speaks to the Soul and to the heart, not so much to the head. Nature is the reflection of the life force. It is the entrance to the subconscious mind and to all learning and relationship to all things. The story speaks to the subconscious mind and teaches many truths but in pictures and symbols. In this way they gave each other knowledge for survival. Nature is like a library for them, a university, a psychology.

The beginning

I will tell you how Hannah described a brief summary of a typical lifetime:

Long ago the giant god snake moved around the land and he made the water holes. The rain god (**Wandjina**) filled them with water for life to come to the earth. The Milky Way above is a masculine thing and holds the spirits of the unborn children. They are reflected in the feminine water like a mirror and from there they become real in this world. A man looking into the water may see the reflection of his child and he may dream about it that night. He will tell his wife and she may also have the same dream accepting it into her inner world and consummating it to become pregnant. The rock pool brings life as light from the stars into this world. This is so true because every cosmologist will tell you that we are ultimately just energy, which is light formed in ancient suns and transformed into stardust which fell upon the earth. The man and the woman dream together and consummate these sacred and ancient things into being.

The newborn child is held until it is eating solid food so it can constantly feel, see, hear, smell and touch the mother with all its senses. It can hear the songs and feel their rhythm; it can listen to the breathing and her heartbeat.

For the child, everything is given a **name** and its **relationship** is defined and explained. When the first teeth come, the child is put on the ground and allowed to explore. They are never punished when they are young and are kept safe by the elder children.

When the second teeth come they are taught all about their **law and culture**. By seven years of age they already know a lot about their law and culture and traditions. They have responsibility and are taught **dream interpretation to understand the message of a dream. Dreams and nature** are the gateway to new learning and wisdom. Inner world and outer world.

Initiation

When the boys start to get hair on their bodies, they are taken away from the women. The girls are never taken away from the women. They always stay with the women. But men come at night and take the boys away by force. The mother cries and tries to fight then she sits in the dust crying and hitting her head with a rock until it bleeds. For her, motherhood is over between her and this boy. He will always respect her but will never sleep in her house again.

Many young men are gathered. Each is given a **Navigator** – a man who is not his father- to teach him about life and the forest and the law and all things. He allows the child to learn by making mistakes, but if the boy does foolish or bad things it is the **Navigator and the parents** who get punished for not teaching the boy the right things. He is taught his relationship to all things, even the stars. He is taught to protect everything that is the world of women, the Motherworld, the feminine, which is all of nature so that the tribe and its culture can continue. He has to learn to hunt, to learn weapons making, food gathering, geography, navigation, songs and art. And many of these things he has already learned from the women as a child.

The aborigines **sing to nature** to make it come alive. By singing to it they stay in relationship with it and its energy and rhythms. Hundreds of stories teach the boys the complex law system.

Then the boys are taken on a long journey to meet all the surrounding villagers. Afterwards, the entire region comes together to celebrate the initiation of the boys into manhood through circumcision and severe scarring of the body. And when he gets his beard, he is ready for marriage and has learned all about the law and the environment.

In the Mankind Project we were taught that by wearing these wounds on the outside for all to see, through scarification, it indicated that a man had touched and understood some of his deepest Shadows.

The initiated man can now sit in the circle with the elders and the married men. But all the men have total respect for anyone older than themselves and cannot offer advice to an older man for to do so is extremely disrespectful. So there is humility and there is respect.

The Girl's story

The girls are always with the women. They are never taken away like the boys are. They are taught how to build shelters, to collect food, cooking, maintenance of the forest, water collection, how to build a fire, hygiene, weather, child-rearing, medical arts, diet, songs, rituals, and intuition and visions. They are attuned to the rhythms of nature. The pregnant woman is taught by the older women what to eat. They rub emu oil onto her belly skin. They prepare the birthing place for her and sing to her and give her reassurance so that the birthing process will be as instinctive and wild as it was ever meant to be.

Significant events during the pregnancy will create the animal name, the animal caste for the child. That animal species will forever be special to the child and he will care for it and have a special relationship with it. He can never eat an animal of this species. So nature is divided up to be cared for in this way under a system of custodianship and stewardship.

The women assist with childbirth but the husband is nearby going through a ritual childbirth of his own in solidarity with his wife. When the child is presented to the village there is a big celebration. The child is checked all over for birthmarks, passed through the smoke of a fire, given its name and animal name.

It is the women who keep the law. The men can make careful suggestions usually when their spirit man dreams and sings a new song of law into being. But women decide what the law is. The men administer the law. The law and punishment must be administered otherwise the powers of nature will destroy the entire community.

Contrasting western and aboriginal education

By eleven years of age a western child is confident, self-centred, domesticated, can read and write and use a computer and understands money. He has little spiritual or mythical knowledge.

By eleven years of age an aboriginal child understands his relationship to all things, the rituals, ceremonies, protocols, dance, songs and stories and survival skills like hunting. He has respect and a healthy fear for each day. He upholds the law, shares everything and contributes to village life.

Marriage

Most marriages were arranged marriages and such an arranged marriage could be set in motion at the birth of a girl. From that day on the man will give presents to the girl's parents and help them. At the time when the rains have come it is time for the older girls to get married and pregnant. Villagers walk the girl for weeks if necessary to her husband's country. There, elders will take the two of them away for two weeks to learn to live together, how to work together and how to be compatible. They hunt together, share stories and camp together.

The wedding night

On the wedding night the villagers from the entire region have set up camps geographically around the village in the same pattern as that of the region from where each one comes from. The married couple are smoked near a fire and taken to a bed of leaves made by the men and women of the village. Here elders care for them discretely for several days before they re-join the camp. Then the new wife ceremonially farewells her family.

It is always the woman who leaves her village to live with the husband. She teaches him her law and customs so he can behave properly whenever he visits her village. And so her new tribe learns to understand, respect and support her own village and tribe.

Death

When the old man is soon to die, he is kidnapped - once again - but this time by the older women. They hold him down and rub themselves all over him. From then on he has returned to the world of women from where he was taken as a boy by the men. He can discuss women's business and sit in circle with them. Women claim the beginning (birth) and the end (death) of all life. They have no need to sit in circle with the men or discuss men's business because they gave birth to all men.

When someone dies there is a lot of crying and beating of themselves with rocks. The spirits go to live on the islands offshore. This is not a nice place for us but the spirits like it there. The aboriginal **spiritman** can visit there and the spirits will teach him new songs about the law to sing to the tribe. The aborigines worship their ancestors and spirits and the spirits appear in their dreams and visions and in their songs and dance.

The dead man is put on a wooden platform and smoked to release his spirit. The body is left there to decompose. His name is not allowed to be spoken for many years and a person with the same name must take on a new name during this time. All of his possessions are taken from his widow and she is given other things to use instead. She is in mourning, and cuts her hair. She is isolated for two years or more until the elders return to the platform to wash and paint the bones in red dust and kangaroo oil.

Stones from around the platform are gathered and brought with the bones back to the village so the elder men can enquire into the cause of death and punish anyone responsible. The bones arrive in a sack and in the light of dawn are pulled on a string strung between two ceremonial logs from the shadows and into the light. It has been said that the string represents the honey bees that fly each dawn to fetch honey and live in hollow logs. So it reminds the people that there is always a sweetness to life even though death is inevitable. At a precise moment the string is cut to release the bones and to symbolically release the spirit to live amongst them once again. The mother keeps the bones for one year and the person becomes alive but in a spiritual and mythical way. The widow ends her mourning and is joyously re-united with her friends and family.

After one year, the men come to collect the bones and take them to a cave near the waterfall or rock pool where the man was first dreamed from the Milky Way into this life. In the cave are spiritual rock paintings of the Wandjina, bringers of rain and of life. His bones are left there with a bladder of water from his sacred water hole, from where the first stirrings of his conception came to be when he was just a celestial reflection of light that caught his father's eye.

Appendix 4: Facilitation advice

Facilitation, leading yourself and leading groups

Here is a bit of advice for facilitation and leading groups which may help you on your own journey, a few things to work on. Why not highlight those that resonate with you most strongly and try to work on them because practice makes the Master. I love the expression: "It's hard to play a guitar badly." Basically things are much easier if we learn to do them well.

There are so many books on the subject of leadership and facilitation but I just want to give you a basic list of things to consider and work with if you start to explore this industry of transformational work, outdoor education and adventure. It is one of the most positive and fulfilling careers you could ever have chosen. As you take each group through a new experience, the group also transforms you into a more self-actualised person. So stick with it and the rewards will come. It is traditionally not a massive source of income so when given the choice, be responsible in financial matters but mainly follow your interests, passions and life's mission over money. Those who just follow money not only become a slave to earning it but usually put their authentic life on hold, and regret it later because although money is so useful it doesn't have as much value as heart. Chasing money can become a neurotic activity if it creates a life unlived and unexpressed.

1. Plan well. Prepare for any possible deficiencies in the system. This is the skill of attention to detail.
2. When given the choice between action and inaction or delaying, always take action. Do not procrastinate.
3. Do not practice the abysmal habits of platitudes and "she'll be right" mentality. That is just self-soothing and usually doesn't conform to reality. People who dish out platitudes have im-

mense power in the moment but they are dishing out false hope. Have a healthy scepticism about everything and everyone and everything people tell you. In other words, believe in yourself first and check things out for yourself. If you hear, "She'll be right..." it's a red light signal for you to go and check and confirm "She'll be wrong..."

4. Spot the 'Swiss Cheese Effect' when things start to align for an impending disaster and warn everyone that mischief is afoot.
5. As a leader, the buck stops with you. This means that you must accept responsibility for your followers and provide for them in every way even if that means denying them things so they can grow. Accept fault for your team's failures. You are their custodian and you are ultimately the custodian of your team's success or failure.
6. You are only limited by your thinking. Life gets better when we learn to think better. Practice thinking better.
7. Practice the skill of creativity. Creativity is a habit, a practice, a skill and it can be learned. And it is always delightful. Every challenge is begging for your creativity so enjoy the conundrums along the way.
8. Life is life... indeed it is a miracle. We only judge it as good or bad depending on what glasses we choose to wear that day. Wear happy Golden Glasses not scratched, rusty unhappy glasses.
9. There are many kinds of leaders but one of the most powerful is the Servant King. He sees himself as the gardener and his followers are the flowers that need to grow. And he is a person with people skills so he can resonate with the energy of another and meet that person where they are at. Like is attracted to like. So develop the skills of mirroring another and becoming the energy they resonate with.

10. All new teams want to know, "Are you one of us, do you understand us, and can you provide us with what we need or want?" This is very important in a cross-cultural setting but applies to all groups and when there is an age discrepancy between you and the group.
11. All teams go through the phases of Forming, Norming, Storming, Performing and Mourning. Help them understand this at the start so they can recognise and negotiate the Storming phase well when it inevitably occurs. And at the end, always finish with a proper goodbye ceremony.
12. 'Every dragon guards some golden treasure.' Go there to the dark places to your fear and talk to the dragons. They always surrender their treasure to the ones who are willing to sit with them and share their pain or their fears.
13. Display great body language. Stand tall and deliver well. Be animated and interesting. In effect, put on the show. Be magnificent in the moment.
14. You have just milliseconds to make a good impression. Step up to people immediately and shake their hands and ask a question of interest to get the connection and conversation going. Asking a question takes the pressure off you giving you time to create a safe social space.
15. Learn great people skills. Build connection immediately with others. It starts with a big welcome. It's in your eyes and body language. So learn to speak as much with your gestures as with your voice.
16. Become great at remembering people's names. Develop a system for encoding their names as you meet them for future recall. Or write them down if necessary.
17. Always have a pen and paper.
18. Develop the skill to feel the energy of individuals and groups. Keep your fingers on the pulse of morale. A Facilitator channels

this energy and plays with it. A leader takes this energy and channels it into action.
19. Learn to ask great questions.
20. Learn to listen well. In a group, one person talks, the rest simply listen.
21. Learn to 'hold the space'… don't allow anyone to talk when someone is silent and trying to find the words to come out with some profound insight or disclosure. Stop them because energy is building for a breakthrough.
22. Learn to set your Ego slightly to one side. Tame it in order to contribute to the Greater Good and to allow your Life's mission to be expressed.
23. Cultivate your soulfulness and connection to all things, to nature and to everyone.
24. Learn psychology so that you can understand the operating systems of your brain and those of others.
25. Love your religion but have a big enough heart and mind to understand and embrace the truths in other religions and the beliefs and paradigms of others. We all stand on hills looking upon the miracle of life. Every hill is different. Why argue about the different perspectives when we can simply delight in them all.
26. Learn the skill of instantly developing a safe social space or container in which other people are free to share and to be.
27. Google a 'Values List' and go through it to find out what you truly value in life. All of your decision making is actually clarifying what you value most at the time of the decision. Your decision in that pivotal moment, your choice, becomes your destiny because the die is cast. And you alone are responsible for this unfolding story of your life.
28. Understand people's pursuit of Pleasure and avoidance of Pain as an underlying primary motivator.

29. Understand the chemical and mental basis for our addictions. They are just the consequences of our subtle choices between Pleasure and Pain and a manifestation of discipline or lack thereof.
30. Without discipline we can never achieve greatness.
31. Develop great checklists for all activities. For example, what to bring when you are packing for an abseiling weekend or what to say in an activity brief. Great corporations have great checklists.
32. Work on your body. Make it something to be proud of. It's an awesome machine so occasionally take it around the block.
33. Wear great clothes. Your appearance will help or hinder whatever you are trying to do in the world of people. And if you catch your reflection and see someone magnificent, well it's like rocket fuel in your life!
34. Develop your voice. Great leaders are mostly great speakers. And even more so if you can sing.
35. Arrive at a venue early and claim it in your mind as your own space and get ready before everyone arrives. Understand all the technology in the venue.
36. Always keep all your kit together. Never let it get spread between vehicles or people or get left behind.
37. Be mindful if you step in to help with a deficiency. If you always are the one dishing out kit to people who haven't planned well enough, you lose those things you prepared for, and you disempower others by teaching them to trust in Rescuers which are another manifestation of the Mother Complex.
38. Always have a head torch, a small raincoat and some thermals in your backpack plus a large plastic bag so if it rains your kit need not get wet.
39. Finish one day at a time. Don't leave things for tomorrow.

40. Develop a discipline such as meditation, Tai Chi, road running, nunchakus, wooden flute, guitar.... whatever. Be good at something.
41. Develop one amazing magic trick. It will bring wonder to others your entire life and get you out of deep water a million times.
42. Understand that inside of you is a bucket of emotional energy. It is the energy you see when you watch people going ballistic cheering at a footy final. That same energy flows down emotional taps such as sadness, happiness, anger, envy, jealousy, depression etc. Learn to control these emotional taps and switch on or off the ones you want to.
43. Learn about projections... how everything we repress, deny or don't know about ourselves starts to control our behaviour, and is behind all our emotions and the stories we tell ourselves about our lives.
44. The events in our lives are stories. Strive to create empowering ones.
45. Understand liminality versus the liminoid.
46. Get rid of negative influences and negative people in your life ie: work with winners. Surround yourself with positive people because company is contagious.
47. Beware of toxic conversations, toxic groups and toxic companies or corporations.
48. Be authentic, open and honest. Speak your truth. In some measure, learn to thrive on rejection.
49. Always be on time. And mostly, start activities on time...neither too early nor too late. Starting too early can put panic into a group. Starting too late means that slackness is acceptable. A timing is an agreement for all concerned.

50. Keep your agreements. If you cannot keep an agreement, simply negotiate a new agreement with those concerned before the deadline expires.
51. If you break an agreement, saying sorry is not enough. Do a simple act of service eg: make everyone a cup of tea to get back into integrity with those concerned. Then they will learn to trust you again.
52. Develop a Vision Board for what you want to come true in the next 6 months and mostly it will in some form or another.
53. Surround yourself with some good mentors in your life to fast track you.
54. Speak in a language other people understand. Slang spoken to a foreigner is cultural blindness.
55. Understand what the group wants and give them what they have come looking for.
56. Meet the group where it's at and attend to their needs: physical, mental, emotional and spiritual, social and soulful.
57. Build an altar by your bedside and kneel there or sit there each day.

Appendix 5: Shackleton's Story

Once upon a time, it is said that a very strange and elusive newspaper article appeared in a London paper. The article has never been found but its legend lives on.

"Men wanted for hazardous journey. Small wages. Bitter cold. Long months of complete darkness. Constant danger. Safe return doubtful. Honour and recognition in case of success."
   Sir Ernest Shackleton

The year was about 1912, some twelve months after Roald Amundsen had beaten Robert Scott by 6 weeks in a race to the South Pole. Amundsen had planned well, even eating all his sledge dogs on the return journey to save carrying extra food. Scott's mission was plagued with bad planning and poor decisions and none of his crew that reached the South Pole made it back alive through the blizzards and snow. Scott and his senior staff were from the British Navy which gave them an air of superiority and distanced him from his men.

Shackleton realised that the next greatest thing to reaching the South Pole was to cross Antarctica on foot. So by 1914 he had his magnificent ship, the Endurance packed with twenty eight men anchored off the British coast and ready to sail. WW1 broke out that evening at midnight and despite offering his ship and crew to help fight the war, he was told by Winston Churchill to continue on the Polar expedition....the reason being that England would need brave explorers and good news to boost the morale of the fighting troops. We all need Heroes to believe in.

Shackleton expected the war to be over in 6 months, but it continued on for five long years claiming 17 million lives and wounding 20 million others. Shackleton was not to know that two and a half years later his men would return from the Antarctic with so much experience at survival and navigation that many of them would play key roles in leadership later in the war. But now they were heading into the Antarctic, a place with no communications to the outside world and they could be lost there forever.

He planned to sail to South America, then down to Antarctica and start the crossing whilst another ship and crew set up food supplies along the journey from the other side nearer to New Zealand. Three months later Shackleton reached a small island called South Georgia which was still about 1000 miles from Antarctica. Here was a small Norwegian whaling station. He waited a month here making friends with the Norwegians and waiting for thick ice to clear in the Weddell Sea ahead.

When Shackleton entered the huge bay from the Weddell Sea, he battled icebergs and the frozen sea for 6 weeks before the temperature plummeted and his ship quickly froze into the ice. The men kept up their morale by playing soccer and hockey on the ice and hunted seals for food. Shackleton constantly led the men well, making excellent plans and decisions and becoming a dear friend to every one of them. The many photos that survive show the love that these men had for each other – every photo has certain magnificence.

But as the ice quickly drifted them far from their intended landing site, the ship became crushed and broken. Shackleton ordered all men to camp on the ice and set about rescuing as much of the supplies as he could. They even swam into the kitchen through holes in the hull to rescue floating food supplies. But one spectacular night after 300 days on the ice it was totally smashed and sank beneath water. All of this was captured in photographs and film that survive to this day.

Dragging three lifeboats, they pulled their supplies across the ice, trying to make it to land 350 miles away. Eventually the ice began to break up. They had to bunny hop between islands of ice and pull the lifeboats onto icebergs to sleep the night. This was perilous. The ice cracked beneath them as they slept creating massive holes which could have killed the men as they slept.

On day 500, five months without their ship, they made a run for Elephant Island. It was a spectacular journey but once there Shackleton knew he must go on and bring help otherwise the men would never be rescued. He chose his best five men and set sail in a small lifeboat and travelled 900 miles across the most treacherous ocean in the world to South Georgia.

Mountainous seas pummelled the boat. One wave was mistaken as white clouds in the blue sky and when it hit them and all the men feared it was the end. They bailed all the way, day and night and many times the boat nearly sank with all the ice and frost that weighed it down so the whole way they had to constantly chip the ice off the boat.

They only had four chances of using their basic navigation equipment to find this tiny island in such a vast ocean but three weeks later they made it. Three men were left there at the beach too weak to continue and Shackleton and two others set off on foot to cross mountains and glaciers for three days to get to their friends at the Norwegian Whaling station. This journey alone was beyond belief…it had never been done before and they had no equipment. In the last stages, they even slid down huge snow slopes, got temporarily lost and finally had no option but to abseil over a huge waterfall one by one into a deep pool below and swim to land in the icy water. They arrived at the station filthy tired but overjoyed. That evening the three men on the shore were rescued but it took three months and four attempts in different ships from South Georgia, the Falkland Islands and Chile to get to the twenty two men on Elephant Island due to ice and breakdowns of the ship motors. But Shackleton persisted and not a man was lost.

Further Reading

Abram, D. (1997). *The Spell of the Sensuous.* New York. Vintage Books.

Armstrong, K. (2006). *A Short History of Myth.* Edinburgh. Canongate.

Bell, H. R. (1998). *Men's Business Women's Business. The spiritual Role of Gender in the World's Oldest Culture.* Rochester. Inner Traditions International.

Biddulph, S. (1994, 1995). *Manhood (Second edition):* An action plan for changing men's *lives.* Lane Cove. Finch Publishing Pty Ltd.

Bly, R. (1991). *Iron John: A Book about Men.* Shaftsbury. Element Books Ltd.

Bly, R. (1988). *A Little Book on The Human Shadow.* HarperCollins Publishers.

Brizendine, L. (2007) London. *The Female Brain.* Transworld Publishers.

Brizendine, L. (2010) London. *The Female Brain.* Transworld Publishers.

Campbell, J. (1972). *Myths to Live By.* Penguin Group.

Doblhofer, E. (1973). *Voices in Stone.* London. Paladin

Dunn, J. (1997). *Painful People: and how to deal with them.* Australia. Harper Collins Publishers Pty Ltd.

Fry, S. (2018) *Heroes: Mortals and Monsters Quests and Adventures.* Australia. Penguin Random House

Gerryn, G.A. (2011). *Men of Honour: A young Man's Guide to Exercise, Nutrition, Money, Drugs, Alcohol, Sex, Pornography and Masturbation.* Sydney. Freedom House Publishing Pty Ltd.

Greene, R. (1998). *The 48 Laws of Power.* London. Profile Books Ltd.

Harris, T. (1973). *I'm Okay You're Okay.* London. Pan Books.

Hillman, J. (1979). *The Dream and the Underworld.* New York. HarperCollins Publishers.

Hillman, J. (1991). *A Blue Fire.* New York. HarperPerennial.

Hillman, J. (1997). *The Soul's Code: In Search of Character and Calling.* London. Transworld Publishers.

Hillman, J. (2004). *A Terrible Love of War.* New York. Penguin Press.

Johnson, R.A. (1993). *Transformation: Understanding the Three Levels of the Masculine Consciousness.* HarperCollins Publishers.

Johnson, R.A. (1993). *Owning Your Own Shadow: Understanding the Dark Side of the Psyche.* HarperCollins Publishers.

Johnson, R.A. (1995). *Lying with the Heavenly Woman: Understanding and Integrating the Feminine Archetypes in Men's Lives.* HarperCollins Publishers.

Johnson, R.A. (1995). *The Fisher King and the Handless Maiden: Understanding the Wounded Feeling Function in Masculine and Feminine Psychology.* HarperCollins Publishers.

Johnson, R.A. (1989). *Ecstacy: Understanding the Psychology of Joy.* HarperCollins Publishers.

Johnson, R.A. (1989). *Inner Work: Using Dreams and Active Imagination for Personal Growth.* HarperCollins Publishers.

Johnson, R.A. (1989). She: *Understanding Feminine Psychology.* HarperCollins Publishers.

Johnson, R.A. (1989). *He: Undestanding Male Psychology.* HarperCollins Publishers.

Johnson, R.A., Ruhl, J.M. (1998). *Balancing Heaven and Earth: A Memoir of Visions, Dreams and Realizations.* HarperCollins Publishers.

Johnson, R.A., Ruhl, J.M. (2000). *Contentment: The Way to True Happiness.* HarperCollins Publishers.

Johnson, R.A., Ruhl, J.M. (2009). Living Your Unlived Life: Coping with Unrealized Dreams and Fulfilling your Purpose in the Second Half of Life. Penguin Books.

Jung, C.G. (1986). *Aspects of the Feminine.* London. Routledge.

Jung, C.G. (1963). *Memories, Dreams, Reflections: An Autobiography.* London. William Collins.

Kauth, B. (1992). *A Circle of Men: The Original Manual for Men's Support Groups.* New York. St Martin's Press.

Matthews, A. (1997). *Follow Your Heart: Finding Purpose in your Life and Work.* Trinity Beach. Seashell Publishers.

Moore, R. Gillette, D. (1990). *King Warrior Magician Love: Rediscovering the Archetypes of the Mature Masculine.* New York. HarperCollins Publishers.

Lashlie, C. (2005). *He'll Be OK: Growing Gorgeous Boys Into Good Men.* Auckland. HarperCollins(NZ)Publishers.

Masters, R.A. (2015). *To Be a Man: A Guide to True Masculine Power.* Boulder. Sounds True, Inc.

Milton, G. (2008)*Paradise Lost: Smyrna 1922: The Destruction of Islam's City of Tolerance.* London. Hodder & Stoughton.

Murdock, M. (1990). *The Heroine's Journey: A Woman's Quest for Wholeness.* Boulder. Shambhala Publications, Inc.

Neumann, E. (1971). *Amor and Psyche: The Psychic Development of the Feminine.* Princeton. Princeton University Press.

Packenham, T. (1991). *The Scramble for Africa.* London. Weidenfeld & Nicholson.

Plotkin, B. *(2008). Nature and the Human Soul: Cultivating Wholeness and Community in a Fragmented World.* Novato. New World Library.

Plotkin, B. *(2003). Soulcraft: Crossing into the Mysteries of Nature and the Psyche.* Novato. New World Library.

Plotkin, B. *(2013). Wild Mind: A Fieldguide to the Human Psyche.* Novato. New World Library.

Riso, R. (1988). *Personaity Types: Using the Enneagram for Self-Discovery.* London. HarperCollins Publishers.

Ritual Theatre: The Power of Dramatic Ritual in Personal Development and Clinical Practice. Edited by Claire Schrader. (2012). London. Jessica Kingsley Publishers

Robinson, M. (2009). *Cupid's Poisoned Arrow: From Habit to Harmony in Sexual Relationships.* Berkeley. North Atlantic Books.

Rovelli, C. (2016). *Reality is not what it seems: The Journey to Quantum Gravity.* UK. Penguin Books.

Ruiz, M. A. (1997). *The Four Agreements: A Toltec Wisdom Book.* San Rafael. Amber-Allen Publishing Inc.

Ruiz, M. A. Mills, J.A. (2004). *The Voice of Knowledge.* San Rafael. Amber-Allen Publishing Inc.

Ruiz, M. A. (2011). *The Mastery of Love: A Practical Guide to the Art of Relationships.* San Rafael. Amber-Allen Publishing Inc.

Ruiz, M. A. Mills, J.A. (2013). *The Circle of Fire.* San Rafael. Amber-Allen Publishing Inc.

Ruiz, M.A. Emrys, B. (2018). *The three Questions: How to Discover and Master the Power Within You.* London. HarperCollins Publishers.

Slater, R. (2003). *29 Leadership Secrets from Jack Welch.* New York. McGraw-Hill.

Stephenson, B. (2006). *From Boys to Men: Spiritual Rites of Passage in an Indulgent Age.* Rochester. Park Street Press.

Thompson, M. (2000). *Speaking of Boys: Answers to the Mosrt Asked Questions about Raising Sons.* East Roseville. Simon & Schuster (Australia) Pty Limited.

Tillet, P. *Consider the Heavens: A guide to Astronomy and its Impact on Our Lives.* Frenchs Forrest. New Holland Publishers.

Wison Learning Library (2004). *The Social Styles Handbook.* NovaVista Publishing.

Zamoyski, A. (2004). *1812: Napoleon's Fatal March on Moscow.* London. HarperCollins Publishers.

Zimmer, H. (1956). *The King and the Corpse.* Princeton. Princeton University Press.

www.ingramcontent.com/pod-product-compliance
Lightning Source LLC
Chambersburg PA
CBHW051533010526
44107CB00064B/2716